The EMERGING EUROPEAN UNION

W9-BBD-292

ICELAND

0   miles   500

0   km   500

Norwegian Sea

SWEDEN

FINLAND

NORWAY

Gulf of Bothnia

North Atlantic Ocean

North Sea

DENMARK

ESTONIA

LATVIA

Baltic Sea

LITHUANIA

RUSSIA

IRELAND

NETHERLANDS

BELGIUM

U. K.

BYELARUSSIA

POLAND (√)

English Channel

GERMANY

LUX.

UKRAINE

CZECH REPUBLIC (√)

SLOVAKIA (√)

Bay of Biscay

FRANCE

SWITZER-LAND

AUSTRIA

HUNGARY (√)

ROMANIA

Black Sea

PORTUGAL

ANDORRA

CORSICA

ITALY

SLOVENIA

CROATIA

Adriatic

BOSNIA

SERBIA

MONTENEGRO

MACEDONIA

BULGARIA

SPAIN

BALEARIC ISLANDS

SARDINIA

Tyrrhenian Sea

GREECE   *Aegean*

TURKEY (√)

ALBANIA

SICILY

Ionian Sea

MOROCCO

ALGERIA

TUNISIA

MALTA (√)

Mediterranean Sea

CYPRUS (√)

Members of the European Union

Associate members of the European Union

(√) Applied for membership in the European Union

The EMERGING EUROPEAN UNION

DAVID M. WOOD
University of Missouri

BIROL A. YEŞILADA
University of Missouri

Longman *Publishers USA*

The Emerging European Union

Copyright © 1996 by Longman Publishers USA.
All rights reserved.
No part of this publication may be reproduced,
stored in a retrieval system, or transmitted
in any form or by any means, electronic, mechanical,
photocopying, recording, or otherwise,
without the prior permission of the publisher.

Longman, 10 Bank Street, White Plains, N.Y. 10606

Associated companies:
Longman Group Ltd., London
Longman Cheshire Pty., Melbourne
Longman Paul Pty., Auckland
Copp Clark Longman Ltd., Toronto

Executive editor: Pamela Gordon
Production editor: Linda Moser
Cover design: David Levy
Compositor: ExecuStaff

Library of Congress Cataloging-in-Publication Data
Wood, David Michael
    The emerging European union / by David M. Wood and Birol A.
Yeşilada.
        p. cm.
    Includes index.
    ISBN 0-8013-1144-6
    1. European Union. 2. European federation. I. Yeşilada, Birol
A. II. Title.
JN30.W66   1996
341.24'2—dc20
                                                95-20347
                                                CIP

1 2 3 4 5 6 7 8 9 10-MA-9998979695

For Mary and Susan

Contents

Preface

T*he Emerging European Union* is a political science text designed for upper division college courses in three fields: (1) comparative European politics, (2) international political economy, and (3) international organizations. It can be used as well for more specialized courses on individual European political systems, particularly those of the United Kingdom (UK), France, and Germany, and on the European Union (EU) and the process of European regional integration.

For comparative politics courses, the book draws the attention of students to how membership in the EU and its predecessor, the European Community (EC), has affected and been affected by, the domestic politics of the member countries. In chapters 1 and 3-6, we highlight the roles played in European integration at various times in the past and especially in the 1990s by the governments of the three largest countries. In chapters 5 and 6, we devote attention to how the emergence of the EU has affected parties, elections, and relationships between governments and parliaments in Britain, France, and Germany.

From the standpoint of international political economy, we treat the EU as the product of fundamental global economic changes, as well as political changes, which have themselves in large part been influenced by changes in the international economy. How this has occurred historically is one of the themes we address in chapter 2 on the evolution of regional integration theory in which economic and political explanations have periodically been stimulated by unexpected developments in European integration. Discussions in chapters 3-5 demonstrate how the international political economy influenced this history. Chapters 7-11 examine policy responses of the EU to changes in the international political economy. In these chapters we examine economic and monetary policies (chapter 7); the Common Agricultural Policy (CAP) (chapter 8); regional, social, industrial, and environmental policies (chapter 9); international trade policy (chapter 10); and foreign and domestic security policies (chapter 11).

For international organizations courses, the EU serves as the unique case of a regional organization that has moved beyond the strictly intergovernmental format of the typical international organization. In every chapter of the book, we examine the ways in which the EU has transcended the status of an international organization by combining intergovernmental and supranational features.

In designing and writing the book, we have been conscious of the fact that the study of the EU does not fit neatly into the traditional substantive breakdowns of political science curricula. In targeting the previously mentioned types of courses, we have tried to include enough substantive material to satisfy instructors looking for a main text on European integration, without going into so much depth that the text will not fit the specifications for a supplementary text. We believe we have produced a text that will effectively cover this variety of needs.

The authors wish to acknowledge the intellectual contributions of colleagues, including Robin Remington, Herbert Tillema, and Walter Johnson at the University of Missouri-Columbia; Leon Hurwitz at Cleveland State University; and Emil Joseph Kirchner at the University of Essex. Beth Robedeau, of the American Bar Association Central and Eastern European Law Initiative, deserves special thanks as a coresearcher in our work on the agenda-setting role of the European Council. The assistance of the European Community Studies Association (ECSA) and of the Delegation of the European Communities in Washington, D.C., is also gratefully acknowledged. Finally, the staff of the Department of Political Science at the University of Missouri-Columbia—Jeannie Bangs, John Green, and Linda Eickmeier—provided immense assistance in the preparation of our draft manuscripts.

We would also like to thank the following individuals who reviewed the manuscript and provided helpful suggestions:

Philip R. Baumann, Moorhead State University

Desmond Dinan, George Mason University

Robert Evans, Bologna Center, Johns Hopkins University

Richard B. Finnegan, Stonehill College

Gary P. Freeman, University of Texas

Norman Furniss, Indiana University

Arthur B. Gunlicks, University of Richmond

Louis D. Hayes, University of Montana

James F. Hollifield, Auburn University

Steven Lewis, University of Wisconsin
Anthony M. Messina, Tufts University
Anthony Mughan, Ohio State University
Jorgen Rasmussen, Iowa State University
Martin Slann, Clemson University
David S. Wilson, University of Toledo

Abbreviations

ACP	African, Caribbean, and Pacific countries (Lomé states)
Benelux	Belgium, the Netherlands, Luxembourg Customs, and Economic Union
CAP	Common Agricultural Policy of the EU
CDU/CSU	Christian Democratic Union/Christian Social Union (Germany)
CEDEFOP	European Center for the Development of Vocational Training
CFSP	Common Foreign and Security Policy
CIS	Commonwealth of Independent States
Commission	Commission of the EU
COREPER	Committee of Permanent Representatives at the EU
Council	Council of Ministers of the EC
CSCE	Conference on Security and Cooperation in Europe
CU	Customs Union
DG	Directorate General
DM	Deutschmark (Germany)
EAGGF	European Agricultural Guidance and Guarantee Fund
EAP	Environmental Action Programs
EBRD	European Bank for Reconstruction and Development
EC	European Community (officially known as the European Communities)
ECB	European Central Bank
ECJ	European Court of Justice

ECSC	European Coal and Steel Community
ECOFIN	European Council of Finance Ministers
ECU	European Currency Unit
EDA	European Democratic Alliance (EP group)
EDC	European Defense Community
EEA	European Economic Area
EEC	European Economic Community
EES	European Economic Space
EFTA	European Free Trade Area
EIB	European Investment Bank
EMI	European Monetary Institute
EMS	European Monetary System
EMU	Economic and Monetary Union
EP	European Parliament
EPC	European Political Cooperation
EPP	European People's Party (Christian Democratic EP group)
ER	European Right (EP group)
ERDF	European Regional Development Fund
ERM	Exchange Rate Mechanism
ESC	Economic and Social Committee
ESCB	European System of Central Banks
ESF	European Social Fund
EU	European Union
EUA	European Unit (currency) of Account
EURATOM	European Atomic Energy Community
EUT	European Union Treaty
FDP	Free Democratic Party (Germany)
FRG	Federal Republic of Germany
GATT	General Agreement on Tariffs and Trade
GDP	Gross Domestic Product
GDR	German Democratic Republic (former East Germany)
GMP	Global Mediterranean Policy
GNP	Gross National Product
GSP	EU's General System of Preferences
IGC	Intergovernmental Conference
IMF	International Monetary Fund
JHA	Justice and Home Affairs
LDCs	Less Developed Countries
LDR	Liberal Democrat and Reformist (EP group)
LU	Left Unity (EP group)
MCA	Monetary Compensatory Account
MEP	Member of the EP
MP	Member of Parliament (Britain)

MRP	Popular Republican Movement (French Christian Democrats)
NAFTA	The North American Free Trade Area
NATO	North Atlantic Treaty Organization
NMBCs	Nonmember (EU) Mediterranean Basin countries
OECD	Organization for Economic Cooperation and Development
OPEC	Organization of Petroleum Exporting Countries
PCF	French Communist Party
PES	European Socialist Party (Socialist EP group)
PDS	Party of Democratic Socialism (Germany)
PS	Socialist Party (French)
QMV	Qualified Majority Voting
R&D	Research and Development Policy
RPR	Rally for the Republic (French Neo-Gaullists)
SEA	Single European Act
Social Charter	Community Charter of Fundamental Social Rights for Workers
SDR	Special Drawing Rights (of the IMF)
SPD	Social Democratic Party (Germany)
TEU	Treaty on European Union (Maastricht Treaty)
TRNC	Turkish Republic of Northern Cyprus
UDF	Union for French Democracy (center-right party)
UK	United Kingdom
UN	United Nations
UNPROFOR	United Nations Peacekeeping Forces in the former Yugoslavia
VAT	Value Added Tax
VER	Voluntary Export Restraint
WEU	Western European Union

chapter 1

Introduction

The subject of this book is the European Union (EU). Until 1993, when the Maastricht Treaty on European Union (TEU) went into effect, what is now the EU was called the *European Community* (EC) (see chapter 5). The initials EC were used instead of EU, and the word *Community* instead of *Union* because it was as the European Community that this regional international organization came more prominently to the world's attention when its powers were substantially expanded during the 1980s. The change in name to European Union is relatively recent. As we will discuss in chapters 2 and 3, the EC had its origins in three regional international organizations that were established in the 1950s—the European Coal and Steel Community (ECSC), the European Economic Community (EEC), and the European Atomic Energy Community (EURATOM). Each significant development in the evolution of the EU has involved the pooling of some governmental functions and powers by the Western European member states. In the three original communities of the 1950s, there were six member states: Belgium, France, the German Federal Republic (FRG, also known at the time as West Germany), Italy, Luxembourg, and the Netherlands. Three new members—Denmark, Ireland, and the United Kingdom (which we will usually call Britain)—joined in 1973. By this time the three separate communities had been combined into what was by then officially called the European Community. In 1981 Greece became the tenth member, and in 1986 the adhesion of Portugal and Spain brought the EC membership to 12. Most recently, on January 1, 1995, three new members joined—Austria, Finland, and Sweden—raising the membership of the EU to 15.

This introductory chapter provides a brief overview of what the EU is in two senses: (1) as a set of governing institutions that collectively make policies to be implemented uniformly over the 15 member states, and (2) how the

1

domestic politics of the members of the EU are related to the politics of the EU. In doing so, the chapter introduces the principal institutions that will feature prominently in the chapters to follow.

THE FRAMEWORK OF THE EUROPEAN UNION

The EU is emerging as something more than the organization of regional economic integration that was called the European Community. According to the Maastricht treaty, the EU is becoming an *Economic and Monetary Union* (EMU) and a *Political Union.* If EMU is achieved as planned, around 2000 or later, it will go beyond the removal of barriers to free trade between the member states. It will mean (1) the pooling of the capacities of the member states to make macroeconomic policies, so that common fiscal and monetary policies will be adhered to by all member states, (2) a common central banking system for the member states akin to the U.S. Federal Reserve System, and (3) a common EU currency replacing the separate currencies of the member states. Supporters of EMU anticipate that it will mean common social, regional, industrial, and environmental policies as well. All of these policy realms will be discussed in later chapters in terms of what has been realized up to now and what is projected by Euro-enthusiasts for the beginning of the twenty-first century. Suffice it to signal for now that EMU and its projected policy implications are being hotly debated within and between the member states.

The meaning of *Political Union* is likewise a combination of what the EU is at present as a result of over 40 years of evolution and of the aspirations for future political integration on the part of those who advocate the creation of a European federated state. At present the EU is a set of specific institutions that bring together the member states in a variety of ways, usually classified as *intergovernmental* and *supranational.* The distinction is similar to that between a *confederation* and a *federation.* Confederations make decisions through a process of intergovernmental bargaining. Federations have decision-making bodies that are independent of the member states. For example, the U.S. Congress is elected by the voters in the states, rather than chosen by the state governments. In the EU, supranational bodies are above the control of national governments acting individually. In the EU, all bodies, whether intergovernmental or supra-national, are collective actors, but the intergovernmental bodies have the upper hand. So the EU is somewhere between a confederation and a federation. We will outline this institutional framework very briefly here (see Figure 1.1), then show how it operates in chapter 6.

Intergovernmental bodies in the EU bring together political leaders or delegates of the 15 member governments. Supranational bodies bring together nationals of the member states who are not accountable to their governments, but deliberate in the name of the EU as a whole or of the European citizenry. The principal intergovernmental institution is the Council of Ministers, in which members of the governments of the 15 member states meet to adopt policy

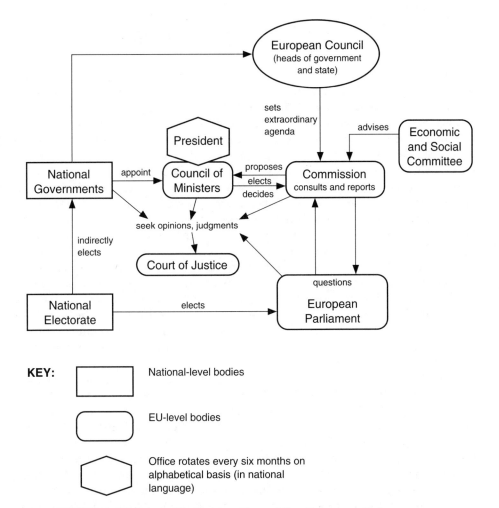

FIGURE 1.1 Basic institutional outline of the European Union

NOTE: This figure does not reflect the growth in the legislative role of the European Parliament that has occurred since the mid-1980s. See Figures 6.1 and 6.2 in chapter 6 for the role of the European Parliament under the cooperation and codecision procedures.

measures applicable to all of them. At its apex, the Council of Ministers takes the form of the European Council, in which it is the heads of state and government[1] who meet at least twice per year to make the most important decisions for the EU. Every 6 months the responsibility for presiding over the European Council and setting its agenda is handed over by one member state to the next through an alphabetical rotation order,[2] which ensures that each of the 15 members will hold the 6-month presidency once every $7\frac{1}{2}$ years. The presidency has some of the agenda-setting powers of the head of state (president) in a presidential system of government, such as in the United States, but these powers are shared with the other 14 governmental heads in the European Council, and with the president of the Commission, who heads one of the supranational bodies of the EU.[3]

The principal supranational institutions of the EU follow the threefold separation of powers familiar to students of American government. The *Executive* (a term used interchangeably with the official title) is the European Commission, a body of 20 commissioners who are nominated by the governments of the member countries (two commissioners for each of the five largest members— Britain, France, Germany, Italy, and Spain—and one for each of the smaller members), and then formally chosen by the Council of Ministers. The Commission is headed by one of the 20 commissioners, the president of the Commission, who is elected by the Council. The president assigns responsibilities to the other commissioners. When this role is played by an effective political personality, such as Jacques Delors, who was Commission president from January 1985 through January 1994, it provides its occupant with the capacity to lead the EU in his or her prioritized directions, assuming that the governments of enough member states are willing to follow. Minimally, this means that leaders of two or three of the largest and strongest members (Germany, France, and Britain) must go along with the president, and be able to bring other members with them. Some national leaders, like François Mitterrand or Helmut Kohl, can provide impetus for the EU in their own right, sometimes moving out ahead of the Commission president.

The other two supranational bodies are the European Parliament (EP) and the European Court of Justice (ECJ). Members of the European Parliament (MEPs) are directly elected by voters in Euro-elections every 5 years. The powers of the EP have been growing steadily since the 1970s. But, as a legislative body, the EP shares powers with the Council of Ministers, which remains the stronger of the two. The ECJ, like the Commission, contains judges who are nominated by their member governments and formally chosen by the Council of Ministers. Through judicial interpretation of the treaties of the EC and EU, the ECJ has established its authority to declare actions of both the EU bodies and the member states to be in violation of EC and EU law, a power akin to judicial review as exercised by the U.S. Supreme Court.

All of these EU institutions will be analyzed at greater length in later chapters, in terms of their respective powers and the degree to which they approximate or fall short collectively of satisfying the criteria for a democratic system of governmental institutions. The terms *intergovernmental* and *supranational* suggest that they will also be analyzed in terms of the extent to which the EU represents a departure from a confederal mode of sharing power among sovereign states and movement toward a federal pooling of sovereignty by states that are no longer fully sovereign. The European Council and the Council of Ministers act as 15-member intergovernmental bodies, trying to find common ground among all member states before making decisions. But in the 1980s and 1990s the practice has been growing, with the encouragement of the Single European Act (SEA) and the Maastricht treaty, to decide matters in the councils by *qualified majority vote* (QMV). This means that, if more than 70 percent of the weighted votes of the member states are cast in favor of a particular course of action, as many as seven small member states could be outvoted and would have to go along with the others. As QMV advances, the sovereign independence of the member states, especially the smaller ones, recedes, and the EU becomes increasingly a supranational arrangement of institutions. The Commission, the ECJ, and the EP are supranational bodies, but they remain dependent upon the intergovernmental bodies to register the consensus among member states necessary to move the EU ahead. Clearly, the member states, individually as well as collectively, are major actors in the EU political process. But some are more major than others, and there are important differences between them that are relevant to the ways they act at the European level.

THE MEMBER STATES

Each of the 15 member states of the EU encompasses a political system with its own set of laws, governing institutions, political parties, elections, interest groups, and subnational levels of government. Increasingly, developments within the EU affect these domestic political systems. For example, with the evolution of the European Council as the principal agenda-setting body of the EU, the significance of national political leaders within their own political systems has grown at the expense of secondary leaders in national-level legislative bodies and political parties.[4] Because summit meetings generate a great amount of media attention, other national-level political actors are made dependent upon the president or prime minister to negotiate effectively with leaders from other countries on behalf of national interests. Successful negotiations of EC package agreements in the 1980s and early 1990s added to the lustre of German Chancellor Helmut Kohl, French President François Mitterrand, and British Prime Minister Margaret Thatcher, all of whom cultivated an image of toughness combined with tactical adroitness in knowing when to make concessions while retaining the principal advantage. Such image management at the EU level undoubtedly contributed to the remarkable longevity in office of all three of these national leaders.

In 10 of the 15 member states, the domestic political regime is a parliamentary system (see Table 1.1). In such a system the head of government and the ministers (department heads) chosen by the head are responsible to a majority in the legislative body, or Parliament. If they lose a vote of confidence in Parliament, it means that they no longer have the support of a majority, and they must resign in order to allow the Parliament to choose a new government. In some parliamentary systems, as in the case of Britain, they may instead call new elections to try to get the support of the electorate for a new Parliament with a favorable majority. Britain is usually cited as the classical example of a parliamentary system.

British voters choose between candidates of political parties in *single-member districts*. The winner of the most votes (a *plurality*) in each district

TABLE 1.1 Systems of government of European Union member countries

Member Country	Year Joining Union	System of Government
Austria	1995	Premier-weak president
Belgium	1958	Parliamentary (coalition govt.)
Denmark	1973	Parliamentary (coalition govt.)
Finland	1995	Premier-weak president
France	1958	Premier-strong president
Germany	1958	Parliamentary (coalition govt.)
Greece	1981	Parliamentary (majority party)
Ireland	1973	Premier-weak president
Italy	1958	Parliamentary (coalition govt.)
Luxembourg	1958	Parliamentary (coalition govt.)
Netherlands	1958	Parliamentary (coalition govt.)
Portugal	1986	Premier-formally weak president
Spain	1986	Parliamentary (minority govt.)
Sweden	1995	Parliamentary (minority or coalition)
United Kingdom	1973	Parliamentary (majority govt.)

SOURCE: Wayne C. Thompson with Mark H. Mullin, *Western Europe 1993,* The World Today Series (Washington: Stryker-Post Publications, 1993).

gains a seat in the House of Commons. The leader of the party that gains a majority of House of Commons seats in the election becomes the prime minister. He or she then chooses a cabinet of fellow parliamentary party leaders to govern the country with the support of the House of Commons majority. The party that wins the election stays in power until defeated in a subsequent election, or (a rare case in Britain) in the event of a loss of a vote of confidence in the House of Commons. Because the two main parties in Britain win most of the parliamentary seats in each election, one of them almost always has a clear-cut majority of seats, which, because of disciplined voting by party members in Parliament, means the party can stay in power for 5 years, or until any time beforehand when the prime minister judges that it would be to the ruling party's advantage to hold new elections.

With some specific differences, the ten EU members that have pure parliamentary systems operate under similar rules. The main distinguishing feature of the British system is that one or the other of its two main parties, Labour or Conservative, is strong enough to win a majority in its own right. In this they are helped by the single-member district plurality electoral system, which encourages voters not to waste their votes on smaller parties, but instead to vote for the candidates of parties with a chance of winning a majority of seats enabling them to form a government. British voters know that the parties that do not get a majority of the seats in Parliament will be on the outside looking in as far as policy making is concerned. Occasionally a minority government is formed in Britain when no party has a majority but the largest party can govern, at least for a short time, with the support of votes from one or more of the smaller parties, such as the Liberal Democrats, who have a handful of seats in Parliament. In other European parliamentary systems, coalition governments are usually formed because it is rare for one party to have a majority. In all of the parliamentary EU countries other than Britain, the electoral system is one or another variant of *proportional representation*, which gives parties a share of seats in Parliament roughly proportional to their shares of the popular vote. Such electoral systems do not penalize voters for voting for smaller parties, unless there are thresholds to keep out the very small parties, such as the 5 percent barrier in Germany.

Britain is one of a minority of member countries in which issues relating to the EU have been sufficiently divisive that they can affect the contests that go on between and within the political parties. In chapters 3–6 we discuss some of the British debates over Europe that have occurred over the past 40 years. From the mid-1950s to the mid-1970s, the fights were over the question of whether Britain should join or (later) stay in the EC. Since the late 1980s, European issues have again arisen, centered on the main elements of the Maastricht treaty: EMU and Political Union. Many Conservatives prefer that the EU remain essentially an intergovernmental union, and they oppose any further extension of EU powers. EMU implies a substantial transfer of economic policy-making capability from the member states to supranational institutions, especially to a new European monetary authority, the future *Eurofed.*

Conservative Prime Minister Margaret Thatcher was adamantly opposed to EMU because it meant to her the abandonment of the British government's capacity to control the domestic economy. The issue helped lead to her fall from power in November 1990, as many members of her own party in Parliament felt that she had become too unyielding on EMU. John Major, her successor as prime minister, agreed to the Maastricht treaty in December 1991, while reserving the right for Britain to opt out of the third stage of EMU's development, when Eurofed and a common currency are supposed to come into being. But there is a segment of Major's Conservative Party in Parliament that is loyal to Thatcher's Euro-scepticism and watches over Major's shoulders, opposing almost every concession he makes to his fellow EU heads of government. Major has lost several House of Commons votes on EU issues since the 1992 election, which reduced the Conservative majority to 21 seats. These were not votes of confidence, so the prime minister was not forced to resign or call new elections. Although British elections must take place at least every 5 years, midway through its term the Parliament elected in 1992 appeared to be nearing the brink of dissolution. Dissolution would mean new elections, and it could still happen if a handful of Major's Conservative colleagues should join the opposition parties in voting against the prime minister on a motion of confidence relating to his European policy. If so, it would be the first time in more than a century that a British prime minister has been defeated on a motion of confidence as a result of the defection of members of his own party. Thus, the intrusion of EU politics into British politics has seriously disrupted the traditional cohesion of a major

British political party, and the political stability of the EU's most stable member has been called into question (see chapters 5 and 6).

By contrast, in another parliamentary member country, Germany, EU politics does not produce serious domestic political divisions. Unlike Britain, Germany has more than two political parties with a reasonable chance of sharing governmental power. Also, unlike Britain, it is very rare for one party to have a majority of seats in the Bundestag (Federal Diet), which is the popularly elected house of the German Parliament, comparable to the House of Commons. The German electoral system operates essentially according to proportional representation rules in translating votes into seats. There are two larger parties, the Christian Democrats (CDU/CSU) on the right, and the Social Democrats (SPD) on the left. Between them is the smaller Free Democratic party (FDP), which has usually held the balance of power between the two larger parties, joining with one or the other of them to give the governing coalition a majority of seats in the Bundestag. As a result of the October 1994 Bundestag election, two other parties of the left, the Greens and the ex-Communist Party of Democratic Socialism (PDS), have seats as well. The governing coalition of Chancellor Kohl's CDU/CSU and their junior partner, the FDP, has a very slim majority as a result of the loss of 57 of the 398 seats they had held after the December 1990 election. But despite the precarious majority, the Kohl government seems unlikely to be defeated on an EU-related issue, because the German political parties are not torn apart on questions of the structure and powers of the EU, as is the Conservative Party in Britain.

German elites and public opinion have for many years been consensual with respect to Germany's role in Europe. German unification (October 3, 1990), which has raised issues between the parties especially on domestic economic policy, has strengthened the resolve of the government and the leading opposition party to maintain solid ties to Western Europe through the EU. Chancellor Kohl has sought to play a leadership role since unification in pushing for a more supranational Europe both in the negotiations over the Maastricht treaty and in those that have involved its implementation. In this, he appears to have enjoyed considerable support among German elites and the public alike (but see chapter 6).

Among the other member countries with parliamentary systems, Denmark and Sweden have shown greater interparty and public disagreement over the question of EU powers than have any of the countries further south, with the possible exception of Greece. As in Britain, the Maastricht treaty proved particularly divisive in Denmark, where the voters failed to ratify the treaty in a 1992 referendum. But a year later, when the Social Democrats who had opposed Danish ratification in 1992 were back in power, the new government supported ratification, the voters were consulted again, and the treaty was ratified. In Sweden in 1994 it was uncertain whether voters would ratify Swedish accession to membership, but, as in Denmark, when the Social Democrats returned to power shortly before the referendum, they supported Swedish entry, and their voters provided the necessary votes for ratification. In these cases, domestic politics appear to be supreme over European politics, in that European issues become chips that are played in the domestic political poker game. In the remaining parliamentary countries—Italy, Luxembourg, Spain, the Netherlands, and Belgium—support for the Maastricht treaty and for the EU generally has been widespread enough that, as in Germany, it is unlikely that the life or death of governments will be decided on EU issues.

The remaining five EU member countries—France, Finland, Ireland, Portugal, and Austria—do not have pure parliamentary systems of government. Nor are they presidential systems like the United States. They have mixed features, elements of both presidential and parliamentary systems, or what Matthew Shugart and John Carey have called "premier-presidential" systems.[5] All of them have directly elected presidents, like the U.S. president, and also premiers, that is, prime ministers, who, like the British prime minister, rest on the support of majorities in directly elected legislative bodies. In the four smaller premier-presidential countries the president plays a relatively passive role, allowing executive authority to be wielded by the prime minister and cabinet. At times of political deadlock the president is available to step in and resolve conflicts, but parties in Austria, Finland, Ireland and Portugal prefer to work out their differences within Parliament rather than to let the president play a stronger role. Thus far in these four countries, EU issues have not been sufficiently divisive to require presidential intervention in the normal political process.

The situation is different in France. One of the original EC members, France has had the mixed premier-presidential form since the formation of the Fifth Republic in 1958. The first president of the Fifth Republic, General Charles de Gaulle (1958–1969), played a strong role in ending the Algerian War that had brought on the fall of the Fourth Republic; and he also took upon himself as president the formulation of French foreign policy, including its policy as a member of the original EEC. He determined who would be his prime minister, a practice followed by his successors until the mid-1980s. This meant that the president was ultimately in control over domestic as well as foreign policy. If he allowed his premier to make decisions, they had to be decisions that followed the president's general policy lines. When conflicts occurred between president and prime minister the latter would have to yield or be replaced by someone more compliant with the president's wishes.

President de Gaulle was, like Margaret Thatcher 20 years later, a Euro-sceptic. As will be discussed in chapter 3, he wanted France to control the development of the EC, or else he would not cooperate with the other member governments. He approved of the economic benefits France gained from membership, but he did not want the EC to infringe upon French sovereignty in more politically sensitive areas. After de Gaulle left office in 1969, his successors gradually became more cooperative with EC partners, while continuing to exercise leadership, usually in tandem with Germany. By the mid-1980s Europe had virtually ceased to be a major issue among French politicians. Public opinion polls showed that the initially sceptical French populace had become comfortable with France's role in the Community.

But an inherent contradiction within the premier-presidential system surfaced in 1986. Prior to the parliamentary elections in March of that year, the Socialist party (PS) of President François Mitterrand, the leading left-of-center party, had a solid majority in the National Assembly, the popularly elected lower house of Parliament. The election proved to be a serious setback for Mitterrand's Socialists. The two principal opposition right-of-center parties, the Union for French Democracy (UDF) and the Rally for the Republic (RPR), gained a bare majority of seats, enough to make it impossible for Mitterrand to appoint whom he wished as prime minister. He was forced to choose the leader of the neo-Gaullist RPR, Jacques Chirac, who then formed his own right-of-center government. Mitterrand and Chirac therefore found themselves locked in what was quickly termed *cohabitation,* meaning that a president of the left and a prime minister of the right were required to live together. This happened because the president is elected for a 7-year term, but the Parliament's term is only five years, so the elections do not coincide. In addition the Fifth Republic Constitution contains the normal parliamentary system feature that enables a majority of the Assembly to vote the prime minister out of office. For the president to name one of his own supporters as prime minister would be to invite repudiation of his choice by the Assembly. But cohabitation was short-lived. Two years later, in 1988, Mitterrand's term came to an end, and he was reelected. He then dissolved the National Assembly, bringing about new parliamentary elections. The PS did not quite win a majority, but it was close enough that a minority government was formed, headed by Socialist Michel Rocard. This election gave the Socialists 5 more years in power, holding both the presidency and the prime ministership. But in 1993 it was time for legislative elections again, and this time the parties of the right overwhelmingly defeated the Socialists, and Mitterrand again had to choose a Gaullist to be prime minister, this time Edouard Balladur, a close associate of Chirac. (The latter had decided this time not to seek the prime ministership). Thus, France entered upon another 2-year period of cohabitation, which ended with the presidential election of 1995. The election of Jacques Chirac to the presidency meant that both the president and the majority of the Assembly (elected in 1993) were of the right.

During cohabitation periods, the consensus across left and right over European policy matters has prevented deadlocks between president and prime minister from occurring on such matters. Both attended meetings of the European Council, but President Mitterrand was recognized by the other leaders around the table as the legitimate spokesman for France. Within France there are dissenting Euro-sceptic voices on both the left and right that challenge Euro-consensus. The possibility exists that one of the three major parties will take up the resistance to a further transfer of French sovereignty to the EU. Polarization over Europe might then be encouraged by the electoral process. In both the presidential and parliamentary elections, a *two-ballot majority* electoral system is used. If no candidate—for president or for a parliamentary seat—wins a majority of votes on the first ballot, a second ballot is held, with lower vote-getters eliminated, to determine the winner.[6] On the second ballot both elections usually work out to be contests between left and right, with the weaker candidates on both sides dropping out after the first ballot and urging their voters to vote for the stronger candidate on their side of the spectrum. Under these conditions, if one of the main parties with a chance of gaining the presidency or a parliamentary majority were to desert the pro-European consensus among French political elites, it could mean that the inherent left-right polarities in French politics might reassert themselves after years of party depolarization. While EU politics has had the effect in Britain of dividing the governing party, but not the entire party system, in French politics they could become the main battleground between left and right, returning French political conflict to an intensity and bitterness that has not been experienced since the Fifth Republic survived the first cohabitation.

In 1992 President Mitterrand unnecessarily and, in retrospect, unwisely put the question of French ratification of the Maastricht treaty to the voters in a referendum. The treaty was ratified by a margin of less than 2 percent. The narrowness of the victory was a serious blow to the idea that the French are in broad agreement with the EU and its goals. Whether the less than overwhelming support for the treaty was a reflection of their true feelings about the EU or was a way of expressing the low esteem with which they held Mitterrand and his Socialists at the time, the message was sent that the political elites should not take the voters for granted when it comes to European questions. In late 1994, Jacques Delors, the president of the European Commission, and a former Socialist finance minister under Mitterrand, was leading the public opinion polls as a potential candidate to succeed Mitterrand in the April–May 1995 presidential election. His closest competitor was Prime Minister Balladur, followed by former Prime Minister Chirac. Balladur and Chirac, once close associates, were now rivals for the support of the Gaullist party for their presidential candidacies. In the early stages of the contest, recognizing that Delors would be the favored choice of French Euro-enthusiasts, both Balladur and Chirac were beginning to make public statements suggesting that France might oppose further steps in the direction of a "federal Europe." For both of them this appeared to be a change of emphasis from pro-EU positions they had been taking since the 1980s. In early December, Jacques Delors publicly announced that he would not be a candidate. Although age was undoubtedly a factor in his decision, it is also possible that Delors recognized that without his presence in the race it would be less likely that the campaign in 1995 would be polarized along pro-EU and anti-EU lines, which would be damaging to the constructive role of leadership France plays in the EU. Nevertheless, it was clear that Europe was once again playing a major role in French politics as it had in de Gaulle's time (see chapter 6).

This brief discussion of the political institutions of the EU and its leading member states has been designed to demonstrate that the politics of the EU goes on simultaneously at two levels, with what happens at each level having an important effect on what happens at the other. Contrary to the formal definition of a federal system, the transfer of powers from the national level to the institutions of the EU has not meant that the national governments have ceased to be involved in deciding how they will be used. In other terms, the question of whether certain tasks will remain in the hands of governments or become part of the domain of EU competence is not a zero-sum contest. The national governments continue to be involved in decisions as to how the powers will be used, and power and influence flows in both directions between the governments and the EU.[7]

In chapter 2 we review the leading theories of European integration, presenting them in their historical context. Chapters 3-5 provide a historical overview of the development of the EU from its origins in the Schuman Plan of 1950 until the ratification of the Maastricht treaty (TEU) in 1992-1993. Chapter 3 outlines the growing political coordination among the member states in the 25-year period up to the mid-1970s, when the European Council was established, a development which, we argue, represented a turning point in the process of political integration. Chapter 4 focuses on the steps toward growing economic and political integration within the EC later in the 1970s and during the 1980s. Chapter 5 traces the steps leading to the agreement at Maastricht in December 1991 on the TEU, as well as the struggle to ratify the treaty in 1992-1993 and the aftermath of that struggle.

Chapter 6 outlines the roles played by the principal agenda-setting and decision-making institutions of the EU: the European Council, the Council of Ministers, the Commission, the EP, and the ECJ. It also considers the extent to which a public EU agenda is taking shape. In this light, the June 1994 EP elections are reviewed, as are recent developments involving the EU and the domestic politics of the leading member states.

Chapters 7-11 look at policy areas in which the EU either has taken over functions previously belonging to the member governments or has served as a forum for efforts to coordinate policies remaining primarily in members' hands. In chapter 7 we examine the developing macrolevel economic policy coordination that has taken place in the European Monetary System (EMS), with its Exchange Rate Mechanism (ERM) that controls monetary fluctuations among member country currencies, and that is being strengthened under the EMU outlined in the Maastricht treaty and scheduled to be completed by the end of the 1990s.

In chapters 8 and 9 we pay attention to important EU internal policies that are necessitated by problems created or made worse by poor economic performance: the CAP in chapter 8; and regional policy, social policy, industrial policy, and environmental policy in chapter 9.

Chapter 10 examines external economic policies of the EU, and chapter 11 discusses foreign and security policy. Under the Maastricht treaty, foreign and defense policies constitute the second pillar of the EU. This pillar is separate from the "EC pillar," or what might be considered the domestic policy of the EU, and does not as yet fully involve some of its members. The steps taken in the Maastricht treaty may produce better planning and more systematic approaches to crises such as those in the Persian Gulf and the Balkans, but foreign and defense policy will remain more squarely within an intergovernmental framework than will economic policy coordination. Finally, the third pillar, internal security policy, is outlined at the end of chapter 11. We present our overall conclusions in chapter 12.

ENDNOTES

1. Whereas the president of the United States is both head of state (the ceremonial leader) and head of government (the chief executive), in most Western European countries there is either an hereditary head of state, like the queen of England, or an elected head (like the German president of the Federal Republic), usually with ceremonial functions and few, if any, powers that can be independently exercised. In such cases the head of government is the effective executive leader, such as the British prime minister and the German chancellor. But see the case of France, discussed later in this chapter.
2. The 15 countries rotate in the alphabetical order of their names according to their native languages. Thus Deutschland (Germany) precedes France.
3. Emil Joseph Kirchner, *Decision-making in the European Community: The Council Presidency and European Integration* (Manchester, England, and New York: Manchester University Press, 1992).
4. Fritz W. Scharpf, "The Joint-Decision Trap: Lessons from German Federalism and European Integration," *Public Administration* 66 (Autumn 1988): 268.
5. Matthew Soberg Shugart and John M. Carey, *Presidents and Assemblies: Constitutional Design and Electoral Dynamics* (Cambridge: Cambridge University Press, 1992), p. 41.
6. For National Assembly elections, if a candidate for an Assembly seat receives a majority (50 percent + 1) of the votes on the first ballot, he or she is declared elected. If there is no first ballot winner, a second ballot is held a week later, and all candidates receiving at least 12.5 percent of the registered votes in the district are eligible to remain in the contest. However, the weaker candidates will usually withdraw in order not to divide the vote on their side of the left-right spectrum, so in most districts only two candidates remain on the second ballot. In the presidential election, again, if a candidate gains a majority of votes on the first ballot, he or she is declared elected. However, if no one wins a majority, then the second ballot, 2 weeks later, is an automatic run-off between the two candidates who receive the most votes on the first ballot. All others are eliminated.
7. Kirchner, *Decision-making in the European Community,* chap. 1.

chapter **2**

The Theory and Practice
of Regional Integration

This chapter reviews the major *theories of regional integration* that have been formulated during the half-century since European integration became more than just a glint in the eyes of a few European visionaries. The student should be given two warnings before we embark on this journey. First, theories of international integration, like all political theories, are produced in order better to understand ongoing political events and to solve distressing political problems that preoccupy political leaders at the same time they are preoccupying the theorists. Thus, they follow the times, and they compete with one another to set the trend. Those theories that receive the most attention are "fashionable" theories; they are not necessarily the ones that will continue to provide inspiration for political thinkers a half-century, or even a decade, later. In this chapter we review several theories with varying degrees of staying power, and we conclude that none of them is sufficient to understand fully where the EU is today, or to explain how it got that way. But we do draw upon those theories that are general enough and strong enough so that each will provide part of the full explanation.

Second, political theorists attempt to do three things: to explain, to predict, and to prescribe. All the theories we discuss in this chapter have done a better job explaining what has happened than predicting what will happen. If they had been better at predicting, they might have stayed in fashion longer. As for prescribing, it is safe to say that they all are directed toward outcomes that are the same as those they predict. For example, if the theorist wants to see a European federal state created, then the theory will be constructed to show how that outcome will be achieved, both by highlighting recent trends that have already moved Europe in the right direction and by showing how a continuation of those trends will lead to the predicted outcome. In this chapter we concentrate on the explanatory and predictive elements of most of the theories, but we do touch on the prescribed outcomes as well. We also compare theory with practice over time.

REALISM AND IDEALISM

Why would nation-states like France or Germany give up any of their sovereign powers to a regional collectivity? To do so would be to do away with flexibility in dealing with unforeseen problems and to make the nation-state vulnerable to decisions and actions by the collectivity that are not in the best interests of that nation-state or its citizens. Many students of international relations insist that the governments of nation-states ordinarily will act rationally in the decisions they take on behalf of their citizens. They will carefully weigh the likely consequences of these decisions in terms of the goals they have adopted for the benefit of the societies they govern. Governments of nation-states are not, from this perspective, expected to do things that run counter to the national interest. The founder of the postwar realist school of international relations, Hans Morgenthau, defined the national interest that governments must protect in terms of the nation-state's power to achieve its objectives. Nation-states, according to Morgenthau, are the most powerful actors on the international scene. They are constantly attempting to maintain and enhance their power relative to one another.[1]

How do we know that nation-states act rationally? Because they seek to maintain and enhance their power, the realists answer. But how do we know that states will always act this way? What if they make mistakes, or their leaders get swept up in some irrational sentiment, like the urge to help others (altruism) or the quest for something like the Holy Grail (idealism)? The answer tends to be that governments do not do such things, and that, even though some of their actions may look a bit peculiar, their leaders have calculated that they are in the nation's best interest, that is, they will enhance the power of the nation-state. Thus, Marshall Plan aid after World War II may have looked to some Americans like incredible generosity emanating from Washington, with the flow of benefits going entirely in the direction of Europe. But realists insist that the United States obtained political benefits far in excess of the economic costs, and that, in fact, within a decade, the economic benefits to the United States were outweighing the original economic costs as well. The result was that, as U.S. leaders had anticipated, the United States gained in its capacity to exercise political and economic hegemony throughout the post-World War II era.[2]

Another school of international relations, once labeled the *idealist* school, and now *liberal internationalism,* acknowledges that nation-states sometimes seek to protect or expand their relative power positions. But it sees this tendency as what leads nation-states to commit acts of aggression and to attempt to strengthen themselves in ways that are likely to provoke countermeasures on the part of other nation-states. This school both hopes and predicts that nation-states will give up such precivilized habits and learn to live with one another peaceably without arming to the teeth. In countering the realists, it argues that there is a higher rationality than the egoistic quest for power, and that nation-states can improve the welfare of their citizens more certainly by burying their short-term differences and reaching accords with one another designed to promote their mutual well-being over the longer run. They ask if it is rational for states to distort the economic division of labor within their societies by building up stores of arms and conscripting young citizens out of the domestic work force. Such policies, they insist, will increase the likelihood that much of the economy and population will be destroyed or left in a weakened position because the mobilization for purposes of defense has led eventually to war. Further, war will disrupt international trade, adversely affecting the economies of many countries. Finally, they believe that institutions of national governments and international organizations can be improved through democratization and the spread of the rule of law, in such a way that the temptation to go to war will be held in check.[3]

Europeans, more than Americans, experienced the destruction and depriva-tion (including the postwar deprivation) of world war. Europeans perceived the danger of Soviet expansion, but as individual states they lacked the capacity to build up their power to meet the threat. Particularly, their economies were in such shambles that the immediate task was to rebuild a peacetime economy, without which an eventual military buildup, if necessary, could not occur. In the meantime, they relied on the United States for military protection and for a jump-start on the way to economic reconstruction and modernization.

There was general recognition in Europe that, in the dangerous circum-stances of the late 1940s, states could not simply abandon the effort to protect themselves. But it was also recognized that they could not each do so apart from the others. Their common tragic experience in the 1930s and early 1940s also suggested to them that World War II itself might have been prevented had there been close coordination between the other European states in defiance of Adolf Hitler's aggressive designs. European idealists and realists in this early postwar period both saw the need to create regional international organizations designed to cope with common problems, especially economic problems, that were getting in the way of each state's desire to improve its own security. Two plans that were gaining support in the late 1940s were *federalism* and *functionalism*. The former attracted the support of nongovernmental organizations and move-ments led by prominent public figures; the latter was pursued more quietly by governmental officials.

FEDERALISM, FUNCTIONALISM, AND "MONNETISM"

Federalists believed that the vulnerable states of postwar Western Europe must join together in a political union in which they would exercise mutual self-help in the face of threats to their common security. By forming a federation of once sovereign states, they could pool their individual capacities to organize their defenses, mobilize their resources and industrial strengths, and guide their economies in the direction of modernization and economic growth. The basic motivation would be political. The purpose of federation would be to concentrate the power of the federating states in a central authority. The authority would be given control over certain economic levers, in order better to accomplish its overriding objective of providing for the collective security of the member states. The states would retain control over those aspects of their domestic affairs that were not seen to be vital for the common effort. But the pooling of sovereignty in the "federal government" would be substantial, and once having given up this sovereignty, each state would be bound to abide by common decisions.[4] As idealists, they believed that political leaders would simultaneously recognize that wars could only be prevented if nations pooled their military resources in a political union dedicated to resolving conflicts among them peaceably.

The closest the states of Western Europe came in the postwar period to attaining such a political union was in the agreements reached by France, West Germany, Italy, Belgium, the Netherlands, and Luxembourg (the original six of the eventual EU) in the early 1950s to establish a European Defense Community (EDC) and a European political community. EDC would bring the armed forces of the six countries under a single multinational commissariat and command structure. The political community would provide institutions for democratic political control over the multinational defense structure.[5] But these plans fell by the wayside in 1954 when the EDC was buried by a vote in the French Parliament. Further concrete steps toward European integration did not follow the federalist blueprint.

In contrast to the federalists, the functionalist school did not outline plans for an elaborate division of political responsibilities between different levels of authority. In a very pragmatic sense, they concentrated on the immediate economic needs facing the survivors of World War II. Functionalists could be found in the British Labour government of 1945–1951.[6] The principal writings on the subject by the intellectual founder of the school, David Mitrany, were produced during the war and immediately afterwards.[7] He was not interested in functional integration of European nations per se, but in the creation of international organizations to fulfill certain specific needs, including whatever set of member states might be willing to join together for very limited purposes. These might include organizing relief efforts for war refugees, regulation of air traffic, formulation and enforcement of international health and safety standards, or promotion of more efficient agricultural methods. Should several such organizations come into being for different purposes, they would comprise different sets of member states, usually including members from different continents and subregions around the globe. They would not all involve a given set of members found in a particular region. That is, they would not gradually become a collective, statelike territorial entity in their own right. Mitrany rejected federalism on the grounds that it would replace the old states with a new, larger one, without necessarily reducing human misery.[8]

Yet Mitrany is generally regarded as the forerunner of an activist movement that theorized about European functional integration and also went on to achieve the first real success in that direction: the European Coal and Steel Community (ECSC). This community was the brainchild of a Frenchman, Jean Monnet, whose career with the League of Nations before World War II, as a liaison figure between France, Britain, and the United States during the war, and as head of the French economic planning commission after the war, had always concentrated on finding very practical solutions to immediate problems, usually problems of an economic nature. Like Mitrany, Monnet believed that, when faced with their own inability to solve problems that could only be solved by international cooperation, states would, although reluctantly, pool limited elements of their sovereignty with one another in international organizations.

Monnetism was more optimistic than Mitrany's pure functionalism. When confronted with nation-state stubbornness, Monnet believed that government leaders could be persuaded to move from a narrow, short-run definition of the national interest to one that acknowledged the long-run benefits to be derived from joining forces with others. And Monnet was a very persuasive individual. Throughout his career he accumulated a rich network of contacts with important people in many countries whom he had found to share elements of his ideas and had convinced to share his goals and support his methods of attaining them.[9] Many of these contacts showed up in positions of governmental authority in Western Europe in the 1950s, and he drew them together into his Action Committee for a United States of Europe. The group was to be successful in mobilizing elite support in Western Europe for the creation of the EEC, the forerunner of today's EU.[10] In the final analysis, Monnet was committed to a regionally specific set of nation-states joining together in what would eventually become a European federation. But his method of attaining it was indirect. Federalism was essentially a political goal for Monnet, ultimately involving a common foreign and security policy, or what is sometimes called *high politics*.[11] But Monnet preferred to begin by attaining consensus among a limited number of states to cooperate in *low politics* policies for economic cooperation and trade.

The concrete problem with which Monnet began was that of overproduction in the European coal and steel industries and the necessity for production to be publicly regulated to avoid the likelihood of a severe depression in these sectors, which would drive producers out of business and threaten the security of the region by diminishing reserve productive capacity. If governments of the producing countries could pool their regulative capacities with respect to these specific industrial sectors into a coal and steel community (limited in scope but strategically crucial), market failure could be avoided. Monnet's plan was officially proposed in 1950 by French Foreign Minister Robert Schuman, and it was popularly given the name of its public initiator: the *Schuman Plan.* The governments of the "European six"—France, West Germany, Italy, Belgium, the Netherlands, and Luxembourg—agreed to form the ECSC with surprising rapidity, and it came into being less than 2 years later. The six invited Britain to join, but the Labour government was suspicious of what looked like longer-run federalist objectives, and Britain stayed out.[12]

Monnet soon linked this single-purpose organization to the goal of an eventual multi-purpose organization of the same members, when he and his associates took the abortive steps to achieve a defense community and a political community.[13] While Monnet envisioned a United States of Europe along federal lines in the future, after the defeat of the EDC in 1954, his practical orientation enabled him to refocus attention upon more immediately achievable goals.

In essence, governmental leaders of Monnetist persuasion formulated a new agenda for the European six in the mid-1950s, which resulted in the creation in 1958 of two new communities: EURATOM and EEC. The first of these achieved only modest results, because of the unwillingness in the final analysis of governments, especially the French, to pool their sovereignty regarding what was considered a vital element of national interest, atomic energy. In contrast, the second, popularly though erroneously called the *Common Market,* achieved remarkable success as a *customs union*[14] in pursuit of its practical economic goals during the first decade of its life. Yet its chances of achieving a political union among the six member states appeared, by the end of that decade, to be at best problematic (see chapter 3 for a fuller discussion of these developments).

THE RISE AND DECLINE OF NEOFUNCTIONALISM

The attainment of economic goals through political means lies at the heart of the scholarly revision of functionalism that came to be called *neofunctionalism.* Its founder was Ernst B. Haas, an American political scientist who had witnessed at first hand the mid-1950s emergence of a new European agenda. Haas was sufficiently impressed by Monnet's strategy and tactics to put them into a theoretical framework that was more elaborate and academic in nature.[15] Haas argued that functional integration would most likely occur if influential and powerful elites were motivated to take decisive steps toward it. These must include governmental and political party leaders, but the politicians could not be expected to take action unless there were pressure exerted from opinion leaders and from the leaders of interest groups, especially those in the economic sector, especially business, labor, and agricultural leaders. He was more skeptical about the potential impact of movements such as the European federalists. He did not disagree with their goal, at least as an ideal, but he felt that mass opinion was likely to be too passive to be moved directly by groups promoting idealistic causes, and political elites were too hardheaded to risk their careers by single-mindedly supporting objectives that were not high on national agendas.[16]

Haas's first major work, *The Uniting of Europe* (1958), was an examination of the experience of the ECSC. Jean Monnet had not only been the originator of the Schuman Plan idea, but had been the first president of the ECSC's High Authority, the executive body to which the six member states had given substantial regulatory powers. Owing to the defense mobilization in which the member states participated in the face of the Korean War (1950–1953), the ECSC began its life when the European economies were on the upswing and the demand for coal and steel was high. By the late 1950s demand for coal had tapered off because of the cheaper energy available in the form of oil, primarily from the Middle East. But in the mid-1950s what was noteworthy was that better access to raw materials, energy, and steel, which the ECSC had fostered, had contributed to rapid economic growth in the six countries, more rapid than that in Britain, which had stayed out of the organization.

In his study of the ECSC, Haas introduced a number of neofunctionalist concepts that he intended as aids in an explanation of the regional integration steps that had already occurred, as well as any further steps that might occur. Two central elements of his neofunctionalist theory are the concepts of *spillover* and *supranationalism*.[17] By spillover Haas meant that, if the tasks of a regional organization were to expand, it would occur as a result of experiences with the tasks the organization was already performing. The ECSC had positive achievements that invited emulation in other spheres; it also had some unintended consequences that had to be addressed. Hence, the EEC came on its heels as an attempt both to produce the same advantages in other sectors and to deal with some of the ECSC's side effects. The motivating forces for integration could be found essentially within the organization itself and its members, in Haas's view.

But Haas emphasized that there was nothing automatic in spillover. Task expansion by the regional organization would require political initiative. What we now call *cross-national networks* were becoming thicker, in terms of frequency and multiplicity of contacts. This process of communication made it possible for elites to address common problems in concrete terms and to discover an "upgraded common interest." The communications net corresponded to neither a federal nor a confederal framework; instead it was *supranational*.[18] Although the principal actors were nationally based, they came together predisposed to find common solutions to their mutual problems, and their method of arriving at decisions was by unanimous consent, avoiding votes, vetoes, and subsequent expressions of antagonism. The bias, Haas found, was in favor of reaching agreements.[19] This was the spirit in which Monnet had operated.

It was also the spirit that guided Walter Hallstein, the West German politician and administrator who became the first president of the EEC commission. Under Hallstein's leadership, the EEC developed a method of decision making that refused to acknowledge the absence of consensus. In the early 1960s, midnight deadlines were imposed upon meetings of the Council of Ministers, and the clock was stopped at a minute before, with the meetings continuing on into the next day or days until agreement could be reached.[20]

With the publication of his later study of the International Labor Organization,[21] Haas gave greater attention to the importance of leadership as a part of his conception of supranationalism. The executive leaders of international organizations can play an important role in "upgrading the common interest" if they use their skills (1) to define an *organizational ideology,* (2) to build a bureaucracy committed to that ideology, and (3) to build coalitions of national actors supporting the leadership and its ideology.[22] Haas saw these attributes as necessary for the organization to be able to expand its functions. Without it, the organization's method of decision making would not be supranational, because an essential element would be lacking for bringing member states together to upgrade the common interest.

In 1965, EEC President Hallstein attempted to force spillover from the economic to the political realm by presenting to the Council of Ministers a plan that would provide for a greater transfer of revenues from the national governments to the EEC, enabling a strengthening of the organization's economic impact. President Charles de Gaulle of France objected to Hallstein's plan and pulled his ministers out of the Council of Ministers for what turned out to be a period of 6 months, from July 1965 to January 1966. Ultimately Hallstein and the governments of the other five countries had to withdraw the budget expansion proposal and concede to France informally, that, counter to the spirit of supranationalism, when a member government considered the vital interests of its country to be at odds with a given proposal to be voted on in the Council, it could insist on the unanimity rule and thereby exercise a veto.[23]

This so-called Luxembourg compromise of February 1966 was not followed by very many actual exercises of the veto, because the practice of deciding by consensus without a vote continued. However, the earlier supranational assumption that consensus would be reached and action would be taken whenever the Council met to decide an issue began to wither away with this French-imposed "empty chair crisis." Although further items on the original Rome treaty agenda were adopted and implemented later in the 1960s, spillover was no longer taking place; that is, new agenda items were not being taken on board in response to the effects of policies already adopted. Efforts continued to be made to move from the concrete commitments of the Rome treaty to more ambitious and far-reaching objectives such as EMU, but the Council of Ministers never got down to the bargaining stage on such projects, because governments were reluctant to make further concessions of sovereignty.

By the early 1970s, neofunctionalists were no longer as optimistic as they had been a decade earlier. Leon Lindberg and Stuart Scheingold conceded that the nation-state had reoccupied the political high ground, and that the regional integration progress that had been made in the 1950s and 1960s had been confined to decidedly low politics realms of economics, especially trade policy and agricultural policy.[24] By the mid-1970s, Ernst Haas observed that "global turbulence" was destroying the coherence of the EC and other regional economic organizations.[25] Supranationalism appeared to have come to an end, or at least to be on hold.[26]

A PAINFUL LEARNING EXPERIENCE

Global Economic Interdependence

As chapters 3 and 4 will show in greater depth, the 1970s were difficult years for regional integration in Europe. Important economic changes were taking place that were to be better understood in the following decade. Advanced industrial countries in the 1970s experienced a slowing down of economic growth, which had been unusually rapid for most of them in the preceding 20 years. Along with slower growth came greater monetary instability, as the U.S. dollar ceased to be a reliable anchor for other currencies, which gained substantially in value relative to the dollar during the 1970s, requiring adjustments in the world monetary order. EC economies suffered the same problems as others, but EC growth was more sluggish than that of Japan and other East Asian economies that were coming to compete with the EC in product areas wherein the Europeans had held comparative advantages before the 1970s. On its own, each member country was finding it more difficult to control unemployment, inflation, adverse trade balances, and monetary instability. Following the oil crisis of 1973–1974, international shocks were hitting domestic economies in all these ways simultaneously.

National economies had, by the 1970s, become highly interdependent. Steps such as erecting trade barriers or devaluing one's currency, if taken unilaterally to adjust to adverse economic developments, could have bad economic consequences for other countries, especially those with whom one had extensive trade links. Such actions taken in the middle and late 1970s by individual EC countries tended to drive the members apart and make it impossible to achieve conjoint action to alleviate the impact of global economic changes on the EC as a whole. Even when common measures were sought, the tendency was often to seek them in larger arenas, or regimes,[27] in the belief that unless the United States and, increasingly, Japan could be brought into the cooperative venture, the problems could not be resolved. Although this may indeed have been true, without joint EC efforts to bring about greater economic cooperation among themselves, the members were vulnerable to strategies of divide and rule. This was particularly the case of the international monetary regime, in which some EC currencies participated in a joint float (the *snake*) vis-a-vis the dollar, while others floated separately against both the dollar *and* the joint EC float; and of the energy regime, wherein some EC members cooperated with the U.S.-led effort to reduce the impact of the Organization of Petroleum Exporting Countries (OPEC) cartel, while an overlapping set sought separate arrangements with OPEC to minimize its impact upon their own economies, irrespective of the consequences for partner countries. In each of these examples, some EC countries were at loggerheads with others, accusing each other of pursuing "beggar thy neighbor" strategies.

Intergovernmentalism in the 1970s and 1980s

Supranationalism in neofunctionalist terms had rested heavily on the notion of mutual recognition by national governments of the economic bases of their political self-interest. But the early successes had come at a time of rapid economic growth in the 1950s and 1960s. By the 1970s, national governments were seeking greater state control over the levers of economic regulation. The EC was unable to act collectively in the face of energy shortages or to curb the rise of unemployment and inflation. Only in the area of monetary regulation was progress made. Following a series of experiments during the 1970s, the governmental leaders of West Germany and France succeeded in 1978 in bringing some of their partner governments along in the creation of the EMS with its exchange rate mechanism (see chapter 4). These decisions were made possible through the development of more effective means of intergovernmental decision making, most notably through the regularization of summit meetings of heads of state and government as the European Council. But the establishment of the EMS did not appear to be much of a success at the time. Britain stayed out of the exchange rate mechanism, and it was not until 1983 that the French Socialist government of François Mitterrand decided that dropping out of the mechanism during hard economic times was not a viable option.

By the early 1980s, the accepted interpretation of the EC was that it was at bottom an intergovernmental organization. It was a period in which the Commission no longer was looked to for major initiatives. Most major policy issues were decided in the European Council in negotiations between governmental leaders. Even obligatory decisions, like those which annually fixed the EC budget and the farm prices under the CAP, could be held up without decision in the Council of Ministers by an intransigent government, often the British government of Prime Minister Margaret Thatcher. Such deadlocks had to await resolution at the next meeting of the European Council, where the heads of government could make commitments to one another that their ministers could not. The prevailing academic view of the way the EC worked was now called *neorealism*—which pointed to the fact that the nation-state was not dead in Western Europe. The member states had come to dominate the EC and had reduced the supranational Commission to a subordinate role.[28]

On the other hand, realists of an earlier day might have been surprised at the extent to which, even at the height of the economic turbulence in the mid-1970s, the governments of the EC member countries had come to regard themselves as partners in a community in which armed conflict between them could no longer be imagined. This acknowledgement had freed them to concentrate on the economic problems that separated them and to cooperate in seeking solutions. Though major decisions were reached with great difficulty, they were made collectively through consultation and bargaining. When disagreements could not be resolved, decisions were postponed. Mechanisms for improving EC decision-making capabilities were evolving during the decade after de Gaulle left the French presidency in 1969. Institutions were developed in the 1970s that followed a design de Gaulle had supported in the 1960s (see chapter 3). This intergovernmentalist design accorded with de Gaulle's assumption as a classical realist that states would pursue their own interests, but that de Gaulle himself might be able to exercise leadership in persuading them that their interests accorded with those of France.[29] It involved regular meetings of EC foreign ministers to discuss mutual foreign policy concerns, and regular "summit" meetings of heads of state and government to discuss major matters of concern to all members and sometimes to reach significant decisions that would advance the cause of regional integration. Although France does not dominate the EU today, the institutional framework of the EU contains important elements drawn from de Gaulle's blueprint.

Light at the End of the Tunnel

At the June 1985 Milan summit meeting, the heads of government of the EC accepted a White Paper that called for completion of the Common Market through adoption of the Single European Act (SEA). The SEA was ratified 2 years later. This major development will be dealt with at greater length in chapter 4, but here it is enough to note that earlier theories of regional integration were unable to predict that the members of the EC would conclude that a more thoroughgoing removal of trade barriers among themselves would be needed to cope with competition from more efficient and technologically up-to-date competitors. This was not a neofunctionalist spillover from one policy domain already engaged in to another. It was not an attempt either to emulate one successful enterprise by embarking on another or to deal with the unforeseen side effects of actions in one domain upon conditions in another. Instead, it involved returning to an already existing policy domain and improving EC performance in line with the original Rome treaty objectives. It was prompted by changes in the world in which the EC finds itself, rather than by processes internal to the EC, as neofunctionalists would have anticipated.

Theorists have sought to explain the SEA in terms of some of the various formulations we have discussed in this chapter, or of combinations of them. Wayne Sandholtz and John Zysman have emphasized the role of business interests in pushing for the liberalization of EC markets, using neofunctionalist arguments in part, especially in the emphasis they put on the leadership of the EC Commission. But they also stress the argument that economic interdependence had superseded the efforts of EC nations or the EC itself to exercise effective economic regulation.[30] On the other hand, Robert Keohane and Stanley Hoffmann have pointed out that, if neofunctionalist spillover were to have occurred, it should have produced something like the SEA earlier, presumably in the 1970s, and that the changes in the global political economy should likewise have produced earlier responses on the part of the EC.[31]

Nevertheless, these authors are in agreement that member states, pursuing their own interests, had to reach some convergence of interests in order for the major departure to take place.[32] This point of view is highlighted by the study of the SEA by Andrew Moravcsik, who argues that it was achieved through an intergovernmental process of bargaining, in which the roles of the Commission and even of the Commission's president were secondary to that of the governments of the leading states: France, Britain, and West Germany. Changes in the domestic political configurations of these countries, especially of France, had cleared the ground for the SEA, according to Moravcsik.[33] But, as we will argue, while the process of setting the agenda for negotiation was essentially intergovernmental in nature, the role of the Commission in the eventual choice between alternatives was substantial as well.[34]

The SEA also included a provision that many of the specific pieces of EC legislation to embody its trade-liberalizing provisions could be adopted in the Council of Ministers by qualified majority vote, rather than requiring unanimity as imposed by the Luxembourg compromise of 1966. This provision made it possible for most of the prescribed legislation to be adopted by the specified deadline of the end of 1992. The SEA also increased the ability of the European Parliament (EP) to induce the Council of Ministers to make changes it wanted in the same body of legislation. These were at least modest supranational outcomes, so if, following Moravcsik, we see the process of negotiation as primarily an intergovernmental one, it is still possible for intergovernmental decision making to produce supranational outcomes.

In 1988, the president of the EC commission, Jacques Delors, resurrected plans originally outlined in 1970 for an EMU of the EC members. In 1990, two intergovernmental conferences were instituted that developed separate parts of the TEU that was adopted at the Maastricht summit of December 1991. The two parts were (1) EMU, which followed rather closely the Delors proposals with provisions for a European central bank, for closer economic and monetary policy coordination, and potentially for a common EC currency, and (2) Political Union, which provided for steps toward establishing common foreign and security policies for what was to be called the *European Union,* extended the principle of qualified majority voting to new policy realms, and added further to the powers of the directly elected EP. (see chapters 5-7 and 11 for more complete discussion of the Maastricht treaty).

These steps taken in the late 1980s and early 1990s moved well beyond what neofunctionalism might have predicted as realizable in such a short period of time. They were much more than an incremental accretion of low politics functions. That they sought EU before giving themselves time to absorb the single market or even to begin the stages envisaged for EMU was due primarily to the events in Central and Eastern Europe, which dramatically altered the stable security equation of the Cold War and which particularly presented them in 1990 with the imminent achievement of German unification. Global political change served as a stimulus to integration. In many ways the "great leap forward" to EU resembled the blueprints of the old discarded European federalism:Seize the opportunity when it arrives, because it may not come again soon.

REGIONAL INTEGRATION THEORY TODAY

Most students of European integration today, including the authors of this text, have concluded that no single theoretical framework can hope to account for the phenomena they study[35] due to the following:

1. Major economic and political events that are beyond the control of the EU as an organization or any of its members acting singly or jointly continue to

occur in defiance of any EU efforts to pursue a stable course of action. The member states are not only dependent upon one another, but if they are to plan ahead for their mutual security and economic well-being, they are dependent upon the rest of the world to stay still long enough for them to agree on and carry out coherent courses of action. Broad theories of international inter-dependence[36] help us to understand the dilemmas the EU faces, but they do not provide answers about what will occur when and with what effects.

2. As a decision-making mechanism, the EU has become much too complex to be captured by any simplifying framework drawing upon familiar ideas that political scientists commonly accept. As discussed in later chapters, the EU has a multilevel character.[37] Different theories discussed above, including realism, federalism, functionalism, neofunctionalism, and complex interdependence, all can find levels or niches within this organizational complexity that work the way the theories tell us they should. In other words, the EU is whatever the theorist wants to make of it; it enables a variety of equally coherent definitions of existing relationships, explanations of how they got that way, and predictions of where they are going, all of which are plausible if one accepts the beginning assumptions. The student should be warned that those assumptions will be selective. With that warning, we briefly present our own working assumptions, the prime justification for which is that they draw generously on whatever concepts and theories seem appropriate for each aspect of the EU to be considered in the remaining chapters.

We expect that for the foreseeable future decisions on the most important matters, especially those involving regional security, will involve an inter-governmental process rather than a supranational one. But this concession to realism does not imply that the EU has not moved and will not move further in a supranational direction, in so far as the *outcomes* of such decisions are concerned. A process of intergovernmental decision making is not incompatible with a willingness to concede sovereignty on important matters if mutual benefits can be perceived by all member governments and what is given up does not offend the deeply held values and norms of citizens of member states. Thus outcomes may be supranational in the neofunctionalist sense, even though decision processes are not. Moreover, the processes themselves may follow neofunctionalist expectations within domains about which there is already longer-standing agreement and where affected interest groups may be brought into agreement.

This process implies a split-level functioning of the EU's institutions in two senses: First, decision making takes place at both the national and the regional (EU) levels. Actions taken at each of these two levels give rise to subsequent actions at the other.[38] Second, decision making at the EU level involves two different sets of *agendas:*[39] (a) the original European Communities agenda established by the treaties which created the three communities in the 1950s (ECSC, EEC, and EURATOM), that is, the *ordinary agenda,* and (b) an agenda of decisions to be taken to modify the original treaties, or what we will call the *extraordinary agenda.* When issues on the extraordinary agenda are resolved in ways that modify the original treaties, as in the case of the SEA of 1986 (Project 1992) and the TEU of 1991 (Maastricht treaty), the ordinary agenda is altered, while the extraordinary agenda is cleared for new items to be placed on it. At the same time, work begins on the processing of the altered ordinary agenda. This distinction will become more meaningful as we discuss the historical steps by which items have been processed on the extraordinary agenda and then passed on to the ordinary agenda (see chapters 3–5). These processes will be dealt with in more analytical terms in chapter 6.

ENDNOTES

1. Hans J. Morgenthau, *Politics among Nations: The Struggle for Power and Peace,* 3rd ed. (New York: Alfred A. Knopf, 1962), pp. 507–509.
2. Robert O. Keohane, *After Hegemony: Cooperation and Discord in the World Political Economy* (Princeton, N.J.: Princeton University Press, 1984), pp. 136–141.
3. Charles W. Kegley, Jr., and Eugene R. Wittkopf, *World Politics: Trend and Transformation,* 3rd ed. (New York: St. Martin's, 1989), pp. 12–15.
4. Charles Pentland, *International Theory and European Integration* (London: Faber & Faber, 1973), chap. 5.
5. F. Roy Willis, *France, Germany and the New Europe, 1945–1967,* rev. ed. (London: Oxford University Press, 1968), chaps. 6 and 7.
6. Stephen George, *An Awkward Partner: Britain in the European Community* (Oxford: Oxford University Press, 1990), pp. 16–22.
7. David Mitrany, *A Working Peace System* (Chicago: Quadrangle Books, 1966).
8. Ibid., pp. 64–65. In a sense, Mitrany foreshadowed the insistence of the British government of Prime Minister John Major in 1991–1992 on his country's right to opt out of some functions to be performed by the emerging EU, such as a common defense and a common monetary policy.
9. See the essays on Monnet in Douglas Brinkley and Clifford Hackett, *Jean Monnet: The Path to European Unity* (New York: St. Martin's, 1991).
10. Leon N. Lindberg and Stuart A. Scheingold, *Europe's Would-Be Polity: Patterns of Change in the European Community* (Englewood Cliffs, N.J.: Prentice-Hall, 1970), pp. 33–34.
11. Pentland, *International Theory,* p. 109. Although the boundary between high politics and low politics fluctuates depending upon who is using the terms and in what context, foreign and defense policy matters are commonly considered high politics and policies limited to particular economic sectors are considered low politics. The grey area in between is occupied by macroeconomic policy, especially monetary policy, which, given its widespread implications for countries' international standing, probably ought to be considered within the high politics realm today. In other words, it is an area, along with foreign and defense policy, over which nation-states are least willing to give up control.
12. George, *An Awkward Partner,* p. 21.
13. George W. Ball, "Introduction," in Brinkley and Hackett, eds., *Jean Monnet,* p. xix; Derek W. Urwin, *The Community of Europe: A History of European Integration since 1945* (London and New York: Longman, 1991), p. 61.

14. A customs union is a regime established between states in which all tariffs and quotas restricting trade between the participating countries have been removed, while common tariffs and quotas are established with other countries. A common market goes further in removing all obstacles to trade among the countries, including such impediments as border controls and government regulations, state purchasing policies, and taxes that discriminate against the producers of one member country against those of another. The SEA of 1987, which provided for the removal of all such obstacles to trade among EC members by the end of 1992, popularly labeled *Project 1992,* represents an effort to approximate the conditions of a true common market among the 12 EC members.

15. Ernst B. Haas, *The Uniting of Europe: Political, Social, and Economic Forces, 1950–1957* (Stanford, Calif.: Stanford University Press, 1958); Haas, *Beyond the Nation State* (Stanford, Calif.: Stanford University Press, 1964).

16. Haas, *The Uniting of Europe,* chap. 1.

17. Ibid., chaps. 8 and 13.

18. Robert O. Keohane and Stanley Hoffmann, "Institutional Change in Europe in the 1980s," in Keohane and Hoffmann, eds., *The New European Community: Decision-making and Institutional Change* (Boulder: Westview, 1991), p. 15.

19. Haas, *The Uniting of Europe,* p. 523.

20. Lindberg and Scheingold, *Europe's Would-Be Polity,* pp. 96–97.

21. Haas, *Beyond the Nation State.*

22. Leon N. Lindberg, "Political Integration as a Multidimensional Phenomenon Requiring Multivariate Measurement," in Lindberg and Stuart A. Scheingold, eds., *Regional Integration: Theory and Research* (Cambridge: Harvard University Press, 1971), pp. 94–95.

23. See John Newhouse, *Collision in Brussels: The Common Market Crisis of 30 June 1965* (New York: W.W. Norton & Co., 1967). See chap. 3 below for further discussion of the "empty chair crisis."

24. Lindberg and Scheingold, *Europe's Would-Be Polity,* pp. 70–75.

25. Ernst B. Haas, "Turbulent Fields and the Theory of Regional Integration," *International Organization* 30 (Spring 1976): 174–212.

26. Dale L. Smith and James Lee Ray, "European Integration: Gloomy Theory versus Rosy Reality," in Smith and Ray, eds., *The 1992 Project and the Future of Integration in Europe* (Armonk, N.Y., and London: M.E. Sharpe, 1993), pp. 32–33.

27. Robert O. Keohane and Joseph S. Nye, *Power and Interdependence,* 2nd ed. (Glenview, Ill.: Scott, Foresman & Co., 1989), pp. 19–22.

28. Paul Taylor, *The Limits of European Integration* (New York: Columbia University Press, 1983).

29. For a discussion of de Gaulle's views, see David M. Wood, "Old Thinking and the New Europe: The Persisting Influence of de Gaulle and Thatcher" (Occasional paper No. 9211, Center for International Studies, University of Missouri-St. Louis, December 1992).

30. Wayne Sandholtz and John Zysman, "1992: Recasting the European Bargain," *World Politics* 42 (October 1989): 95–128.

31. Keohane and Hoffmann, "Institutional Change," pp. 19 and 23.

32. Sandholtz and Zysman, "1992," 111–113; Keohane and Hoffmann, "Institutional Change," pp. 23–24.

33. Andrew Moravcsik, "Negotiating the Single European Act," in Keohane and Hoffmann, eds., *The New European Community,* pp. 41–84.

34. The distinction between setting the agenda and choosing between alternatives is that of John W. Kingdon, *Agendas, Alternatives, and Public Policies* (Glenview, Ill., and London: Scott, Foresman & Co., 1984), pp. 3–4.

35. This conclusion is exemplified by the eclectic approach taken by David R. Cameron, "The 1992 Initiative: Causes and Consequences," in Alberta M. Sbragia, ed., *Euro-Politics: Institutions and Policymaking in the "New" European Community* (Washington, D.C.: The Brookings Institution, 1992), pp. 23–74.

36. Keohane, *After Hegemony;* Keohane and Nye, *Power and Interdependence.*

37. Dale L. Smith and James Lee Ray, "The 1992 Project," in Smith and Ray, eds., *The 1992 Project,* pp. 6–10.

38. Ibid., p. 9.

39. Kingdon, *Agendas, Alternatives, and Public Policies;* David M. Wood, Birol A. Yeşilada, and Beth Robedeau, "Windows of Opportunity: When EC Agendas Are Set and Why," (Paper presented at the Third Biennial Conference of the European Community Studies Association, Washington, D.C., May 27–29, 1993).

chapter 3

The Rome Treaty and Its Original Agenda (1957–1975)

In this chapter, and in the two that follow, we review the history of the EU from the adoption of the Treaty of Rome to the present. The current chapter takes the story up to the mid-1970s, chapter 4 carries it to the end of the 1980s, and chapter 5 brings it through 1994. (See Box 3.1 for a list of governments in France, Germany, and Britain from the beginning of the EEC until 1994.) In all three chapters, we relate the political developments that occurred within the major member states and at the level of the European institutions to the policy decisions made in implementing the original agenda of the EC and in bringing new items onto the agenda. Changes occurring in the larger world relevant to changes in the EU are taken into account as well. We begin with the mid-1950s and the decision by the original six to create a customs union (CU).

When the original six member states of the EC agreed in 1957 to the Treaty of Rome, establishing the EEC, they set an agenda for themselves and the new EEC institutions that was expected to preoccupy them for at least a decade. The principal items on this agenda were the first steps toward economic integration, involving the freeing of trade among the six economies and the establishment of a common trading policy with respect to the rest of the world. The principal areas of trade they had in mind were manufactured goods and agricultural products, although eventually there were to be, among other projected developments, free movement of persons and capital, a common transportation policy, a common monetary regime, and a common social policy.[1] Ultimately the six countries envisaged an evolution from an economic community to a political union. But, while these goals above and beyond the new trade and commercial regime were mentioned in the Treaty of Rome, or in the case of political goals, hinted at in the treaty's preamble, they were not considered by the drafters of

---

**BOX 3.1 Successive governments in France,
Germany, and Britain, 1958–1995**

French Presidents and Supportive Parties and Coalitions

Charles de Gaulle, 1958–1969, Gaullists, assorted center and right support

Georges Pompidou, 1969–1974, Gaullists, assorted center and right support

Valéry Giscard d'Estaing, 1974–1981, Giscardist center-right, Gaullist RPR

François Mitterrand, 1981–1986, Socialists, Communists until 1984

François Mitterrand, 1986–1988, Cohabitation with Prime Minister Jacques Chirac's RPR-UDF coalition

François Mitterrand, 1988–1993, Socialists, center-left

François Mitterrand, 1993–1995, Cohabitation with Prime Minister Edouard Balladur's RPR-UDF coalition

Jacques Chirac, 1995 (next elections by 1998), RPR-UDF coalition

*German Chancellors and Supportive Parties and Coalitions
(Chancellor's Party First)*

Konrad Adenauer, 1949–1963, CDU/CSU, FDP

Ludwig Erhard, 1963–1966, CDU/CSU, FDP

Kurt-Georg Kiesinger, 1966–1969, CDU/CSU, SPD

Willy Brandt, 1969–1974, SPD, FDP

Helmut Schmidt, 1974–1982, SPD, FDP

Helmut Kohl, 1982–1995 (next elections by 1998), CDU/CSU, FDP

British Prime Ministers and Their Parties

Harold Macmillan, 1957–1963, Conservative

Sir Alec Douglas-Home, 1963–1964, Conservative

Harold Wilson, 1964–1970, Labour

Edward Heath, 1970–1974, Conservative

Harold Wilson, 1974–1976, Labour

James Callaghan, 1976–1979, Labour

Margaret Thatcher, 1979–1990, Conservative

John Major, 1990–1995 (next elections by 1997), Conservative

---

the treaty as priority items on the initial agenda. The new trading bloc was to be created by 1970, before most of the further steps were to be taken.[2]

When we refer to the agenda of the EU, we have in mind the issues that are being actively addressed by its decision-making organs. Under the Treaty of Rome, the timing of proposed legislative measures envisaged by the treaty is within the job definition of the Commission. In the early years, the steps taken to create the CU and the CAP (see chapter 8) were developed by the Commission as proposals and sent to the Council of Ministers for action, that is, placed on the Council's agenda. These proposals were what, at the end of chapter 2, we called the ordinary agenda, because in putting them on the Council's agenda, the Commission was simply fulfilling its responsibilities under the Rome treaty. However, during the first decade, there were occasions when items that had not been authorized by the treaty, or over which member governments disputed the right of the Commission to make proposals, were placed on what we have called the extraordinary agenda. An example given prominent attention in this chapter was the 1965 set of proposals by Commission President Walter Hallstein that touched off the famous empty chair crisis.

A BRIEF PERIOD OF CONSENSUS

The Six in 1957

In chapter 1, we discussed in very general terms the domestic politics of members of today's EU and how domestic politics and EU politics interact. Now we look at this interaction with respect to the original EEC. In 1957, the commitment to the original agenda was shared by political leaders and ruling political parties in all six of the original EEC countries. For the most part, the leaders were centrists in the party politics of their countries. Most were either Christian Democrats of the center-right, Social Democrats of the center-left, or Liberals variously located between center-left and center-right. In France and Italy, these political parties of the broad center coexisted between strong Communist parties of the extreme left and nationalist parties on the far right, which did not share the agenda of the centrists for European policy or for foreign and domestic policy in general. In West Germany and the three Benelux countries, extreme parties were weak—and were even outlawed in the case of the West German Communist and neo-Nazi parties.

The pro-European centrists in the six countries shared an acceptance of the Europe of the 1950s as it was and sought to make the best of it. What they had accepted in particular was the existence of the Cold War and the dominant role played by a hegemon[3] on either side of the politically divided continent: the Soviet Union to the east and the United States to the west. They were motivated to organize their part of Europe to make their economic, and ultimately their political, development less dependent upon their hegemon, the United States. For the time being, at least, little could be done about the Soviet hegemony. The creation of the EEC and the priority it gave to reorganizing trade relationships was a realistic way of putting Europe in a more self-sufficient position, economically, if not, politically.[4]

Support for and opposition to the EEC among parties ranged from left to right for four countries: France, West Germany (FRG), Italy, and Britain (see Table 3.1). Among the six member countries, support for the new Community and its

TABLE 3.1 Positions on European Economic Community issues of parties in four countries, 1950s

Country	Left-Anti	Left-Pro	Center-Pro	Right-Pro	Right-Anti
France	Communists	Socialists	MRP, Radicals	Independents	Gaullists
FRG		Social Democrats	FDP	CDU/CSU	
Italy	Communists		Christian Democrats	Liberals	Neofascists
		Socialists	Social Democrats, Republicans		
Britain	Labour		Liberals		Conservatives

KEY: *Pro* refers to pro-EEC, *Anti* to anti-EEC. Parties placed between two categories (e.g., West German Social Democrats between Left-Anti and Left-Pro) reflect ambiguity or internal division regarding the EEC during the decade. Initials: *FRG*, Federal Republic of Germany; *MRP*, Popular Republican Movement (French Christian Democrats); *FDP*, Free Democratic Party (German Liberals); *CDU/CSU*, confederation of German Christian Democratic parties: Christian Democratic Union (national)/Christian Social Union (Bavaria only).

agenda was weakest in France in 1957. The extreme parties of both left and right in France were more strident in their opposition to European integration than were their counterparts in Italy. Communists in all West European countries accepted the leadership of the Soviet Communist Party in officially opposing integration as essentially a means by which the United States maintained its hold on its allies and capitalists enriched themselves at the expense of the working class.[5] For the French Communist Party (PCF), European integration had special significance as an American-backed means by which German capitalists would gain control over the French economy. Throughout the 1950s, the PCF was unalterably opposed to each new initiative in the process of European integration: whether ECSC, EDC, European Political Community, or EEC.[6]

On the French right, the principal opposition to French membership in these various communities was provided by General Charles de Gaulle and the Gaullist movement that supported him. The Gaullists were weaker at the time of the Rome treaty than they had been during the debates over Europe earlier in the decade. De Gaulle himself was in semiretirement. Nevertheless, his views concerning France's role in Europe were well-known and were echoed by political figures and writers both inside and outside the Gaullist movement. De Gaulle had his own agenda for Europe, which he was to put into play after he returned to power in mid-1958.[7] He rejected the notion that the division of Europe between East and West was necessarily frozen, especially if this meant that France must subordinate its own interests to the wishes of the United States. De Gaulle saw the EEC as potentially destructive of the France that he knew and loved, and especially of the leading role in Europe that France could claim as America's influence declined.[8]

In West Germany by 1957, the political party system, at least as represented in Parliament, consisted almost exclusively of parties of the center-left and center-right, all officially committed to the EEC and its agenda, although the SPD on the center-left had only recently endorsed the new Community. Earlier in the

1950s, the SPD had opposed the ECSC and the EDC as helping to solidify the division between East and West Germany, making reunification impossible in the foreseeable future. By contrast, Christian Democratic Chancellor Konrad Adenauer had pursued a policy of acceptance of the division of Europe and the consequent division of Germany as unalterable for the time being. Through membership in the Western European and Atlantic organizations, Adenauer sought to strengthen West Germany's economy, political structure, and national security while options in the East were closed off by Soviet power and policy. During the mid-1950s, the opposition SPD came around to a positive position on European integration.[9]

The British Problem

Although the established centrists of the six gave solid support to the EEC and its original agenda, there was not a clear Euro-center in the British political party system in the 1950s. Britain was invited in 1955 to the Messina conference, where plans were laid that were to result in the Rome treaty. But they arrived as skeptical observers, assuming in view of the EDC debacle that little would come out of the talks. When it became clear that the six were indeed going to create a CU, Britain sought to entice them over to a broader plan for a European free trade area, that would be looser and without the pretensions to political integration that the six had in mind. The British were set against anything that resembled European federalism, even in the distant future. But, while there was sympathy in some of the six for the British plan, the desire to move ahead with a stronger form of market integration prevailed in each country, and the treaty was duly signed and ratified. Britain then took the free trade area concept to smaller countries outside the six—Denmark, Sweden, Norway, Austria, Switzerland, and Portugal—and the European Free Trade Area (EFTA) was formed in 1960.[10]

   In a free trade area, each member state can choose its own level of tariffs to impose upon goods from nonmember countries, whereas states in a CU have the same tariff levels imposed by all members on goods from outside the union. Without a common barrier to goods from outside, the markets of countries wanting to restrict such trade are wide open to goods entering first through their low-tariff partners.[11] Opposition to the proposed CU was widely shared by leaders of both of the major British political parties, Conservative and Labour. The weak center Liberal Party was the only one taking a positive position. The prevailing British view in 1957–1960 was that membership in the EEC would interfere with economic and political links Britain enjoyed with the United States and with member states of the British Commonwealth. Britain had a world role; membership in the EEC would narrow its focus to one region, albeit an important one. Leaders of both British parties believed that Britain had a special relationship with the United States, meaning that U.S. policymakers listened to British advice, and that it was therefore not necessary for the British to join with other medium-sized powers to help them enhance their collective influence with the hegemon. There was also a deeply ingrained suspicion of French motives, as well as a belief that the British system of parliamentary sovereignty was unique and superior to institutional frameworks found on the continent of Europe.[12]

These attitudes on the part of the British government meant that the EEC and its agenda had a British problem. The six could move ahead with their agenda, but if they were to go much beyond the initial priorities, that is, begin to develop a new (extraordinary) agenda, it would become even more difficult to reach an accommodation that could bring Britain into the Community. If the six indeed saw the EEC as a step in the direction of a stronger, more independent Europe, able to operate on a plane of equality with the major world players, then it was reasonable that they would want Britain, which was still regarded as a major power in the world, to join them. This was the dilemma facing the Euro-centrists. For Charles de Gaulle, the British problem was quite different. For the other five EEC members, France under de Gaulle was soon to become a problem in itself.

THE STRUGGLE TO CONTROL
THE EXTRAORDINARY AGENDA

In May 1958, the French Fourth Republic was embroiled militarily in a colonial war against the Algerian independence movement. Weak centrist governments in Paris vacillated in their policies toward the war, as they had done earlier in the 1950s in the process of losing French control over Indochina. On May 13, a revolt broke out in Algiers and other cities, which was led by civilians, but was taken over by French Army generals in what was essentially a military coup directed against the government in Paris. After a few days of uncertainty, the leaders of the revolt called upon the politicians in Paris to hand power over to General de Gaulle.[13] When President René Coty called upon de Gaulle to become prime minister, the General expressed his willingness to do so, but on the condition that he would oversee the writing of a new constitution, which would be presented to the French voters for their approval. On September 16, 1958, the constitutional referendum was overwhelmingly supported by the voters, and the Fifth Republic came into being. In December 1958, de Gaulle was elected the first president of the Fifth Republic.

From 1958 to 1962, when he brought the war to a conclusion by granting Algeria its independence, de Gaulle was a dominant leader willing to take extraordinary measures to defeat threats to his government and to his policy of gradually yielding independence to Algeria. But, although Algeria was a continuing concern during this period, the General also began his efforts to change the agenda of the EEC to suit his purposes.

The Clash of Grand Designs

In the summer of 1961, two events occurred that were to reveal what de Gaulle's agenda for the EEC would be.[14] The first was his success in getting his fellow EEC government leaders, meeting in Bonn in July, to put on their own agenda a proposal for greater political cooperation, which he had been advancing in one form or another since 1959. The heads agreed at Bonn to ask an ad hoc commission chaired by a close associate of de Gaulle, Christian Fouchet, to draft proposals for a treaty to establish a union of states, which were presented to the six governments in November 1961. By then, the second event had occurred, the August 1961 application of the Conservative British government headed by Prime Minister Harold Macmillan for membership in the EEC, which was followed by the similar applications by two of Britain's EFTA associates, Denmark and Norway, and one nonaligned state, the Republic of Ireland.

The French proposals considered by the Fouchet commission envisaged that major political decisions on foreign and defense policy matters, as well as on cultural and scientific matters, were to be taken unanimously by the heads of state and government meeting at the summit. In essence, the proposals anticipated the amendment of the Treaty of Rome to create a political union, with a new agenda and agenda-setting mechanism. There would be a separate European Political Commission comprising officials of the six foreign ministries, who would reside in Paris and coordinate agendas for meetings of foreign ministers and of the heads, leaving the EEC Commission in Brussels with the ordinary economic agenda-setting role assigned it by the Treaty of Rome.[15]

There was a potential link between these proposals and British entry, in that this more forthrightly intergovernmental mode of decision making was much more congenial to the British government than the mode envisaged in the Rome treaty. Already some decisions of the EEC Council of Ministers were officially being taken by simple majority, and the treaty indicated that this would be true of most Council decisions by 1966. If Britain and the others were to enter the EEC, they would have to accept majority decisions taken on the ordinary agenda. But the Fouchet plan for political union would ensure that any extraordinary agenda items, especially those involving matters of political significance that would threaten British autonomy, could be vetoed by Britain, even if supported by all of the other members. At least on this narrow basis, de Gaulle and the British shared an intergovernmentalist view of the Community's future. But the Fouchet proposals were too intergovernmentalist to suit the Euro-centrists in other EEC countries, especially the Netherlands and Belgium, and negotiations were broken off in 1962.[16]

Nevertheless, de Gaulle's vision for Europe differed from the British vision in a fundamental sense. The Macmillan government did not want to be drawn into political obligations in Europe that would interfere with their ties with the United States and the Commonwealth. However, Britain was showing slower economic growth than were the six, which is what moved the Macmillan government to reverse direction and seek EEC membership. They recognized that the CU had produced more dynamic economic results in the first years of the EEC than had their own free trade area, but they were throwing in only half a towel. They certainly did not want economic integration to spill over into political integration. As F. S. Northedge has observed, "For continental Europeans who had looked forward to the opportunity to build a united Europe during the long years of Nazi occupation, bodies like the Council of Europe, the Coal and Steel Community, the Economic Community, were the fulfillment of a dream.

For Britain, joining organizations such as these represented the disappointment of expectations, of hopes of better things. In their inmost thoughts the British were never really convinced about the merits of European unity: unity was all right as a slogan, . . . but it was not a programme for practical action."[17]

De Gaulle's idea had been for his proposed system of political cooperation to extend far enough to bind member countries to commonly agreed projects, so long as these would be projects of French inspiration, following de Gaulle's own vision of Europe's political future. He believed that he had brought Chancellor Adenauer with him in this objective through the personal relationship they had established in 1959, which was to lead to a Treaty of Friendship between France and Germany signed by the two leaders in January 1963. With France and Germany coordinating their foreign policies in line with de Gaulle's vision, it should be a simple matter to bring the smaller and weaker members of the six along with them. If Britain, and perhaps three others likely to follow the British lead, were to join the EEC, there would be another grand design competing with de Gaulle's, a design he believed to be of American inspiration.[18] Accordingly, he vetoed British entry in January 1963, which cancelled the entry bids of the other three as well. Ironically, his veto of British entry helped to undermine the position of Chancellor Adenauer in West Germany. Before the year was out there was a new chancellor in Bonn, Ludwig Erhard, an "Atlanticist" who did not wish to play games in world politics according to French rules.[19]

The Empty Chair Crisis

A further irony of the refusal by France to allow Britain to enter the EEC was that it left France in a smaller organization, most of the other members of which continued to harbor preferences for an EEC that would eventually move beyond the Rome treaty in a supranational direction. As noted previously, by 1966 major decisions of the EEC Council of Ministers were to be by majority vote. For the first 7 years of the Community's life, most such decisions were taken either by unanimous consent or by QMV, the latter according to a formula that was designed to protect the smaller countries from the possibility of the bigger countries joining against them. Commission President Walter Hallstein had followed a pattern of encouraging the Council to continue its deliberations without voting until it was possible to register unanimous consent. Sometimes this meant that one country would give up more than the others, but Hallstein strove to adjust his agenda items in such a way as to have something for everyone. A useful method was to combine measures into package deals so that on different issues countries would make concessions to each other. The package would then be accepted in its entirety, sometimes after days of negotiation among the ministers. Even after majority voting came to be applicable in formal terms across a wide array of decisions, this same style of consensus building would ensure that there would be no big winners or big losers.[20]

Much of the bargaining activity in the first half of the 1960s had involved a three-way struggle between France, West Germany, and Italy over the establishment of the CU and the CAP. In the crisis that began on June 30, 1965, at stake in economic terms was France's interest in a CAP that would benefit farmers to the detriment of consumers and taxpayers in all six countries, because of the higher farm prices and budgetary contributions that would have to be paid to compensate farmers. West Germany had farmers who would benefit as well, but it was less interested than France in the CAP. As a strong exporter of manufactured goods, West Germany was vitally interested in establishing a CU, as it would give German industries assured markets for their products, with protection from imports from non-EEC countries. Italy, which in the early 1960s was experiencing a rapid shift of its active population from farming to manufacturing, expected to have to pay for the CAP out of the uncertain proceeds from the sale of its manufactures in the markets of the EEC, and wanted side payments in the form of regional assistance and a lessened share of budget contributions. A package that involved putting both the CU and the CAP into place, while providing side payments to Italy seemed to the Commission to be an obvious way of moving the Community ahead toward economic integration. The French government, which rested on the farmers' electoral support, appeared to have a high stake in achieving just that. Therefore, Commission President Hallstein believed he could up the ante with proposals that would enhance political, as well as economic, integration, without General de Gaulle being able to stop him. In this he reckoned without de Gaulle's commitment to his own plans and his seemingly invulnerable domestic political position.[21]

The initial significance of the date June 30, 1965, was that, pursuant to regulations mandated by the Rome treaty, the system for financing the CAP had to be put in place by that time, or the EEC farm program could not operate.[22] Hallstein presented his proposals to the Council of Ministers in March 1965. Those proposals relating to CAP financing involved the collection of levies on imports of farm goods from non-EEC countries into the EEC, and their disbursement to farmers in the member countries to compensate for the lower prices they were getting worldwide for their products. The other two features of the proposals were in effect an assertion of the Commission's right to control not only the ordinary, but also the extraordinary agenda of the EEC. The CAP was to come fully into being by July 1, 1967, but the CU for manufactured goods was not to reach its completion until 1970. In an effort to gain the support of West Germany and other members expecting to benefit more from the CU than from the CAP, Hallstein proposed accelerating the CU so that its completion would coincide with that of the CAP in 2 years. This proposal was linked to another proposal to route the proceeds of agricultural levies and customs duties to the Commission for it to administer as the EEC's own resources. The Commission would remit to the six governments a portion of this amount, but it would keep a part for itself to be spent according to the provisions of the annual budget adopted by the Council of Ministers.[23] Although no amendment to the Rome treaty was required by this proposal, it would have meant a very substantial increase in the funds available to the Commission, above what had been expected by the member states.

But the third Hallstein proposal departed from any that was laid down in or could be implied from the Rome treaty, requiring amendments to two treaty articles.[24] Because the six governments could join forces against the Commission and interfere with its planned uses of its newfound largesse, it was proposed that the EP[25] could make amendments to the Commission's annual draft budget by simple majority vote. If the Commission approved such an amendment, the Council of Ministers could turn it down only if five of the six members voted to do so. Although this appeared to increase the Parliament's budgetary powers, it would also enhance the ability of the Commission to control the whole process, because it was also proposed that the Commission could propose amendments to the Parliament's amendments, which could be accepted by a four-sixths majority of the Council.[26] If accepted, the proposed procedures would mean that France and West Germany could be outvoted in the Council by the less powerful member states, and the will of the supranational bodies would then prevail over that of the two strongest states.

The proposals received an angry reaction from the French government.[27] For de Gaulle, the assertion by the Commission president of the authority to impose extraordinary agenda items upon the Council of Ministers was unacceptable. His earlier proposals for regular political cooperation among the governments of the six member countries had rested on the assumption that the Rome treaty was a restrictive document that authorized only those powers and functions explicitly stated in it, and that any extension of EEC powers beyond those authorized by the treaty could only be made by the six governments deciding to amend the treaty or even to reach a new contract. The problem for de Gaulle was that, with the imminent arrival of majority voting, the Commission could make proposals that would go beyond the French interpretation of the treaty, and France could be outvoted in opposition to them. President Hallstein obviously considered the Rome treaty permissive of extensions of the competence of EEC institutions in directions that were by a broad interpretation compatible with the intent of the treaty. The five member states other than France ranged along a continuum between the French position and that of the Commission.[28]

Just before the June 30, 1965, deadline for achieving a system for CAP financing, the French foreign minister called an end to the Council of Ministers meeting that was deliberating over the Hallstein package.[29] In the first instance, this signified a French veto of the package. Six months still remained until the installation of more generalized majority voting, a rules change that was mandated by the treaty and would presumably be placed automatically on the Council's agenda. It soon became clear that by refusing to send his ministers to Council meetings, de Gaulle was forcing at least a postponement in the ordinary agenda of the Rome treaty, attempting to force the others to accept a continuation of the unanimity rule in defiance of the intent of the framers of the Rome treaty.[30]

In January 1966, the French ministers returned to their seat on the Council of Ministers. De Gaulle had been unexpectedly taken to a second ballot in the French presidential election of December 1965, failing to gain a majority on the first ballot as a result of strong showings by François Mitterrand, the candidate of the Left, and a relatively unknown centrist candidate, Jean Lecanuet. The latter had the endorsement of Jean Monnet, and may also have benefited from the votes of many farmers who punished de Gaulle on the first ballot for producing the EEC crisis, thus jeopardizing the CAP and its expected benefits to French agriculture. Although de Gaulle easily won the second ballot runoff against Mitterrand, a dent had been made in his invulnerability.[31]

For their part, the five other member governments were readier for a compromise by early 1966. While the question of who won and who lost in the crisis has long been disputed, it seems clear that on the most fundamental point at issue, whether the EEC would remain basically an intergovernmental organization or take a significant step toward supranationalism, intergovernmentalism was sustained by the Luxembourg compromise. First, the original Rome treaty budget procedure remained intact, with the Parliament having no more than an advisory role. EEC budgets would continue to be controlled by the Council of Ministers, which would make the final determination as to how much of the EEC's "own resources" would be retained by the states and how much allotted to the Commission to be spent for EEC purposes authorized by the Council. Second, the ability of the Commission to put items on the agenda of the Council of Ministers was restricted by the requirement that they must first be shown to the representatives of the six governments permanently residing in Brussels (see discussion following). Third, regarding voting in the Council of Ministers, a vague formula was mutually accepted that permitted the change from unanimity to majority voting to take place as scheduled in the treaty, but which stated that where "issues very important to one or more member countries are at stake," ministers will seek to reach solutions with which all can be comfortable.[32] From the standpoint of the Euro-centrists in the various governments, this statement simply formulated what had been the practice up to mid-1965; from de Gaulle's standpoint, it legitimized the continued right of a state to veto unacceptable EEC initiatives. From whichever perspective, the compromise cut the wings of the Commission and its president and ruled out a reading of the Rome treaty which suggested that, from January 1966, ordinary and extraordinary agenda decisions might be taken when a majority viewpoint prevailed over French resistance, if for no other reason than the existence of an implied threat that France would repeat its empty chair procedure.[33]

ACCOMPLISHMENTS IN THE MIDST OF DIMINISHING EXPECTATIONS

Completing the Original Agenda

It is significant that, from 1966 on, further efforts on the part of the Commission to initiate an agenda item had to be accepted by all member governments. Should a single government be opposed or even just uncertain about a new departure promoted by the Commission, it could block the Council of Ministers from considering the measure. Although this was not stated explicitly in January 1966, in fact, out of the Luxembourg compromise there arose a procedure whereby ambassadorial level permanent representatives of the member governments residing in Brussels (the Committee of Permanent Representatives, or COREPER) work closely with the Commission in examining and modifying Commission proposals to be sent to the Council. This development has had the twin effects of (1) smoothing the way for proposals once they reach the Council, by removing obstacles of lesser importance, and (2) keeping items off the Council's agenda that are likely to be rejected at the Council level by one or more governments. The senior national civil servants in COREPER are thus the gatekeepers for the EC's ordinary agenda, playing a key role along with the Commission both in agenda setting and in defining the alternatives[34] of issues to be addressed by their political superiors in the Council of Ministers.[35]

During the remainder of the 1960s, the EEC completed a number of the tasks on its ordinary agenda with relatively little controversy.[36] In 1967, the executives of the ECSC, EURATOM, and EEC were merged into one, establishing the European Communities.[37] The preferred term in Brussels has been *European Community* (singular). De Gaulle had the satisfaction of seeing President Hallstein replaced by a competent, but less far-reaching new Commission president, Jean Rey, a Belgian. In 1968, the CU for manufactured products was completed, 18 months early and with all six members, including France, having lowered their tariffs according to the accelerated schedule. The previous year, the Commission assumed responsibility for negotiating on behalf of all six members in the Kennedy Round of General Agreement on Tariffs and Trade (GATT) negotiations. Beginning in 1967 and completed in 1973, all six countries adopted a common value-added tax (VAT), a step that was designed to reduce disparities between the six markets in the prices ultimately charged consumers for the same goods.

After de Gaulle

In May 1968, the presidency of Charles de Gaulle was dealt a severe blow by the outbreak of a student revolt, which started in Paris and spread to other French cities, followed by a general strike by French workers. With the considerable help of his prime minister, Georges Pompidou, de Gaulle managed to weather the storm and order was restored in June. But de Gaulle's personal authority had been seriously weakened, as was confirmed in April 1969 when a referendum he presented to the voters was defeated, partly because a segment of his majority, led by former Finance Minister Valéry Giscard d'Estaing (last name usually shortened to Giscard) opposed it. In response, De Gaulle resigned as president and returned to his country home to write his memoirs, until his death the following year. A new presidential election was held in June 1969, which Georges Pompidou won rather easily over a severely divided opposition. He appointed a fellow Gaullist as his prime minister. Giscard, who led his own smaller and moderately pro-EC party, returned to his previous post as finance minister.

As a Gaullist, Pompidou had no sympathy for supranationalist designs for the EC, but he was willing to take steps to remove the animosities between

France and its EC partners that had accumulated during the de Gaulle years.[38] He made it clear that he would not automatically turn his back on a renewal of the British application for membership in the Community.[39] The issue of EC expansion returned to the extraordinary agenda, along with a number of other items designed to move beyond the original Rome treaty agenda, when Pompidou called for an EC summit meeting at the Hague in December 1969. This was the first such summit to be held since the early de Gaulle years, and it was to be the first of four meetings that can now be seen as forerunners to the regularly scheduled European Council meetings that have taken place since they were instituted in 1975.[40]

The Hague Summit did not produce the full array of results that had been hoped for, especially by the Euro-centrists who were still in command of the five, but it did set in motion the first concrete actions that successfully went beyond the Rome treaty. Pompidou decided to take these steps in part because of the growing significance of West Germany in the affairs of Europe. From 1966 to 1969, the CDU monopoly of power in the FRG had given way to a Grand Coalition of the CDU/CSU[41] and the opposition SPD, now led by Willy Brandt.[42] On EC matters the SPD under Brandt had become Euro-centrist, verbally in favor of steps toward European integration, but usually preferring to wait until France was willing to take the initiative in favor of them. As foreign minister in the Grand Coalition government, Brandt had begun to fashion a new *Ostpolitik* for the FRG, designed to reopen contact with the East Bloc countries, especially with the other part of divided Germany, the German Democratic Republic (GDR).[43]

In the parliamentary elections of September 1969, an emerging center-left coalition of the SPD and the smaller FDP defeated the CDU/CSU, and Willy Brandt became the new chancellor. From the point of view of his EC partners, this change in the West German government augured a change in the direction of the FRG's principal foreign policy preoccupations. At a time when West Germany was emerging as one of the strongest and most dynamic world economies, Pompidou feared that its government would turn its back on the EC and fashion a separate foreign policy toward the East. Bonn might be tempted to use its considerable economic power to lessen the opposition of the Soviet Union to closer relations between East and West Germany, which could be a step in the direction of German reunification. It was still too close to World War II for Pompidou to look favorably on such a prospect, which was a consideration that influenced him to promote the Hague Summit. In fact, Brandt preceded Pompidou in calling for an opening of the EC to Britain. Beyond this, however, he left EC affairs largely to his ministers of finance, economics, and agriculture, who were dealing with the principal EC preoccupations other than expansion during the early-to-mid 1970s.[44]

The Hague Summit produced a declaration of support for negotiations with Britain over the terms of entry. Conditions soon came to be ripe in Britain for a new effort. In June 1970, the Conservatives returned to power, unexpectedly defeating the Labour Party of Prime Minister Harold Wilson. The new prime minister was Edward Heath, who was one of the most unambiguous Euro-centrists to be found at the highest level of British politics.[45] Heath, in fact, had been the chief British negotiator during the first bid to enter the Community in 1961-1963. His Conservative Party had come a long way from the Macmillan days; there was now only a small fringe on the party right wing that opposed entry in 1970, whereas there was a sharp division that cut straight through the middle of the Labour Party on the issue.[46] Negotiations of the British entry went smoothly in comparison with the earlier attempts. The main issues involved Britain's budget contribution, a problem exacerbated by the fact that the benefits going to Britain's small but efficient farm sector would be outweighed by the cost to the British consumer of higher priced food. But the issues involving CAP and the British contribution to the EC budget were fudged in the formula established for gradually phasing in the new member's obligations.[47] Heath was able to get the Treaty of Accession through the House of Commons, and Britain joined the EC in 1973, along with Ireland and Denmark, both of which ratified the treaty after comfortable "yes" votes in popular referenda. On the other hand, the fourth applicant, Norway, failed to ratify the treaty after a negative referendum vote, with farmers and fishing communities voting heavily against accession.[48]

In addition to paving the way for enlargement of the Community, the Hague Summit approved the financial provisions for CAP through establishment of the EC's own resources by national contributions out of collection of agricultural levies and industrial customs duties.[49] The EP obtained a say in the use to which these funds would be put, an arrangement France had opposed since the empty chair crisis, but now Pompidou stepped back from de Gaulle's negative position. At the summit, it was also agreed that EMU would be achieved by 1980.[50] In 1970, the Council of Ministers appointed a committee headed by Luxembourg Prime Minister Pierre Werner to sort out the competing proposals for EMU. The Werner Plan presented to the Council later in the year included proposals for coordination of economic and monetary policies and for an eventual common currency. But when the global monetary crisis began in 1971, the plan was shelved indefinitely.

As long as France's partners were willing to take an intergovernmental approach to achieving cooperation in the foreign policy realm, the French were all for it, as likewise were the British, poised on the brink of joining the EC. Following the Hague meeting, the six foreign ministers commissioned a report by a committee headed by Belgian diplomat Étienne Davignon. The Davignon report on European political cooperation, which came to be called *EPC,* recommended regular meetings of the six foreign ministers wearing their hats as guardians of national interests rather than as the EC Council of Ministers deliberating on general EC policy matters. The plan was to develop habits of regular contact and collaboration between the member countries to allow Europe to speak with a single voice in diplomatic questions, thus raising the potential of France, Germany, and the others to influence matters normally controlled by the superpowers. In fact, although confined to the member states, EPC would not be an integral part of the EC, or of Community institutions. The early steps to EPC paved the way for more significant moves toward political cooperation taken in the mid-1970s after the Community was enlarged to nine members.[51]

In general, the Hague Summit represented the opening of a new extra-ordinary agenda for the EC. But it was an agenda that bore little evidence of the sort of Commission initiative taking and power aggrandizement that had been attempted under President Hallstein. Heads of government, foreign ministers, and career diplomats were in the forefront of the new steps being taken. In two cases, the consequences of the new steps were essentially intergovernmental: (1) the entry of Britain into the EC strengthened the hand of intergovernmentalist France in the Council meetings, as the new, if temporary, axis of power within the EC was the Pompidou-Heath combination, since West Germany was momen-tarily preoccupied with matters to the east; and (2) the new procedures for EPC were decidedly intergovernmentalist, with the Commission having no more than the right to express its views on agenda items initiated by the governments.[52] However, the completion of CAP and the new budget provisions strengthened the supranational elements of the Community.

The Rise of the European Council

The Hague Summit of 1969 can be regarded as a prototype of the agenda-setting summit meetings that began to be held in the 1970s. The next major package deal was reached at the Paris Summit of December 1974, at which the practice was established of holding thrice yearly summit meetings, that is, meetings of the heads of state and government—the European Council—whose presidency rotates among the member countries every 6 months, as was the already existing practice in the Council of Ministers.[53] This practice was the contribution of the new French President Valéry Giscard d'Estaing, who was not a Gaullist but was a center-right Gaullist ally. Giscard was elected president in May 1974, succeeding Georges Pompidou, who had died the previous month. The European Council had the support of the new German chancellor, Helmut Schmidt, who had replaced his fellow SPD leader Willy Brandt in March 1974.

Giscard and Schmidt had already established a good working relationship before becoming their countries' leaders. Both had served as finance ministers under their predecessors at a time when intense efforts were being made to cope with the monetary chaos of the 1971–1973 period (see chapters 4 and 7). They were both of a practical bent with little sympathy for the European visionaries found in the Commission, the EP, or in the governments of some of the other member countries.[54] They could be considered Euro-centrists not in their desire for a supranational Europe—both were pragmatic intergovernmentalists—but in the priority they gave to Europe over other foreign policy concerns. They wanted to see the states of the EC move together in an effort to resolve the severe economic problems of the mid-1970s and to meet the challenges of political change occurring on the continent because of the declining hold of the hegemons over their respective blocs. Both recognized that France and West Germany working together held the key to the growing influence of the EC in

Europe and in the larger world, and neither was looking for an edge over the other.[55]

Shortly before Schmidt and Giscard took the controls of their governments, in the general election of February 1974 power shifted back in Britain from the Conservatives under Edward Heath to the Labour Party headed by Harold Wilson. Whereas Heath had fit the pragmatic Europe-first mode of the new French and German leaders, Wilson, with an uncertain majority in Parliament and with an economy in shambles, was necessarily more preoccupied with Britain than with Europe, and he tended to view European issues in the light of their significance for British domestic politics and economics.[56] This attitude foreclosed any EC leadership role for Britain, leaving the field open to his French and German counterparts, but it also made him a source of irritation to them, as his view of what was politically expedient often worked at cross purposes with what they considered best for Europe, and therefore for France and West Germany.

Wilson's strategy in domestic politics was to use the EC as a means of strengthening his own moderate or social democratic wing of the Labour Party against its left wing. The Labour left, led by Industry Minister Tony Benn, was calling for Britain to leave the EC and threatening to use the issue to siphon off some of Wilson's support base elsewhere in the party. To counter this danger, Wilson promised in the election campaign of February 1974 that, if elected, Labour would renegotiate the Treaty of Accession terms by which Britain had entered the EC in 1973. After winning the election, Wilson signaled to the other EC members that he wished to renegotiate the terms of British membership, failing which Britain would not remain in the Community. The partners reluctantly agreed in principle, but while Wilson managed to gain some minor advantages for Britain out of the negotiations, he claimed for purposes of home consumption that he had gained more for Britain than the facts justified. Although Chancellor Schmidt lent the British considerable assistance in the negotiations, he had little patience with Wilson's tactics.[57]

At the December 1974 Paris Summit, the renegotiation was Wilson's highest priority. He accepted other elements of the package deal Giscard and Schmidt were putting together, including increased regional assistance at the insistence of Italy and Ireland and direct elections of the EP, which had been promoted by the smaller member countries. At the first regularly scheduled European Council meeting, held in Dublin in March 1975, he further irritated his fellow heads by filling the agenda to overflowing with the British renegotiation. In the end, Wilson declared the modest Dublin concessions to be a victory and went on to win a strong "yes" vote in the referendum held in Britain to give advisory approval to the agreements reached.[58]

The heads agreed at the December 1974 Paris Summit to pursue an EC regional policy to give economic assistance to the poorer regions of the member countries. This agreement represented side payments that France and West Germany made to Italy and Ireland in particular, although it was also a policy that the British Labour government supported in the hope that British regions would benefit as well. It represented a departure from the Rome treaty, as was the decision to create regular European Council meetings. Simon Bulmer and Wolfgang Wessels point out that "a key difference from earlier summits was that the commitments were not just pious hopes but had been based on the details of policy as well. . . . The EC's position had been stabilised; its relevance to the 1970s was confirmed."[59]

The decision at the Paris Summit to put direct elections of the EP on the agenda of the Council of Ministers was not so much a departure from the original Rome treaty agenda as it was a long-delayed removal of French resistance to direct elections, which had stood in the way of fulfillment of the treaty for the 15 years of Gaullist rule. It was one of the specific elements of the intergovernmentalism versus supranationalism debate between the Gaullists and the Euro-centrists in France wherein Giscard sided with the latter. Beginning in 1978, there would be regular elections for all seats in the EP every 5 years. Giscard was able to put together an ad hoc Euro-centrist majority in the French National Assembly against the combined opposition of the Communists and Gaullists to enable direct elections to be held in France. With French resistance to direct elections removed, the British became the footdraggers, as the slow process of adopting the electoral law by the British Parliament in the face of left-wing Labour and right-wing Conservative opposition caused the first Euro-elections to be delayed in all nine countries until June 1979.[60]

The European Community in the Mid-1970s

The principal innovations in the EC during the first half of the 1970s were set in motion in one fashion or another by the Hague Summit of December 1969 and were rounded off by the Paris and Dublin summits 5 years later. They confirmed the significance of the empty chair crisis and the Luxembourg compromise of the mid-1960s. It was now clear that additions to and alterations of the original Rome treaty agenda could be undertaken only on the initiative of the heads of government. With the establishment of the European Council, a regular procedure became available for agenda items to be introduced by the heads.[61] This role fell especially to the French president and the West German chancellor, both of whom were in strong political positions after coming to office in the spring of 1974.

The domestic preoccupations of the British government made it possible for Schmidt and Giscard to chart new courses in EPC. In the mid-1970s, EPC was becoming a vehicle by which the EC-nine could take foreign policy positions that were at least gently at odds with the priorities of the United States. Through EPC, the heads probed alternatives to the American pro-Israel position in Middle East questions. More concretely, EPC followed along the lines of reducing tensions between Eastern and Western Europe that de Gaulle had pioneered in the late 1960s with his policy of detente and that Brandt had dramatically achieved in the 1970s with his ostpolitik. In 1975, the Conference on Security and Cooperation in Europe (CSCE) was held at Helsinki, which brought together the states of Western and Eastern Europe, including the Soviet Union, plus the

United States and Canada. A declaration was produced that outlined steps for reducing tensions and accelerating human contacts between East and West. The nine EPC states acted essentially as one under the leadership of the government currently holding the 6-months presidency of the EC Council. The process was strictly intergovernmental because EPC existed outside the Rome treaty framework. Major initiatives to be taken in CSCE negotiations were decided upon in meetings of the nine foreign ministers under general guidelines given at summit meetings.[62]

With respect to the ordinary Rome treaty agenda, beyond the emplacement of the final elements of the CU and the CAP, the Rome treaty provided only very general guidelines to what should happen next. The budget was often the object of intense conflict between the Commission and the Council, between the EP and the Council, and between individual member states within the Council, but somehow budgets were produced, and the ability of the EP to influence parts of them increased. In 1975, a treaty amending the Rome treaty was adopted. It gave the Parliament for the first time the ability to reject the budget outright, and it created a Court of Auditors to monitor the use by the EC of its revenues. Appointment of members of the Court was subject to review and endorsement by the EP.[63]

But the EC in this period was better known for its abortive ordinary agenda items, many of which were proposals by the Commission for harmonizing the separate technical standards that acted as barriers to inter-EC trade, preventing the CU from having its full economic effect. Although some of these, including some with environmental significance, were adopted by the Council of Ministers in the 1970s, many were buried by COREPER or delayed in the Council of Ministers as a result of individual governments implicitly exercising a veto under pressure by economic interest groups that might be adversely affected by harmonization.[64] Movement on these blocked agenda items would await the achievement of the package deal in the mid-1980s that brought about the SEA with its Project 1992 measures for liberalization of trade and harmonization of regulatory regimes affecting trade between the member economies.[65]

On the other hand, below the surface of public attention, a process was going on in the 1960s and 1970s by which the interpretation of the Rome treaty's ordinary agenda was being expanded without reference to the intergovernmental bodies created by the treaty or emerging after the 1965–1966 crisis. The European Court of Justice (ECJ) was in the process of establishing a body of EC constitutional law in a case-by-case fashion, much as the Supreme Court of the United States under John Marshall did in the early nineteenth century. Without challenging the member governments directly, in the 1960s the ECJ asserted the principle that the Rome treaty had the status of a constitution and therefore that its provisions were superior to the laws of the member states. It also granted to "individuals" (usually companies registered in the member states) the right to challenge actions of the member states considered to be in violation of the Treaty of Rome. This led in the 1970s to the declaration that, when actions of the member states were in conflict with lawmaking actions of the EC taken in pursuit of the Rome treaty, EC law would prevail.[66] These assertions would have had little effect if the courts of the member states had refused to accept them, simply regarding the treaty as an international agreement among sovereign states that were competent individually to interpret its meaning for themselves. But gradually in the 1960s and 1970s, national courts did cite decisions of the ECJ as authority for upholding EC law in the face of resistance by national governments and parliaments.[67]

The opinions of the ECJ did not, in and of themselves, have the effect of expanding the ordinary EC agenda, unless the more politically oriented EC bodies were willing to use them for that purpose. The Court could not by itself force new EC legislation. Either the Commission might use an ECJ interpretation of the treaty as justification for a new legislative departure, or a member government might take the initiative in trying to get the other governments to take a course of action implied by something the ECJ had declared. But the 1970s were years of Commission caution and of serious disagreement among the member governments on many policy issues. Nevertheless, the eventual reopening of both the ordinary and the extraordinary agendas in the 1980s was to benefit from a less restrictive interpretation of the treaty than had emerged in the previous decade. The ECJ's work had helped to create the new atmosphere.[68]

CONCLUSION

By the end of 1975, much of the primary work which the six original EEC members had agreed upon in the Treaty of Rome had been accomplished. The CU and the CAP were in place. Differences in conception about how the institutions were to function, which had come to a head in the mid-1960s crisis, had been smoothed over in practice. At least for the time being, intergovernmentalism had come to prevail over supranationalism, not least of all because of the entry of intergovernmentalist Britain, the major holdout of the 1950s, along with Denmark and Ireland. To be sure, direct elections to the EP had been agreed upon and the Parliament had gained a greater role in the budgetary process, but these modest supranational advances were counterbalanced by intergovernmentalist gains in the institutionalization of summit meetings and in the forms established for EPC. And the arrival of EMU, heralded in 1969, had been shelved indefinitely.

What supranationalists regarded as logical extensions of the CU—monetary union and a true common market with all barriers to trade removed—seemed further away from realization than ever in the mid-1970s. Dissatisfaction was growing in particular with what CAP had become, a highly expensive program that was costly to consumers and which, given the waning importance of agriculture in advanced industrial economies, constituted much too large a share of the EC budget. For Britain, a net food importer, agricultural exporting countries like France and the Netherlands were getting too large a share of the British consumers' and taxpayers' pounds. Three major issues were thus holdover items on the EC agenda for the period covered by the next chapter (1976–1989): monetary union, the internal market, and the intertwined issues of CAP and the British share of the EC budget.

ENDNOTES

1. "Preamble and Selected Articles of the Treaty Establishing the European Economic Community, March 25, 1957," in Howard Bliss, ed., *The Political Development of the European Community: A Documentary Collection* (Waltham, Mass.: Blaisdell Publishing, 1970), pp. 47–66.
2. Lindberg and Scheingold rank decision-making functions of the EEC as of 1968 according to the mix of Community-level and national-level decisions involved. The highest rank received was for functions wherein there was policy making at both levels, but where "Community activity predominates." The two functions in this category were "agricultural protection" and "movement of goods, services, and other factors of production within the customs union." For the 20 other functions listed, decision making was either exclusively or predominantly at the national level. Leon N. Lindberg and Stuart A. Scheingold, *Europe's Would-Be Polity: Patterns of Change in the European Community* (Englewood Cliffs, N.J.: Prentice-Hall, 1970), p. 71.
3. Keohane defines hegemony as leadership in political, economic, and security matters that a state is able and willing to exercise over other states. Robert O. Keohane, *After Hegemony: Cooperation and Discord in the World Political Economy* (Princeton, N.J.: Princeton University Press, 1984), p. 39. Benefits of this leadership are mutual, although not necessarily evenly balanced, for both leaders and followers (ibid., p. 128).
4. Derek W. Urwin, *Western Europe since 1945: A Political History,* 4th ed. (London and New York: Longman, 1989), pp. 131–134.
5. Roy Godson and Stephen Haseler, *'Eurocommunism:' Implications for East and West* (New York: St. Martin's, 1978), pp. 97–99.
6. F. Roy Willis, *France, Germany and the New Europe, 1945–1967,* rev. ed. (London: Oxford University Press, 1968), pp. 98–99, 140–141, 262–264.
7. Extensive analyses of de Gaulle's strategy in Europe within the context of his general world view are found in Philip G. Cerny, *The Politics of Grandeur: Ideological Aspects of de Gaulle's Foreign Policy* (Cambridge: Cambridge University Press, 1980); Alfred Grosser, *The Western Alliance: European-American Relations since 1945* (New York: Vintage Books, 1982); Stanley Hoffmann, *Decline or Renewal? France since the 1930s* (New York: Viking Press, 1974); Edward Kolodziej, *French International Policy under de Gaulle and Pompidou: The Politics of Grandeur* (Ithaca, N.Y.: Cornell University Press, 1974).
8. Hoffmann, *Decline or Renewal,* pp. 301–302.
9. William E. Paterson, *The SPD and European Integration* (Lexington, Mass.: Lexington Books, 1974), chaps. 3–5.
10. Stephen George, *An Awkward Partner: Britain in the European Community* (Oxford: Oxford University Press, 1990), pp. 26–28.
11. John Pinder, *European Community: The Building of Union* (Oxford and New York: Oxford University Press, 1991), pp. 45–46; Dennis Swann, *The Economics of the Common Market,* 5th ed. (Hammondsworth: Penguin Books, 1984), p. 22.
12. F. S. Northedge, "Britain and the EEC: Past and Present," in Roy Jenkins, ed., *Britain and the EEC* (London and Basingstoke: Macmillan, 1983), pp. 15–37.

13. For accounts of the Algerian war and the transformation of the Fourth Republic into the Fifth Republic, see Edgar S. Furniss, Jr., *France, Troubled Ally: De Gaulle's Heritage and Prospects* (New York: Frederick A. Praeger, 1960); Roy C. Macridis and Bernard Brown, *The De Gaulle Republic: Quest for Unity* (Homewood, Ill.: Dorsey Press, 1960).

14. Derek W. Urwin, *The Community of Europe: A History of European Integration since 1945* (London and New York: Longman, 1991), pp. 103-107.

15. Suzanne J. Bodenheimer, *Political Union: A Microcosm of European Politics, 1960–1966* (Leyden: A.W. Sijthoff, 1967), pp. 59-60.

16. Ibid., pp. 92-99. The West German government sought unsuccessfully to reach a compromise between the French position and that of the others. Jan Werts, *The European Council* (Amsterdam: North Holland, 1992), pp. 23-25.

17. Northedge, "Britain and the EEC," p. 26.

18. Britain was seen as a trojan horse supporting US interests within the EEC. Miriam Camps, *European Unification in the Sixties: From the Veto to the Crisis* (New York: McGraw-Hill, 1966), p. 3.

19. Werner J. Feld, *West Germany and the European Community: Changing Interests and Competing Policy Objectives* (New York: Praeger, 1981), pp. 50-51.

20. Urwin, *The Community of Europe*, pp. 82, 110.

21. John Newhouse, *Collision in Brussels: The Common Market Crisis of 30 June 1965* (New York: W.W. Norton & Co., 1967), pp. 67-71.

22. Ibid., pp. 56-57.

23. Camps, *European Unification in the Sixties*, pp. 38-43.

24. Ibid., p. 43.

25. According to the Treaty of Rome, what we are consistently calling the European Parliament was officially named the Assembly. The members of the Assembly themselves called it a Parliament from an early stage, although its powers were very weak under the treaty. It could propose budget amendments to the Council of Ministers, but the Council was "under no obligation to accept any amendments," and could adopt its original version of the budget by qualified majority. Ibid., p. 44.

26. Ibid., pp. 43-45.

27. Newhouse, *Collision in Brussels*, p. 77.

28. Camps, *European Unification in the Sixties*, pp. 81-85.

29. Urwin, *The Community of Europe*, p. 111.

30. Werts, *The European Council*, p. 28.

31. Camps, *European Unification in the Sixties*, pp. 95-101.

32. Ibid., p. 112.

33. Ibid., p. 113.

34. John W. Kingdon, *Agendas, Alternatives and Public Policies* (Glenview, Ill., and London: Scott, Foresman & Co., 1984), p. 4.

35. Newhouse, *Collision in Brussels*, pp. 161-165.

36. Urwin, *The Community of Europe*, pp. 130-132.

37. Willis, *France, Germany and the New Europe*, p. 361.

38. F. Roy Willis, *The French Paradox: Understanding Contemporary France* (Stanford, Calif.: Hoover Institution, 1982), pp. 10, 105.

39. In 1967, the government of Prime Minister Harold Wilson made a second effort to bring Britain into the community. For a second time, the bid was turned down by General de Gaulle. George, *An Awkward Partner*, pp. 37-38.

40. Simon Bulmer and Wolfgang Wessels, *The European Council: Decision-Making in European Politics* (Basingstoke and London: Macmillan, 1987), p. 1.

41. The CDU/CSU is a confederation of two Christian Democratic parties. The CDU is active in all German states except Bavaria, and the CSU is the Christian Democratic party exclusively in Bavaria. They act for most purposes as a unit in government and politics at the national level, although the CSU is regarded as more conservative than the CDU, and does not fit our Euro-centrist designation. In the de Gaulle years, its leader, Franz Josef Strauss, was considered a "German Gaullist," meaning that he believed West Germany should join de Gaulle's France in exercising dual leadership of the EC, ridding it of supranational elements and moving the six beyond the sphere of American influence. Willis, *France, Germany and the New Europe,* p. 330.
42. Urwin, *The Community of Europe,* pp. 137–138.
43. Wolfram F. Hanrieder, *Germany, America, Europe: Forty Years of German Foreign Policy* (New Haven and London: Yale University Press, 1989), pp. 196–198, 283–285.
44. Ibid., pp. 285–296.
45. George, *An Awkward Partner,* p. 49.
46. David Butler and Uwe Kitzinger, *The 1975 Referendum* (New York: St. Martin's, 1976), pp. 17–20.
47. George, *An Awkward Partner,* p. 56.
48. Urwin, *The Community of Europe,* pp. 140–145.
49. For discussions of the Hague Summit, see Bulmer and Wessels, *The European Council,* pp. 28–30; Urwin, *The Community of Europe,* chaps. 9 and 10.
50. Rainer Hellmann, *Gold, the Dollar, and the European Currency Systems: The Seven Year Monetary War* (New York: Praeger, 1979), pp. 20–22.
51. *European Political Co-operation (EPC),* 5th ed. (Bonn: Press and Information Office of the Federal Government, 1988); Wolfgang Wessels, "New Forms of Foreign Policy Formulation in Western Europe," in Werner J. Feld, ed., *Western Europe's Global Reach: Regional Cooperation and Worldwide Aspirations* (New York: Pergamon, 1980), pp. 12–29.
52. *European Political Co-operation (EPC),* p. 28.
53. Bulmer and Wessels, *The European Council,* pp. 11–13.
54. Urwin, *The Community of Europe,* p. 173.
55. Bulmer and Wessels, *The European Council,* pp. 41–42.
56. George, *An Awkward Partner,* pp. 74–78.
57. Ibid., pp. 82–87.
58. Ibid., pp. 87–95; Butler and Kitzinger, *The 1975 Referendum,* pp. 39–47.
59. Bulmer and Wessels, *The European Council,* p. 46.
60. Urwin, *The Community of Europe,* pp. 167–168; Dominique Remy with Karl-Hermann Buck, "France: The Impossible Compromise or the End of Majority Parliamentarism?" pp. 99–125; Mark Hagger, "The United Kingdom: The Reluctant Europeans," pp. 204–238, in Valentine Herman and Mark Hagger, eds., *The Legislation of Direct Elections to the European Parliament* (Westmead: Gower, 1980); David M. Wood, "Comparing Parliamentary Voting on European Issues in France and Britain," *Legislative Studies Quarterly* 7 (February 1982): 101–117.
61. Bulmer and Wessels, *The European Council,* pp. 17–21.
62. *European Political Cooperation (EPC),* pp. 95–97; William Wallace, "Political Cooperation: Integration Through Intergovernmentalism," in Helen Wallace, et al., eds., *Policy-Making in the European Community,* 2nd ed. (Chichester: John Wiley & Sons, 1983), pp. 378–380. See chapter 11 for the evolution from EPC to the CFSP of today's EU.

63. Helen Wallace, *Budgetary Politics: The Finances of the European Communities* (London: George Allen & Unwin, 1980), pp. 77–91, 102.

64. Alan Dashwood, "Hastening Slowly: The Community's Path Towards Harmonization," in Wallace, et al., eds., *Policy-Making in the European Community,* pp. 184–187; Thomas Sloot and Piet Verschuren, "Decision-making Speed in the European Community," *Journal of Common Market Studies* 29 (September 1990): 79–80; Bulmer and Wessels, *The European Council,* p. 5.

65. Alberta M. Sbragia, "Asymmetrical Integration in the European Community: The Single European Act and Institutional Developments," in Dale L. Smith and James Lee Ray, eds., *The 1992 Project and the Future of Integration in Europe* (Armonk, N.Y., and London: M.E. Sharpe, 1993), pp. 101–104; Helen Wallace, "The Council and the Commission after the Single European Act," in Leon Hurwitz and Christian Lequesne, eds. *The State of the European Community: Policies, Institutions and Debates in the Transition Years* (Boulder: Lynne Reinner, 1991), pp. 24–25.

66. Anne-Marie Burley and Walter Mattli, "Europe Before the Court: A Political Theory of Legal Integration," *International Organization* 47 (Winter 1993): 66; G. Federico Mancini, "The Making of a Constitution for Europe," in Robert O. Keohane and Stanley Hoffmann, eds., *The New European Community: Decisionmaking and Institutional Change* (Boulder: Westview, 1991), pp. 180–181.

67. Martin Shapiro, "The European Court of Justice," in Alberta M. Sbragia, ed., *Euro-Politics: Institutions and Policymaking in the "New" European Community* (Washington: The Brookings Institution, 1992), p. 127.

68. David R. Cameron, "The 1992 Initiative: Causes and Consequences," in Sbragia, ed., *Euro-Politics,* pp. 52–53.

chapter 4

From Euro-Pessimism to Renewed Euro-Optimism (1975–1989)

$\mathbf{B}$y the mid-1970s, optimism about the future of the EC was in short supply. Governments of the EC member countries were exhausting their political capital in attempting to grapple with the problems of energy shortages, monetary instability, and stagflation, all of which were visited on them by a turbulent global economy over which they had little control and about which they lacked a common understanding.[1]

Within the EC, the leadership potential of the European Commission and its president had seriously eroded in the years since the confrontation between Commission President Hallstein and French President de Gaulle. Yet there was a strong sense that the economic problems of the member countries could be coped with more effectively if they could work together to solve them, rather than pulling in different directions. In the late 1970s and early 1980s, leadership was found that energized both the supranational and the intergovernmental institutions of the EC sufficiently that new advances were made on the extra-ordinary agenda. By the mid-1980s, Euro-pessimism was giving way to renewed Euro-optimism, which was to prevail for the rest of the decade. It emerged first in the business sector; then, as economies recovered, it affected political elites as well.

In the 1980s, advances were made toward both political and economic integration, and two further expansions of the EC occurred, in 1981 (entry of Greece) and 1986 (entry of Portugal and Spain). Expansion of the EC to include three Mediterranean countries, less developed economically than most existing members, provided considerable impetus for the effort to complete the common market that resulted in adoption of the SEA. In discussing these and other developments, we show how the extraordinary agenda was processed and the problems of exchange rate instability, internal market blockage, and budgetary distortions were converted from extraordinary into ordinary agenda items. First, we review briefly the steps that had been taken toward economic integration up to the mid-1970s, which must be understood to comprehend the motivations for the steps taken thereafter.

THE ROME TREATY AND ITS IMPLEMENTATION

The Rome treaty, which set up the EEC, came into effect on January 1, 1958. It is a long document containing 248 articles. Article 3(a) called for the elimination of internal trade barriers in the form of tariffs and quotas on manufactured products, creating a free trade zone covering the six countries. Article 3(b) provided for the creation of a common external tariff schedule for the member states, which would establish a CU. And Article 3(c) required the members to abolish all other restrictions and obstacles to freedom of movement of peoples, goods, and services, creating a common market.[2] For this purpose, Article 3(h) called for the harmonization of member state laws to facilitate realization of the common market, which was to be achieved over a period of 12 years (by 1969). Article 3(d) called for the establishment of a CAP among the member countries which would remove barriers to trade in agricultural goods between the members and regulate trade in farm products with the rest of the world. From 1958 to 1969, the six member states proceeded to construct the basic elements of economic integration projected by the treaty. Although they did not achieve a common market, an effort which was to be resurrected with the SEA, they did create a CU and a CAP. The CU was completed in 1968, with the removal of tariffs and quotas on manufactured goods between the member states, and the consolidation of a common external tariff for manufactured goods produced in non-EEC countries.

Although agricultural production was a declining component of the national product of the member countries, and was a smaller portion of gross national product (GNP) in each country than the manufactured product, the political support of farmers was cohesive and was often crucial to the parliamentary support of governments in power. The economic status of less efficient farmers in Europe was vulnerable in the face of lower priced farm products that could invade the markets of the six unless farmers were protected. In all six countries, governments protected their farmers with subsidies and price support systems, which guaranteed that they could compete with imported farm products, including products of the other member countries' farmers. Such state support ran counter to the idea of a common market, but farmers in all six countries, even highly industrialized West Germany, were too strong politically to allow governments to give up agricultural protectionism. Barriers against trade in farm products among the six countries were removed, but farmers insisted that they remain in place and even be strengthened against agricultural goods that would otherwise invade the EEC market from the United States, Canada, Australia, and other more efficient agricultural producers.

According to Article 39 of the Rome treaty, the objectives of the CAP were to increase productivity, ensure a fair standard of living for the agrarian population, stabilize markets, and guarantee a steady supply of food and other agricultural goods at reasonable prices to the consumers. The CAP was to reflect and increase economic interdependence among the six. For example, while France needed markets for its agricultural products, West Germany was in need of food imports, which included northern grains; meat and dairy products from the Benelux countries and northern France; and vegetables, fruits, and other Mediterranean products from Italy and southern France. In turn, West Germany wanted access to the markets of the other countries, especially France, for its manufactured goods. While the CAP was to be an expensive plan, particularly for the Germans, EEC leaders felt it was important to guarantee self-sufficiency in this area in view of the wars that had visited Europe twice in the century. Also, besides being an agricultural price support system, CAP was designed to help in the restructuring of Western European agriculture by encouraging fewer, larger, and more efficient farms.[3]

As we have seen in the case of the empty chair crisis, securing agreement among the six countries in support of CAP was not easy. Particularly vexing was the issue of how to finance CAP, as it was recognized that it would take up the lion's share of the EEC budget, at least in the early years. It still constitutes about one-half of the budget today.[4] The Commission saw it as an opportunity to gain greater financial independence of the member governments, but de Gaulle thwarted this aim, and although large CAP sums flow through the Commission's accounts, it has very limited discretion over how they are spent. But though the Commission lacks power to allocate these resources, the formulas used to determine how CAP monies are raised and distributed are not neutral in their effects. In general, the greater the proportion of a member country's economy that is taken up by agricultural production for the export market, the more its net receipts resulting from the CAP will be; the lower the share, the greater the country's net budgetary contribution to the Community budget. Germany has always been a net budgetary contributor because of its strong economic status, as well as net CAP contributions, as has Britain, with a weaker economic base but relatively large CAP-related contributions. Even France, because of the diminishment of its farm sector and the addition of less-industrialized members that gain from the system (Ireland, Greece, Portugal, and Spain), has become a net contributor[5] (see chapter 8 for further discussion of CAP).

As the barriers to trade between the member countries in manufactured and agricultural goods came down, the six economies became more vulnerable to fluctuations in one another's economic fortunes. A recession in, say, France would mean a lessening of demand for products of the other countries, which had become dependent on France's economic good health to market their products in France. The same effect could be produced if the value of the French franc vis-a-vis the U.S. dollar should be lessened (devalued) under the Bretton Woods monetary system of the 1960s, and therefore lessened vis-à-vis currencies of other member countries that remained at a fixed rate of exchange with respect to the dollar. French consumers of products of other EC countries could not buy as much with their francs as before the devaluation, and the French demand for products of the other countries would decline. Under the Bretton Woods system, such maladjustments could work themselves out because demand for the now cheaper French imports would rise in the other countries, increasing the demand of holders of these harder currencies for francs, and therefore returning the franc to its original value. The point to remember, though, is that interdependence in trade brought with it monetary interdependence.

FROM BRETTON WOODS
TO THE EUROPEAN MONETARY SYSTEM

The collapse of the Bretton Woods monetary regime in the early 1970s represented the first of a series of external economic shocks to the EC testing the member countries' seriousness in achieving economic integration. Under Bretton Woods, the United States was required to buy and sell unlimited amounts of gold at the official price of $35 per ounce. In the latter half of the 1960s, the United States began running balance of payments deficits because of overspending on the war in Vietnam and President Lyndon Johnson's War on Poverty at home. To finance these efforts, the U.S. Treasury was rapidly creating money, European holdings of which equaled and then exceeded the value of gold the United States government held in reserve. Confidence in the dollar dropped, and holders of dollars sought to exchange them for more reliable currencies, thus furthering the balance of payments deficit. The final blow to the Bretton Woods system came when the United States ran an alarming balance of payments deficit in 1971 that accompanied the first U.S. trade deficit of the twentieth century. Rather than waiting for its trade partners to knock on the door to exchange dollars for gold, the Nixon administration took the initiative and abrogated the U.S. obligation to the Bretton Woods system.[6]

Because the value of every EC currency was denominated in dollars, the loss of stable exchange rates with the dollar threatened the stability of the EU countries' exchange rates with one another. Their values had to be adjusted and readjusted by trial and error, affecting the stability of trade relations among the members as well. Inflationary pressures on some of the currencies, such as the French franc, the Italian lire, and the imminent newcomer, the British pound, were particularly high. By 1972, these currencies were floating in value against the dollar and, more importantly, against the major stable European currency, the German Deutschmark (DM). By trial and error, the EC-nine developed a joint float against the dollar, called the *snake,* in which each pledged to keep its currencies floating within a fairly narrow range against the floating dollar, which meant that the other EC currencies would remain within a band against the DM as well (see chapter 7). Stronger EC currencies were able to do this; others could not and moved in and out of the snake in their struggle to avoid the severe economic consequences of having currencies that were seriously overvalued, meaning a danger of trade and payments deficits.[7] These problems were less severe for a large and still relatively self-sufficient country like the United States in the early 1970s, but for the smaller, interdependent economies of Europe, getting their monetary policies right was absolutely crucial for their economic well-being. This was becoming apparent to national leaders, who began to perceive that the idea of an EMU, which had been initially put forth in the Werner Plan, then set aside with the onslaught of the monetary crisis, might have had some merit after all. The extended crisis had both necessitated and made possible a learning experience for governments and even their highly qualified economic advisers. By 1977, some of the leading actors were rapidly moving up the learning curve. [8]

The first leader to speak out was Roy Jenkins, a former British chancellor of the exchequer (i.e., finance minister), who became the president of the European Commission in 1977. In his Jean Monnet lecture in Florence in October 1977, Jenkins proposed the creation of an EMU. The reasons he gave for such a venture reflected the disillusionment of many economists with the conventional assumption of a trade-off between inflation and unemployment, or the belief that policies designed to get rid of one would only bring on the other. Jenkins took the monetarist position that monetary stability (low inflation) was necessary to stimulate more efficient and competitive industry across the EC, in turn reversing the reduced employment not only in the aggregate, but in the countries and regions of the EC where industry had been less efficient.[9] The timing of his speech was ripe, because political leaders of some of the member countries were coming to similar conclusions as they contemplated their political prospects at home. At the Brussels European Council meeting in December 1977, the Belgian government head, following Jenkins's lead, persuaded his colleagues to reaffirm their support for the idea of EMU, but without adopting the Jenkins proposal as official policy.[10]

Then, in February 1978, German Chancellor Helmut Schmidt told Jenkins that he favored a major step toward EMU involving an EC-wide monetary bloc with a common currency pool. Schmidt was preoccupied at the time with what he considered to be irresponsible economic management by the Carter administration in the United States, which was allowing the dollar to float downward in value to reduce its balance of trade deficits with other countries by pushing up the value of their currencies vis-à-vis the dollar. To protect the DM against a gain in value that could be damaging to German exporters, Schmidt wanted to tie the EC currencies closer together to keep the DM from rising in value relative to those of Germany's principal trade partners, whatever might happen to the DM-dollar exchange rate.[11] This protection could be accomplished by a plan that would more reliably link EC currencies to one another than could the snake, still subject to dollar fluctuations. On the political side, Schmidt was concerned that upcoming state-level elections in Germany could result in a two-thirds majority for the opposition Christian Democrats in the Bundesrat (upper house of Parliament), and thus seriously hamper with its veto power his government's legislation. Already, the ruling coalition's majority in the Bundestag (lower house) had been reduced to ten seats in the 1976 parliamentary elections. He needed a way of showing the electorate that his government was able to take initiatives in their economic interest.

Schmidt was also signaling, in essence, that Germany would prefer sharing economic leadership in Europe with other European countries, especially with France. The French president, Giscard d'Estaing, was a supporter of EMU, but he faced legislative elections in March 1978 and was trying to pick up votes from both his left and right. Overt support for EMU or for a less ambitious project such as Schmidt was advancing would bring criticism from both the Socialist left on economic policy grounds and the Gaullist right on grounds of loss of French sovereignty. But following the election success of his coalition, these inhibitions were removed, and Giscard sought to portray France as being as committed to monetary discipline as was Germany.[12] In both countries, monetary values are seen as symbolic of national prestige, and it is believed that the state's willingness to protect the currency is an indication of self-assurance and political strength.[13] In April 1978, at the Copenhagen meeting of the European Council, the two closely allied leaders agreed to propose a joint project that would lead to more stability of exchange rates in Europe. Three months later, at the Bremen Summit, experts were given the mandate to work out a stronger version of the joint float against the dollar, creating a new European unit of value (later called the *European Currency Unit,* or *ECU*) that would help the EC currencies themselves replace the dollar in interventions to adjust currency values. The final EMS plan emerged from the Brussels Summit held in December 1978. It came into being in March 1979 with all but Britain as members. Italy and Ireland, which were originally reticent about joining, were enticed into the system with side payments by the richer members.[14]

PRIME MINISTER THATCHER AND THE BUDGET ISSUE[15]

British hesitancy in joining EMS was symptomatic of the same general reluctance to take new steps toward integration along with the "Europeans" on the continent that had kept Britain out of the original Communities in the 1950s, and had moved de Gaulle to refuse British entry to the EEC in the 1960s. A year after British entry in 1973, the same reluctance, by British voters as well as their public officials, had forced Prime Minister Wilson to the political calculation that a Labour Party victory could be bought only at the price of a promise to renegotiate the terms of British entry (see chapter 3). Memories of past British glory, long-standing rivalry and, at times, enmity with France, and more recent brutal experiences with Germany were not easily erased in Britons' minds. Because of their attachments to special relationships with the United States and with other areas of the world colonized by British subjects and still linked in the Commonwealth of Nations—Canada, New Zealand, and Australia—the British could not completely identify themselves with their neighbors across the

Channel. The EMS proposal could be perceived as solidifying the EC against the threat posed by an American government that had ceased to shoulder the responsibilities of hegemony and was looking out for its short-run economic interests. Although Washington endorsed EMS, the British Labour government under James Callaghan (who had replaced Wilson as prime minister in 1976) preferred to stay out of the line of fire in case of a future exchange rate war between the Carter administration and the EMS leaders, Schmidt and Giscard. Besides, there was strong resistance to further British commitments to the EC from those within the Labour Party who had campaigned for a "no" vote in the 1975 referendum over continued British membership.[16]

The Callaghan government was at odds with its EC partners over another issue that, once again, reached down to the roots of the British difference. From the British point of view, the CAP was simply unfair. It was seen, first of all, as a mechanism by which taxpayers in EC countries like Britain that were net food importers were subsidizing not only the farmers of other EC countries, but the governments of those countries, which were relieved by CAP of part of their responsibility for maintaining farmers' incomes. Second, it was seen as a factor adding to both external dislocations (high oil prices) and internal strains (budgetary deficits, high labor costs) that had produced runaway British inflation in the mid-1970s.[17]

To alleviate British economic problems with a loan from the International Monetary Fund (IMF), the Callaghan government had been forced to cut back in government spending in 1977 and impose limits on wage increases of their working class supporters in 1977–1978. In the face of all their economic hardships, British consumers were having to pay higher prices than they were used to for food, much of which came in very visible form into their grocery stores from France, Holland, and Denmark. Yearly negotiations with EC partners over CAP prices and budgetary contributions provided the Callaghan government with constant reminders that its political problems at home were made more difficult by policies of an organization that many of their supporters felt should not have been joined in the first place. In the winter of 1978–1979, large scale strikes broke out in Britain, as trade unions rebelled against "their own" government's wage restraint policy. In the May 1979 general election, Callaghan's Labour Party was defeated by the Conservatives, whose leader, Margaret Thatcher, then became the new prime minister.

Although the rise of Margaret Thatcher is usually seen as ushering in a new era in British politics, as far as British policies toward the EC were concerned, Britain did not turn around and become more cooperative under her premiership —quite the contrary. Although Callaghan had ruffled feathers in EC circles from time to time, Thatcher employed the politics of confrontation as a personal style. Like de Gaulle, she appeared intractible in negotiation, but her style was not aloof and inscrutable. She jumped right into the middle of the fray, and her adversaries knew where she stood, but they were no happier with the positions she took than de Gaulle's opponents had been in the 1960s.[18] On the CAP-budget issue, she made it very clear that, in the opinion of her government, the existing arrangements were unfair, and that Britain would not countenance further progress toward EU as long as the unfairness remained. Her stances and the persistence with which she argued them often angered her fellow government heads. By May 1982, the mutual antagonism got to the point that, when Britain's minister of agriculture sought to evoke the 1966 Luxembourg compromise to block a Council of Ministers decision on CAP that would add to Britain's budgetary contribution, he was overruled by the Belgian presidency, who was strongly backed by France, and upheld by the other members, leaving Britain in isolation. Thatcher decided not to insist on the veto by following de Gaulle's empty chair precedent, and thus a precedent was set supporting majority rule in Council voting.[19]

From the standpoint of the Commission in Brussels and the original six member governments, Britain had never accepted true European goals and norms. Obviously, Britain resisted the goals of economic, monetary, and political union, and the others recognized that any moves they might make in this direction would elicit a British veto, or else a British refusal to take part, as in the EMS case. But Thatcher's claim of unfairness in the CAP and budget discussions was seen by her fellow heads as a repudiation of norms that the Community had developed over the past 30 years. The term *Community* reflected the belief of political elites in France, West Germany, Italy, and the Benelux countries that members had joined in the desire to engage in a cooperative effort to solve problems they could not solve on their own. Policies that the six had put in place prior to Britain's entry constituted what was called in French the *acquis communautaire*, that is, that body of established laws and practices that made them a true community. This body had been accumulated through long and painful negotiations, involving the give and take of members who were ill-disposed to reexamine them at such a late date. When Britain joined the Community, it had accepted the acquis communautaire and its consequences, including its budgetary consequences. This acceptance did not mean Britain could not work to improve the CAP. None of the member countries would insist that the CAP was perfect and should not be reformed. But until agreement could be reached on CAP reform, the budgetary arrangements would have to continue.[20]

It was not lost on Thatcher that France, which was one of the members most resistant to an accommodation with Britain over the budget, had always fought its own corner fiercely, even when the rest of the EC membership was aligned on the other side. But, while he was still German chancellor, Helmut Schmidt sought to find ways to bring the British and the French together on the issue. According to Thatcher, he had pointed out to her that "the CAP was a price which had to be paid, however high, to persuade members like France and Italy to come into the Community from the beginning." In her memoirs, Thatcher was to observe: "Although I had had serious disagreements with him, I always had the highest regard for Helmut Schmidt's wisdom, straightforwardness and grasp of international economics. Sadly, I never developed quite the same relationship with Chancellor Kohl. . . ."[21] In October 1982, a coalition of Helmut

Kohl's CDU/CSU and the liberal FDP replaced the coalition of Schmidt's SPD and the FDP. The centrist Free Democrats had changed sides, foresaking the center-left coalition for a new one of the center-right.

Both Helmuts, Schmidt and Kohl, had to deal with Margaret Thatcher's demand for a fairer mechanism involving the British budget contribution. On the one hand, they could sympathize with her argument that British taxpayers should not be subsidizing the French and other governments, because Germany was itself the largest net contributor to the EC budget. Thus, Kohl joined Thatcher in resisting a lifting of the budget ceiling within which the EC had to operate. But he was also cognizant that an important component of his electoral support as a Christian Democrat and that of his coalition partner, Free Democrat Foreign Minister Hans-Dietrich Genscher, came from West German farmers, who were more dependent on CAP than were British farmers. So he resisted Thatcher's call for CAP reforms that would reduce payments to inefficient farmers, as well as her call for reform of the budget structure, because any substantial reduction in the British contribution would have to be picked up mainly by his own government.[22]

On the French side of the triangle, a major change in government occurred in May 1981, when Socialist François Mitterrand was elected president, defeating the incumbent Giscard d'Estaing. Although his party won a majority in its own right in legislative elections held in June, the government that Mitterrand chose included four Communist ministers, along with ministers drawn from the left wing of the Socialist Party, meaning that traditional French left-wing hostility to European integration now had a voice in the French cabinet. In the first 2 years of his presidency, Mitterrand and his ministers were preoccupied with an ambitious and radical program of domestic socioeconomic reforms that included nationalization (bringing into the state sector) of leading multinational industrial firms and banks and a reflationary strategy to reduce unemployment. By 1983, it was clear that this program was too expensive and was threatening France's capacity to maintain its position in the EMS, with continual pressure being put on the franc that could only with great difficulty maintain its value vis-à-vis the strong DM. Left-wing members of Mitterrand's government were calling for France to pull out of the Exchange Rate Mechanism (ERM) of EMS; but in March 1983, Mitterrand decided to stay in, although the consequence would be a reversal of the socioeconomic reforms and a serious austerity program to defend the franc within the ERM.[23]

With his majority in disarray and his own popularity in decline, Mitterrand needed a success on the international scene to divert attention from the failure of his government's economic policies. He was ready to foster progress on the European front, a prospect which appealed to him anyway, because he had always been a Euro-centrist. He found his target in a number of proposals for both economic and political integration that were being given attention by the Commission and the EP at the time, although they were by no means new. The main opportunity appeared in early 1984 when France assumed the 6-months EC Council presidency, affording Mitterrand a chance to play a leadership role.[24]

To bring about a policy success at the European level, Mitterrand had to find a way to mollify the British prime minister. The obvious way was to make concessions to her regarding the British budget contribution.

In two summit meetings during the French presidency, at Brussels in March 1984 and Fontainebleau 3 months later, an agreement was reached to reduce the British budgetary contribution in such a way as to reflect more accurately (and fairly, from the British viewpoint) the relative British economic position measured in terms of per capita income. This agreement meant an approximately two-thirds reduction in the British CAP-mandated contribution. At Brussels, confrontation prevailed over cooperation, as Chancellor Kohl refused to make up for the British reduction with a sizeable increase in the German contribution, the Italians and French held up payment of a rebate to Britain that had been agreed to in 1983, and Britain threatened not to pay its agreed-upon 1984 contribution.[25] But threats to consider dividing the EC into a fast-track and a slow-track set of member states, with Britain in the slow track, may have put Thatcher in a more conciliatory mood by the time of the Fontainebleau Summit in June. Mitterrand's commitment to resolving the issue was manifested in his willingness to assume a major part of the financial burden that Germany was refusing, enabling Kohl to accept part of it as well.[26] Agreement on the British budgetary contribution received the headlines, while significant steps that were made at Fontainebleau toward what was to become the SEA went largely unnoticed.

THE SINGLE EUROPEAN ACT

The Fontainebleau Summit well illustrates the value of instituting regular summit meetings. They had become a means by which progress could be made in economic and political integration whenever favorable national and international circumstances coincided with the turn of the right member in the Council presidency. Such convergence has opened windows of opportunity[27] such as those provided by the change in French economic policy shortly before it became France's turn to set the agenda for the European Council.[28] At Fontainebleau, the heads of government made the single market their first priority in the quest for economic union. This meant a commitment to removing barriers to the exchange of goods and services and to the movement of labor and capital among the member countries. These were barriers that had continued to exist after creation of the CU or that had been erected more recently, preventing the CU from becoming a true common, or single, market.

Among the factors converging to make realization of the single market more attractive to the heads of government were international and national economic conditions, especially increased Japanese and American competition in both international markets and in the EC market itself.[29] This competition was focusing the attention of European business leaders on their disadvantageous position with respect to economies of scale. Cooperation among the business leaders began after a roundtable discussion of the European multinationals sponsored by

Commission Vice-President Étienne Davignon. The aim of this meeting was to encourage cooperation in high-tech industries and creation of a single market to revitalize industry in Europe.[30] It is also important to recognize that by the mid-1980s some degree of monetary stability had been achieved through the EMS, as member governments, including as noted the French, acknowledged the value of monetary discipline imposed by their ties to the DM.[31] However, the influence of business elites on the member governments is uncertain, because it appears that they became vocal only after the Fontainebleau Summit had signaled the support of the governments. Similarly, the strong push by the Commission to promote single market legislation after French Finance Minister Jacques Delors became its president in January 1985 postdated the setting of the agenda.[32] As far as agenda setting is concerned, Delors may have been important as French finance minister in influencing Mitterrand to take the initiative in the first place, but the Commission's subsequent role in selecting policy alternatives and in making sure that the single market idea took wing was of great importance, as was the support of Euro-business.

After Delors was chosen the new president of the Commission, he assigned a British colleague, Lord Cockfield, the Commissioner for the Internal Market, the task of preparing a White Paper that included a list of 300 measures needed for achieving a true common market. He also laid out a timetable to be followed by the EC members to complete adoption of these measures by December 31, 1992, thus the name *Project 1992*. Some 279 measures were eventually agreed upon and mandated by the SEA. Scheduled to be removed were a wide array of laws and government practices of the member countries that served as barriers, often but not in all cases deliberate barriers, to intra-EC trade. These included, among others, bureaucratic procedures imposing delays in movement of goods and persons at borders between member countries; differences in standards for manufacturing products, which made illegal the sale in one member country of goods produced in another; government procurement policies discriminating against products from other member countries; conflicting taxes and levels of taxation making for differences in price of the same goods produced in different countries; and differences in the price of services involved in moving goods and persons from one country to another.[33]

The Commission's efforts to identify the barriers to trade and the measures needed to remove them were crucial to a successful outcome. It also played an important role along with Euro-businesses after the SEA was adopted in publicizing and popularizing the internal market, thereby disseminating confidence that the EC would be able to bring its objectives to a successful conclusion. But the three principal actors whose policy commitments converged initially to set the agenda for the SEA at Fontainebleau were Kohl, Mitterrand, and Thatcher. Once the budget issue was successfully managed, the heads gave the Commission the task of working out the details of the single market, which was facilitated by the fact that the Commission had already prepared substantial parts of it for presentation to the Council of Ministers. The legislation had languished at the level of the Council, still under the pall of the Luxembourg compromise. But now, instead of the glacial progress that trade liberalization legislation could make on a piecemeal basis, the inclusion of many items in one omnibus package of reforms appealed to the free trade neoliberalism of Margaret Thatcher and her government and to important leaders of the German governing coalition. The addition of the French Socialist government provided the momentum necessary to shift from the expectation that a veto would be exercised to the opposite expectation. But, just to be on the safe side, the SEA included further measures to give the achievement of the single market a nudge in the right direction.

Institutional reforms were a part of the SEA package as well as trade liberalization. Emphasis should be placed on the role played by the EP in continually urging that steps be taken toward political union, modest versions of which found their way into the SEA. Following the first direct elections to the EP in June 1979, Altiero Spinelli, an Italian MEP, founded and led a cross-party group of MEPs, known as the Crocodile Club.[34] This group became the driving force behind EP demands for institutional reform to make the EC more democratic and politically accountable. The Crocodile Club's proposals were brought together as a draft European Union Treaty (EUT) to amend the Rome treaty. The resolution supporting the EUT was adopted by the EP by an absolute majority of 237 to 31, with 43 abstentions, on February 14, 1984, 4 months before the Fontainebleau Summit.[35] As support for the single market idea began to build, Spinelli argued that institutional reform should be attached to it. Otherwise the single market proposals might fail in the face of different governments vetoing different proposals. The most central provision of the EUT was therefore the abolition of the veto in the Council of Ministers. But another important proposal that saw the light of day in the SEA was that of a cooperation procedure between the EP and the Council of Ministers that would make it more difficult for the Council to ignore EP-proposed amendments.[36]

The EUT was one of two influential initiatives that preceded the SEA and contributed elements of institutional reform to it. The other was the Solemn Declaration on European Union adopted by the European Council at the Stuttgart Summit in June 1983. This step, taken at the initiative of German Foreign Minister Genscher and Italian Foreign Minister Emilio Colombo, may be seen as the presentation of an alternative to the direction the EP was promoting. The EUT initiative included an effort to curtail the agenda-setting role of the European Council,[37] whereas the Solemn Declaration explicitly stated that the European Council "'initiates cooperation in new areas of activity'" and gives "'general political guidelines for the European Communities and European Political Co-operation.'"[38] It was an intergovernmental statement, downplaying the role of the Commission, especially in its call for greater intergovernmental cooperation in foreign policy making. But it also envisioned a modest increase in the role of the EP in decision making, a step which had the enthusiastic support of both the German and Italian governments, if not the French and British. Instead of the abolition of the veto as advocated by the EP, it suggested a voluntary discontinuation of its use in the Council of Ministers, which could be accomplished by governments abstaining instead of voting negatively, a practice already occurring in the Council of Ministers' meetings.[39]

At Fontainebleau, at the same time the single market reached the extra-ordinary agenda, the European Council added to the extraordinary agenda the institutional reforms that were to become part of the SEA at the urging of President Mitterrand. Earlier in the year, Mitterrand had held discussions with Altiero Spinelli, who evidently influenced the French president to add his weight to the increase in EP powers.[40] Mitterrand induced the heads at Fontainebleau to appoint a committee of governmental representatives to take both the EUT and the Solemn Declaration and work out a version of EUT that would be acceptable to the ten governments. This committee, headed by Senator James Dooge of Ireland, reported to the Milan Summit a year later, recommending that an Intergovernmental Committee (IGC) be formed to draft what the Dooge report called a *Treaty on European Unity*, but which became, after approval at the Luxembourg Summit of December 1985 and subsequent signing (1986) and ratification (1987), the Single European Act.[41]

This less-imposing name for the Rome treaty revision symbolizes the fact that the institutional changes in the SEA came closer to those advanced in the intergovernmental Solemn Declaration than to those in the more supranational EP proposals. The SEA institutionalized the European Council, with what was more a description of existing practice than a proposal for institutional change. The cooperation procedure for internal market legislation gave the EP more leverage over measures adopted by the Council of Ministers (see chapter 6). Elimination of the veto in the Council of Ministers applied under the SEA only to a restricted range of policy measures mainly involving the internal market. The SEA did not make the EP a coequal half of a bicameral parliament, but the opportunities the institutional reforms opened up for the EP have been used to the Parliament's advantage (see chapter 5).[42] The compromise had the full support of the French and German governments, and what might be called the resigned acceptance of Prime Minister Thatcher, whose first priority was the trade liberalizing features of the SEA. She later wrote that there was "no escape" from QMV, "because otherwise particular countries would succumb to domestic pressures and prevent the opening-up of their markets."[43]

An additional reason the years 1984 and 1985 were years of opportunity for economic and political integration was that negotiations were going on between the EC-10, which had included Greece since 1981, and Spain and Portugal, regarding the terms of entry of the latter two countries into the Community. This entry was accomplished in 1986, bringing to 12 the number of member countries, and adding to the poorer countries and regions that were part of the Community. As in other expansions, special provisions were made for the newcomers to ease them into the full system of obligations and benefits of the existing membership. From the beginning, however, the new members would take their places in the EC institutions, giving them the opportunity to influence agenda setting and policy making for the future. As the phasing-in

period was completed, Spanish agricultural goods and labor-intensive manufactured products would compete in the existing EC market, while the Iberian
countries would be an expanding market for the more sophisticated northern
manufacturers. The French government was uneasy about the expansion, but
Chancellor Kohl strongly pushed for it to occur as soon as possible. In the years
immediately preceding their entry, the members already in place perceived the
necessity before the new members entered to deepen the EC by completing the
common market and by making the institutions more efficient in the face of a
larger membership through reduced opportunity to use the veto. In the final
analysis, the entry of Spain and Portugal was part of a complex package agreement to which the two new entrants were parties, but which also included the
internal market, institutional reform, CAP and budgetary reform, and advances
in assistance to the poorer regions of the EC.[44]

In response to the desires of the new members, the SEA specifically targeted
regional issues, recognizing that redistribution of economic resources from the
richer to the poorer areas of the EC was essential to achieve harmonious
economic integration. In line with the SEA mandate, the members reached an
agreement in 1988 to double the size of the structural funds directed to the
poorer regions before the completion of Project 1992. Moreover, they revised
the mechanism and strengthened the specifications by which funds were to be
distributed, giving the EC more control over the process, so that domestic
political motives would have less effect in determining the allocation (see chapter 10).[45]

The SEA also contained revisions of the sections of the Rome treaty concerned with social policy, an area which had been given relatively little attention
aside from ritualistic statements of aspirations by the Commission and the
European Council. One of these had been the concept of a Social Area put forth
in 1981 by the new Socialist government of France, and later adopted in the
form of the Social Charter proposed by Jacques Delors. Basically the argument
was that some degree of uniformity in Community-wide social standards was
desirable because in an increasingly competitive environment, caused by the
creation of the single market, countries with lower standards of social protection
—minimum wages, social security, working conditions, status of trade unions—
would undercut other members that provide higher standards, resulting in loss
of market shares and company relocation, known as social dumping.[46] The
references to social policy harmonization in the SEA were brief, but they paved
the way for the Social Charter, which became a protocol to the Maastricht treaty
of 1992 (see chapters 5 and 10).

THE DELORS INITIATIVES OF 1987–1989

By the beginning of 1988, Europe and the larger trading world were awakening
to the potential significance of the single market. This awakening was partly
because of the early successes registered by the strategy adopted in the field of

product standards regulation, which allowed mutual recognition by each country of the regulatory standards prevailing in the others, so that borders were opened to goods previously excluded from countries with tougher standards but satisfying the standards of the country of origin.[47] It was also a result of the efforts by the Commission, supportive media, and business interests to publicize projections of rapid economic growth that would result from implementation of the single market, as the world economy was on an upswing. Some assistance may have been given to the upward trend by increased business confidence influenced by the pro-single market propaganda. Whatever the reasons, the late 1980s witnessed the zenith of the Commission's influence within EC policy-making circles, as the prestige of its president reached heights never achieved by his predecessors.[48] In essence, Jacques Delors, with the support of Chancellor Kohl and President Mitterrand, gained the initiative in setting the extraordinary EC agenda for a period that lasted until the upheavals in Central and Eastern Europe that began in late 1989.

In February 1987, Delors presented what became known as his package, a combination of measures designed to reduce the complex of issues between members states over CAP and the budget. The Delors package included three components: (1) the creation of new budgetary resources by additions to member contributions from sources other than their CAP obligations, (2) reform of CAP to reduce spending obligations and the CAP share of the EC budget, and (3) enhancement of the system of redistribution favoring poorer states and regions.[49] This package represented an effort by Delors to bring Margaret Thatcher into the consensual center of the EC, because it answered her call for greater control over CAP spending and a shifting of revenue obligations from those based on food imports to those reflecting the relative strength of members' economies. Although the package made little headway at summits held in 1987, when Germany took over the Council presidency in January 1988, the Kohl government was willing to lend its weight to support the Delors package, even though it would have an unfavorable effect on German farmers' incomes. The Delors package was adopted in February 1988 at an extraordinary Brussels Summit called by Kohl to clear the ground for progress on single market legislation and for initiating a new effort to achieve EMU.[50]

In the later 1980s, the surge of optimism that accompanied the early days of SEA was further sustained by the solid performance of the EMS. By 1987, exchange rates within the ERM had become remarkably stable, and inflation rates had dropped from double figures in most EC countries in 1982 to less than 5 percent for all ERM members, while three of the four EC members not in the ERM were above that figure (see chapter 7).[51] To the Delors Commission and the Mitterrand government, the time seemed ripe to broach the issue of EMU again. EMU was put on the extraordinary agenda at the June 1988 meeting of the European Council at Hanover, with Chancellor Kohl presiding. The agenda-setting decision was to establish a committee headed by Delors to elaborate upon the report and produce a document that could serve as a basis for revision of the Rome treaty.[52]

The Delors report on EMU, known as the Delors Plan and officially presented to the member governments in April 1989, proposed a gradual process of economic and monetary unification.[53] The plan stated that Stage 1 would begin on July 1, 1990, and include liberalization of capital markets, enlarged ERM membership, and coordination of monetary policies by the EC Committee of Central Bank Governors. Stage 2, which would require revision of the Treaty of Rome, would include creation of a European system of central banks (ESCB) similar to the American Federal Reserve System. This institution would set monetary policy but would leave its execution to the national central banks. Furthermore, currency realignments would only be allowed under exceptional circumstances. Finally in Stage 3, exchange rates would irrevocably be fixed, national central banks would be replaced by the ESCB, and the process of economic integration would culminate in the adoption of a single European currency.[54] The Delors Plan, therefore, envisioned a zone of monetary stability for Europe through monetary union, financial market integration, and economic union.

Of the major member states, France was the most enthusiastic about moving ahead to EMU. From the French standpoint, the dominant position of the Bundesbank in aligning ERM currencies around a strong DM meant that severe restrictions were placed upon French economic policy making, especially limiting the ability of the French government to counteract recession and unemployment. EMU would make monetary policy subject to the collective decision making of the ESCB, thus reducing Bundesbank control and giving the Bank of France, and therefore the French government, more influence.[55] To Chancellor Kohl, the idea of moving ahead to EMU was acceptable, although he had to set aside Bundesbank objections in giving the Delors Plan his government's approval.[56] To Margaret Thatcher, whose irritation with Delors had been stimulated the year before by statements he had made envisaging substantial transfers of sovereignty to the Community, EMU was far from acceptable (see chapter 5). Delors's own enthusiasm for EMU was based on his expectation of precisely such a transfer of sovereignty to EC institutions. The Delors Plan effectively put EMU on the extraordinary agenda for the early 1990s.

CONCLUSION

There were three policy areas central to the EC's extraordinary agenda during much of the period under discussion in this chapter: (1) the system of exchange rates between EC currencies, (2) the CAP and the budget, and (3) the internal market. Considerable progress was made from 1975 to 1989 in finding more effective policy instruments for managing all three of these problem areas. The regularization of summit meetings, which began in 1975, was important for allowing agenda setting to occur in all three cases when the opportunities appeared, and the gradual movement away from the use and threat of the veto made progress easier on the third of these issues after adoption of the SEA. The establishment in 1978 of the EMS's Exchange Rate Mechanism set a precedent that was to become more significant 15 years later: the inclusion of some EC members in the ERM, with other members opting to remain outside. This type of arrangement came to be called "two-speed Europe", or "the Europe of variable geometry." It was to become a prominent feature of the Maastricht treaty, especially in the provisions for EMU, the Social Charter, and the Common Foreign and Security Policy (CFSP, see chapter 5).

The issue of how to achieve better monetary coordination in the face of the exchange rate crises of the 1970s was placed on the extraordinary agenda by the German chancellor, with the help of the French president, and after a verbal boost by the Commission president. The success of the ERM, especially the recognition by a French Socialist president that France was better off staying in it, helped pave the way for the breakthrough of 1984-1985 that was spearheaded by President Mitterrand and resulted in the adoption of the SEA. The trade liberalizing features of the SEA had the enthusiastic support of the British and German governments, but the British prime minister only allowed the SEA on the agenda when her budgetary concerns were dealt with, and she only reluctantly accepted the institutional changes in the SEA that made decision making in the Council of Ministers easier and enhanced the influence of the EP. Once the issues dealt with in the SEA were placed on the agenda by the European Council at Fontainebleau, the Commission played an important role in working out the principal policy alternatives to best achieve the single market, while the institutional changes in the decision-making process were worked out by an intergovernmental body with input from the EP and the foreign ministers. Implementation of the SEA then followed the Rome treaty pattern, whereby the Commission set the ordinary agenda by preparing legislative measures, and the Council of Ministers determined whether they would be modified and adopted.

By the late 1980s, the prestige and influence of the Commission president was at an all-time high. Delors played an important role in fostering agreement on a package of CAP and budget reforms, largely resolving the principal British complaint about the way the EC worked. During the German presidency in the first half of 1988, Chancellor Kohl helped to push the Delors package through the European Council and followed this up by sponsoring the return of EMU to the extraordinary agenda. Delors was given the assignment of heading the committee to work out the stages of EMU, about which he already had decided opinions. With the Delors Plan, reported in April 1989, the stage was set for another major revision of the Rome treaty, which will be the primary focus of the following chapter.

ENDNOTES

1. Robert O. Keohane and Stanley Hoffmann, "Institutional Change in Europe in the 1980s," in Keohane and Hoffmann, eds., *The New European Community: Decision-making and Institutional Change* (Boulder: Westview, 1991), pp. 5-8.

2. Dennis Swann, *The Economics of the Common Market* (London: Penguin Books, 1992), p. 12.
3. Stephen George, *Politics and Policy in the European Community,* 2nd ed. (London: Oxford University Press, 1991), pp. 134–135.
4. Andrew Scott, "Financing the Community: The Delors II Package," in Juliet Lodge, ed., *The European Community and the Challenge of the Future,* 2nd ed. (New York: St. Martin's, 1993), p. 78.
5. Michael Shackleton, "The Budget of the EC: Structure and Process," in Lodge, ed., *The European Community and the Challenge of the Future,* 2nd ed., p. 94.
6. Robert S. Walters and David H. Blake, *The Politics of Global Economic Relations,* 4th ed. (Englewood Cliffs, N.J.: Prentice-Hall 1991), pp. 74–77.
7. Francesco Giavazzi and Alberto Giovannini, *Limiting Exchange Rate Flexibility: The European Monetary System* (Cambridge, Mass.: MIT Press, 1989), pp. 26–27.
8. David M. Wood and Birol A. Yeşilada, "Learning to Cope with Global Turbulence: The Role of EMS in European Integration" (Paper presented at the Annual Meeting of the Midwest Political Science Association, Chicago, April 18–20, 1991).
9. Robert A. Isaac, *International Political Economy: Managing World Economic Change* (Englewood Cliffs, N.J.: Prentice-Hall, 1991), p. 58.
10. John Pinder, *European Community: Building of a Union* (Oxford: Oxford University Press, 1991), pp. 124–125.
11. Ibid., p. 125.
12. Jonathan Story, "The Launching of the EMS: An Analysis of Change in Foreign Economic Policy," *Political Studies* 36 (September 1988): 401.
13. Stanley Hoffmann, "Europe's Identity Crisis Revisited," *Daedalus* 123 (Spring 1994): 5.
14. David M. Wood, Birol A. Yeşilada, and Beth Robedeau, "Windows of Opportunity: When EC Agendas Are Set and How?" (Paper presented at the Biennial International Conference of the European Community Studies Association, Washington, D.C., May 27–29, 1993, pp. 14–16).
15. See Box 3.1 on p. 32, which lists the changes in government occurring in France, Germany, and Britain during the period covered in this chapter.
16. Pinder, *European Community,* p. 129.
17. Stephen George, *An Awkward Partner: Britain in the European Community* (Oxford: Oxford University Press, 1990), pp. 132–133.
18. David M. Wood, "Old Thinking and the New Europe: The Persisting Influence of de Gaulle and Thatcher" (Occasional paper No. 9211, Center for International Studies, University of Missouri-St. Louis, December 1992).
19. George, *An Awkward Partner,* pp. 149–150; Margaret Thatcher, *The Downing Street Years* (New York: Harper Collins, 1993), p. 257.
20. George, *An Awkward Partner,* p. 134.
21. Thatcher, *The Downing Street Years,* p. 257.
22. Ibid., pp. 538–541.
23. Peter A. Hall, *Governing the Economy: The Politics of State Intervention in Britain and France* (Oxford: Oxford University Press, 1986), pp. 198–202.
24. Andrew Moravcsik, "Negotiating the Single European Act," in Keohane and Hoffmann, eds., *The New European Community,* pp. 51–52.
25. Ibid., pp. 55–56; George, *An Awkward Partner,* pp. 154–155.
26. Moravcsik, "Negotiating the Single European Act," pp. 56–57; George, *An Awkward Partner,* pp. 155–159.

27. See Wood, Yeşilada, and Robedeau, "Windows of Opportunity," where the application of Kingdon's concept to EC agenda-setting is developed. John W. Kingdon, *Agendas, Alternatives, and Public Policies* (Glenview, Ill., and London: Scott, Foresman & Co., 1984), chap. 8. For a thorough study of the Council presidency that frequently takes note of the opportunities provided by changes in the presidency, see Emil Joseph Kirchner, *Decision-making in the European Community: The Council Presidency and European Integration* (Manchester and New York: Manchester University Press, 1992).

28. This incident illustrates that the timing of changes in domestic politics of the member countries can affect the willingness of a government taking over the presidency to put new items on the extraordinary agenda. Moravcsik, "Negotiating the Single European Act."

29. There has been a considerable amount of work devoted to the process by which the Single Market came into being. See especially Paul Taylor, "The New Dynamics of EC Integration in the 1980s," in Juliet Lodge, ed., *The European Community and the Challenge of the Future* (New York: St. Martin's, 1989), pp. 3–25; Moravcsik, "Negotiating the Single European Act"; David Cameron, "The 1992 Initiative: Causes and Consequences," in Alberta M. Sbragia, ed., *Euro-politics: Institutions and Policymaking in the "New" European Community* (Washington: The Brookings Institution, 1992), pp. 23–74.

30. Cameron, "The 1992 Initiative," pp. 54–55.

31. John T. Woolley, "Policy Credibility and the European Monetary System," in Sbragia, ed., *Euro-politics,* pp. 157–190.

32. The later arrival of both international business leaders and Jacques Delors has been pointed out by both Moravcsik, "Negotiating the Single European Act," p. 65; and Cameron, "The 1992 Initiative," pp. 49 and 51.

33. Paolo Cecchini, *The European Challenge 1992: The Benefits of a Single Market* (Aldershot, U.K.: Wildwood House, for the Commission of the European Communities, 1989), pp. 1–7.

34. Juliet Lodge, "Ten Years of an Elected European Parliament," in Juliet Lodge, ed., *The 1989 Election of the European Parliament* (New York: St. Martin's Press, 1990), pp. 7, 14.

35. Juliet Lodge, "European Union and the First Elected European Parliament: The Spinelli Initiative," *Journal of Common Market Studies* 22 (June 1984): 378.

36. Ibid., pp. 381–394.

37. Ibid., p. 391.

38. Quoted in Simon Bulmer and Wolfgang Wessels, *The European Council: Decision-making in European Politics* (Basingstoke and London: Macmillan, 1987), p. 77.

39. Cameron, "The 1992 Initiative," pp. 54–55.

40. Lodge, "Ten Years of an Elected European Parliament," p. 15.

41. Cameron, "The 1992 Initiative," pp. 23–24.

42. Lodge, "Ten Years of an Elected European Parliament," pp. 17–21.

43. Thatcher, *The Downing Street Years,* p. 553.

44. Moravcsik, "Negotiating the Single European Act," pp. 54–55; Alberta M. Sbragia, "Introduction," in Sbragia, ed., *Euro-politics,* pp. 16–17.

45. Judith Tomkins and Jim Twomey, "Regional Policy," in Frank McDonald and Stephen Dearden, eds., *European Economic Integration* (London: Longman, 1992), pp. 107–109.

46. Beverly Springer, *The Social Dimension of 1992* (New York: Praeger, 1992), chap. 4.

47. John Pinder, "The Single Market: A Step towards European Union," in Lodge, ed., *The European Community and the Challenge of the Future,* 1st ed., p. 98.
48. Peter Ludlow, "The European Commission," in Keohane and Hoffmann, eds., *The New Europe,* pp. 116-121.
49. Loukas Tsoukalis, *The New European Economy: The Politics and Economics of Integration* (Oxford: Oxford University Press, 1991), p. 62.
50. Kirchner, *Decision-making in the European Community,* p. 99.
51. Cameron, "The 1992 Initiative," p. 48.
52. Kirchner, *Decision-making in the European Community,* p. 102.
53. Peter Ludlow, "Introduction: The Politics and Policies of the EC in 1989," in Centre for European Policy Studies, *The Annual Review of European Community Affairs 1990* (London: Brassey's, 1991), p. xli.
54. *The Economist,* "How to Hatch an EMU," April 22, 1989, p. 45.
55. David R. Cameron, "British Exit, German Voice, French Loyalty: Defection, Domination and Cooperation in the 1992-93 ERM Crisis" (Paper presented at the Third International Conference of the European Community Studies Association, Washington, D.C., May 27-29, 1993, p. 13).
56. Ludlow, "Introduction," p. xiii.

chapter 5

European Union in the 1990s

In the present chapter, we examine the major developments that produced the Maastricht treaty (TEU), ratification of which in 1993 meant the transformation of the European Community into the European Union. In addition to sketching the 5-year process by which the EU came into being, we outline the major institutional changes entailed by the transformation of the Community into the Union. Finally, we discuss the steps in 1994 leading to expansion of the EU.

THE QUEST FOR POLITICAL UNION

At any given time in the history of the EU, the four most powerful actors in determining the direction it would take have been the president of the Commission and the heads of state or government in the French Republic, the United Kingdom, and the Federal German Republic. All of these have been political figures with political support behind them, engaged in building and maintaining coalitions among themselves and with the leading political actors of the other states of the EC. In general, when the EC has moved ahead on its extraordinary agenda it has been because of the coalescence of the French president and the German chancellor with the Commission president (Giscard and Schmidt with Jenkins in 1978, and Mitterrand and Kohl with Delors in 1988–1989); or it has been because the British prime minister has achieved his or her aim in exchange for conceding certain aims of the French and German leaders (Heath with Pompidou and Brandt in 1970–1971, Wilson with Giscard and Schmidt in 1974–1975, and Thatcher with Mitterrand and Kohl in 1984–1985).

In none of the pivotal periods prior to the 1990s, when new items were placed on the extraordinary agenda and decisions were reached, can it be said that the EP was a key actor in setting the agenda or in choosing between alternatives.[1] The Parliament was, at most, one among many seekers of influence over the process by which the extraordinary agenda was set at the summit. But throughout the 1980s, following the first direct elections to the EP in June 1979, the influence of the EP grew, especially as it was brought to bear on the issues of institutional reform leading to Political Union.

Following ratification of the SEA in 1987, the EP turned its attention to making sure the new institutional arrangements for bringing about the single market would work effectively. This required an effort on the part of the EP to demonstrate its desire to make the new institutions work with all due speed and to stay within the limits of what could realistically be attained in asserting its prerogatives vis-à-vis the Council of Ministers. The EP's preoccupation with good behavior in pursuit of SEA-authorized legislation continued beyond the direct elections of June 1989 into the 1989–1994 Parliament. As a consequence of these preoccupations and of the swift-moving international events of 1989–1990, it was to enjoy limited influence over the agenda-setting and decision-making processes that eventuated in the TEU signed in Maastricht in early 1992 and ratified in the fall of 1993. These processes were dominated by the previously identified four leading actors, and some supporting players, for example, the governments of Spain, Ireland, Italy, Luxembourg, and the Netherlands, when they held the Council presidency in 1989–1991. Nevertheless, the Treaty on European Union which the EP had proposed in 1984 provided a distant inspiration for many of the elements of the Maastricht treaty, including even the name for the new entity built on an expanded institutional basis of the EC, the new European Union.

THE MAASTRICHT STRUGGLE

The new EU which came into being in late 1993 rests on three pillars, one of which is the former EC of the Rome treaty as modified by the SEA. The other two pillars establish the common foreign and security policy (CFSP) and cooperation in the fields of justice and home affairs (JHA), which overlap institutionally with one another and with the EC pillar. This institutional framework is discussed at greater length later in this chapter.

Economic and Monetary Union on the Agenda

As the Maastricht treaty was being formulated and negotiated, the three pillar arrangement was not immediately apparent. In fact, the first steps on the road to Maastricht, in the years from 1988 to 1990, brought to the extraordinary agenda EMU and the Community Charter of Fundamental Social Rights for Workers (the Social Charter), both of which were conceived to be extensions of EC powers that would be necessitated by the opening of the single market (see chapter 4). EMU involved specification of a series of three stages leading to the creation of an EC-wide central banking system and potentially a single currency. Both EMU and the Social Charter, which was designed to achieve uniformity in social provisions, conditions of employment, and industrial relations, were put on the extraordinary agenda on the initiative of Delors, Kohl, and Mitterrand at the Hanover Summit of June 1988. Both of these packages of proposals were opposed by Margaret Thatcher, but she had greater difficulty in holding up progress on EMU at the summits held in 1988 and 1989 than on the Social Charter. After his reelection victory in March 1988, President Mitterrand joined Delors in giving strong support to EMU, succeeding in bringing along Chancellor Kohl, who overrode the objections of the Bundesbank, much to Prime Minister Thatcher's disappointment.[2] At the June 1989 Madrid Summit, pressed hard by her foreign secretary and chancellor of the exchequer not to leave Britain in an isolated position, Thatcher conceded the creation of an IGC to draft treaty amendments that would provide for an EMU.[3] At the Strasbourg Summit in December 1989, it was agreed to convene the IGC at the end of 1990.[4]

Prime Minister Thatcher's opposition to EMU was based on an unwillingness to see an EC central bank and single currency that would take away Britain's capacity to conduct its own monetary policy. She was even opposed to the idea of Britain's pound sterling being brought within the ERM of the EMS, which her chancellor of the exchequer, Nigel Lawson, was advocating from the middle of the 1980s. The argument between Thatcher and Lawson, which eventuated in the latter's resignation in October 1989, was on the rather technical ground of how best to control inflation. Prime Minister Thatcher's governments since 1979 had followed the monetarist premise that inflation is caused by an increase in the national money supply, and that it can therefore be controlled by controlling the money supply. Lawson had come to the conclusion that money supply could not be effectively controlled and that a more effective means of achieving monetary stability would be to anchor sterling to the strong DM through membership in the ERM. Since the Bundesbank pursued an effective counter-inflationary policy by controlling interest rate levels, Britain could do likewise by following the German lead, as France, the Netherlands, and even Ireland were doing. The prime minister disliked tying Britain's hands in this way. If the Bundesbank raised or lowered German interest rates, Britain would have to do likewise to keep the sterling-DM exchange rate within ERM limits, regardless of the effects on the British economy. Given her strong aversion to a loss of British sovereignty, this step was inevitably resisted by Thatcher, as was the proposed EMU, the latter because it meant that a Euro-version of the Bundesbank would be controlling British macroeconomic policy. While it would not exclusively be German control over the British economy, in some ways it would be worse, because German counterinflationary instincts might be diluted in the larger EMU by the inputs of the French and the governments of the economically less solid member countries. In October 1990, a year after Lawson's resignation, Thatcher finally allowed his successor, John Major, to take sterling into the ERM, but she did so with great reluctance.[5]

Thatcher's inability to forestall the French-led drive toward EMU, as well as her capitulation to the Treasury's desire to join the ERM, reflected the weakness of her position within the parliamentary Conservative Party by 1989–1990. Growing inflation and unemployment since the Conservatives' 1987 general election victory had been accompanied by a loss in support for the Conservatives and especially for the prime minister in public opinion polls. Thatcher had added to her unpopularity with her insistence upon implementation of a highly unpopular local tax, officially called the *community charge,* but referred to by its opponents as the *poll tax.* The community charge was put into effect in the spring of 1990, touching off demonstrations and even rioting. Conservative members of Parliament (MPs) were made uneasy about their reelection prospects with Thatcher still at the helm. The European issues with which she was preoccupied were of much less interest to voters, but there was a growing number of Conservative MPs who felt she was too intransigent on the EMU issue.[6] When she made it clear in a speech to the House of Commons that Britain would hold out alone against the version of EMU that was emerging from the IGC, her former Foreign Minister Geoffrey Howe resigned from her Cabinet and gave a speech of his own that undoubtedly swung some Conservative back-benchers against her. These defectors combined with others wishing to find a more electable prime minister to deny her a majority in a vote of the parliamentary party of November 22, 1990. She resigned 6 days later, and John Major, with her support, became prime minister after outdistancing two opponents on a second vote of the Conservative MPs.[7] While it was generally expected that Major would follow the broad outlines of Thatcher's policies, it was also clear that an important obstacle to the achievement of a treaty on European union had been removed.

Political Union on the Agenda

The other institutional innovations of the three pillars of the eventual Maastricht treaty were of a more strictly political nature, if the term is taken to include internal and external security concerns as well as institutional changes. These concerns did not reach the extraordinary agenda until after the late 1989 upheavals in Central and Eastern Europe that resulted in the collapse of Communist regimes and, of immediate concern for the EC, the October 1990 unification of Germany. The desire of the FRG itself and of its EC partners to anchor the new Germany solidly into the EC framework propelled the EC-12 to join monetary and political union into a single project, which reached its fruition in the agreements at the Maastricht Summit of December 1991.

When the Berlin Wall was pulled down in November 1989, there was general rejoicing throughout the EC, because it represented a victory for Western values supporting democracy and market economies. But when Chancellor Kohl began in late November openly to advocate early unification of the two Germanies, doubts began to be raised privately and hinted at publicly, by both Prime Minister Thatcher and President Mitterrand. Conversely, Commission President Delors gave

German unification early support, as did U.S. President George Bush. In meeting with Mitterrand in December 1989 and January 1990, Prime Minister Thatcher expressed her opposition to unification on the grounds that a larger, more powerful Germany would upset the balance within Europe by gaining excessive influence over the newly emerging east-central European states. Britain and France should join forces as they had done in the past in the face of a strengthening Germany, and attempt to prevent or at least slow the pace of German unification. Although agreeing with Thatcher in principle, Mitterrand was pessimistic about the chances of preventing unification, and thought it best to exercise damage control by strengthening the EC, thus locking the new Germany into a cooperative mode. Thatcher opposed this view, believing that it was precisely within the EC that Germany's hegemony would assert itself, and that it was important for Britain and France to develop links with the east-central European countries, looking toward a widening of the EC before attempting to deepen it through further political integration.[8]

This position of the British prime minister was, in fact, the opposite of the view Jacques Delors was then taking, which was that the EC should strengthen itself internally, especially by achieving EMU, before expanding either to include the Alpine and Scandinavian countries of the EFTA or the east-central European countries that were being widely mentioned as potential candidates for EC membership: Poland, Czechoslovakia, and Hungary.[9] Mitterrand decided that, to keep the Franco-German coalition together and to keep Germany from going off in adventuresome directions to the east, it was best to continue supporting Delors's strategy. Chancellor Kohl enthusiastically endorsed it as well, and Thatcher found herself again facing a bloc of the other three principal EC actors solidly arrayed against her. During the course of the early months of 1990, she lost her arguments regarding both German unification and the direction the EC should take.[10]

Adoption of the Maastricht Treaty

By the time John Major became the British prime minister in November 1990, Political Union had been placed on the EC agenda. Among its strongest supporters were the governments of Ireland and Italy, which held the Council presidency during the two halves of 1990. But the most important initiative was taken by Mitterrand and Kohl, who jointly sent a letter to Irish Prime Minister Charles Haughey, asking him to convene a special meeting of the European Council in April to consider ways to strengthen political cooperation among EC members. After the meeting was called, Belgium weighed in with a set of proposals designed (1) to strengthen the powers of the EP, (2) to improve decision-making efficiency throughout the EC, (3) to give greater recognition to the principle of subsidiarity,[11] and (4) to move toward a common foreign policy. Jacques Delors, after initially calling for more far-reaching reforms, endorsed these more incremental approaches to Political Union prior to the April summit meeting.[12] Before the April summit, Mitterrand and Kohl sent a letter to the other heads calling for the European Council to set up a second IGC to examine Political Union. At the summit meeting, the EC foreign ministers were asked to study this proposal and report back to the regular June 1990 summit.[13]

At the second Dublin Summit, the decision was reached to commission an IGC for Political Union, which would begin its work in December in parallel with the IGC for EMU. Britain, still under Margaret Thatcher's leadership, again resigned itself to working within the IGC framework to minimize the federalizing features of the treaty that would emerge.[14]

The agenda-setting effort in the case of Political Union was essentially the result of external events that moved the French and German heads to push for Community deepening. The role of the Commission president, unlike his initiative-taking in the EMU case, was more that of adjusting his position to what had been agreed upon by Mitterrand and Kohl, who had themselves played the supportive role vis-à-vis Delors's EMU initiative. But in both cases, a coalition of France, Germany, and the Commission was able to outweigh Britain, although Prime Minister Thatcher succeeded in keeping the Social Charter off the decision agenda, at least for the time she remained in office. The role of the EP in providing a list of reforms that found their way into the Belgian proposals, thus refining the options that the IGC on Political Union was to consider, should also be mentioned as a facilitating influence, although not in itself decisive.

Negotiation of the treaty in the two IGCs went on during 1991, under the Council presidencies of Luxembourg and the Netherlands, whose governments sought to find compromises regarding the most troublesome issues. The central issues eventually hedged in the treaty were as follows:

1. Whether to fulfill the EP's maximalist objective of achieving coequal status with the Council of Ministers as one of the two chambers of a bicameral legislative body
2. Whether the EC institutions would acquire competence in the defense policy sphere, rivaling the North Atlantic Treaty Organization (NATO), to which all of the EC members but neutral Ireland belonged
3. Whether all member states should be committed to reaching the third stage of EMU, including the creation of a common currency
4. Whether all member states should be committed to the Social Charter, broached by Delors in 1988

On all of these issues, Britain took a negative stance, joined on the defense issue by smaller countries, Ireland, Denmark, and Greece; on the powers of the EP by France; and on the third stage of EMU by Denmark, the Bundesbank, and a growing percentage of the German public, though not by the Kohl government. On the Social Charter, Britain was isolated even from its usual ally, Denmark, which had a strong commitment to an EC social policy to raise the other EC member countries up to the same level of social provision as prevailed for Danish citizens.

At the Strasbourg Summit in December 1991, the treaty was agreed upon by all 12 heads of state and government. British prime minister Major successfully held out for weak language regarding an EC defense policy, for Britain's right to opt out of a single currency, and for the Social Charter to be separated from the main body of the treaty, applicable to the other 11 countries, but not to Britain. On the issue of legislative powers, Italy and Germany were able to get more for the EP than Britain and France wanted, but less than the maximalists in the EP itself were seeking. A *codecision* procedure was introduced to make it more difficult for the Council of Ministers to ignore EP amendments to legislation, and a larger portion of the votes in the Council itself were now subject to QMV than was true under the SEA (see the following discussion and chapter 6).

Ratification

The Maastricht treaty was signed by the 12 foreign ministers on February 7, 1992.[15] It was expected that ratification could be completed by the end of the year, so that the beginning of the EU would come about at the same time as Project 1992 was scheduled to enter into effect. However, for this to occur, it would be necessary for all 12 member states to ratify the treaty, a process that turned out to be a great deal more difficult than was originally anticipated. Although putting together the treaty had been a difficult process, it was made possible by the skills of the negotiators, many of whom were national-level civil servants with years of experience working together on a wide variety of EC issues. The governments that approved the treaties had all made concessions to one another, such as the mutual concessions by Britain in being willing to sign a treaty that contained many distasteful provisions and by the other 11 members in conceding the various escape clauses that Prime Minister Major felt were necessary to sell the treaty to the House of Commons. Still, the treaty emerged into the light of day without having been subject to much serious scrutiny below the level of elites specialized in the matters under negotiations and the attentive public in the private and public sectors who followed accounts in the specialized press. The general public had little idea of what was emerging and certainly lacked an understanding of the intricacies.

In 9 of the 12 member countries, this isolation of the decision makers from the general public did not pose a serious difficulty for the ratification process. Eight parliaments succeeded in ratifying the treaty by large majorities before the end of 1992: the Belgian, Greek, Italian, Luxembourgeois, Dutch, Portuguese, Spanish, and German. In Ireland, a referendum was held in June, and the treaty was ratified with a 69 percent "yes" vote. But the treaty received a severe referendum setback in Denmark earlier the same month when 50.7 percent of those voting judged the treaty unacceptable. This vote put the later ratifications under a cloud of uncertainty, but the 12 foreign ministers met a few days later and agreed that the ratification process should go on, assuming that the Danes would reconsider. Meanwhile, to demonstrate strong support for the treaty, François Mitterrand declared that ratification in France, which would normally have been accomplished simply by a parliamentary vote, would likewise be subject to a referendum.

Mitterrand's decision proved to be a miscalculation. Left-wing and right-wing opponents of the treaty, weak in Parliament, were able to stir up hostility to the treaty in French public opinion. The issue of German unification and the potential of German hegemony within the EC influenced some voters to vote against the treaty and others to vote for it. But, as in Britain, the issue of loss of French sovereignty was played up by the Communists on the left and the National Front on the right, who also played to fears of an opening of French borders to additional immigrants with the creation of an EC citizenship superseding French citizenship. In other words, the opposition brought the implications of the treaty down to a human level, stressing the negatives, while the positive aspects emphasized by the supporters tended to be more abstract and impersonal, of interest to specialists and not to ordinary citizens. Mitterrand could not claim that the barely positive outcome—a 51 percent "yes" vote—represented a resounding endorsement of the treaty. But, in any event, France had ratified the treaty.

With the referendum surprises in Denmark and France, Euro-pessimism came out of retirement. The optimism of the late 1980s and early 1990s now seemed to have been misplaced. Important sectors of opinion in all three of the major countries were expressing disagreement with the treaty. In addition to the near repudiation by France, polls in Germany were revealing that 70 percent opposed giving up the DM in favor of a single EC currency.[16] In the British House of Commons, which had provided a 336 to 92 majority for the treaty in its preliminary reading in May, opposition on the Conservative Party backbenches was growing, and from the House of Lords, Margaret Thatcher, now Baroness Thatcher, was lobbying for an antiratification vote by Conservatives in an attempt to force the Major government to reverse its position in support of the treaty.

Coincidentally, on July 1, 1992, Britain assumed the presidency of the EC Council for the latter half of the year. Britain's term of office had not passed its halfway point before the EMS experienced a crisis in September 1992. This crisis had been brought on by the Bundesbank's effort to keep the DM strong by raising interest rates. Other central banks and governments were forced to follow suit in order not to have to devalue their currencies. Reluctant to slow British economic growth by raising interest rates, the Major government was forced to take the pound out of the ERM. Opposition to the treaty was given further stimulus by these events, since arguments the government had made on behalf of joining in the first two stages of EMU were seriously undermined by this evidence of the inability of the member states to coordinate their macroeconomic policies, a capacity that would have to be developed anew if EMU were to succeed (see chapter 7).

By October, it was clear that the treaty could not be ratified before the end of 1992. Called by Major to deal with the monetary crisis, a special Birmingham Summit was held in mid-October. Addressing the problem of ratifying the treaty, the heads issued a statement designed to assure Britain and Denmark that the treaty would be interpreted in practice so as not to trample over the sovereign rights of the member states. Major took this assurance to the House of Commons, and on November 4, gained a majority of three on a vote supporting Maastricht, although not formally ratifying the treaty.[17] Major promised that British ratification would await the outcome of the Danish process. In December, the regular summit under the British presidency was held in Edinburgh and agreed upon a series of assurances designed to help the Danish government get a successful result from a second ratification referendum. Among the concessions made were commitments (1) to increase the openness of decision making, especially in the Council of Ministers; (2) to give real meaning to the principle of subsidiarity, that is, to make sure that the EC would not take on new policy-making functions in areas that are best left to the national, or even subnational, governments; and (3) immediately after ratification, to begin the process of negotiation leading to the membership in the EU of Denmark's Nordic neighbors: Sweden, Finland, and Norway. These same concessions to Denmark were likely to make Prime Minister Major's task easier as well.

During the same month of December 1992, both houses of the German Parliament voted overwhelmingly to ratify the treaty, but a challenge to the treaty's constitutionality was lodged in the Federal Constitutional Court, which did not rule favorably until late October the next year, making Germany the last member state to ratify the treaty. Denmark held a second referendum in May 1993, with a favorable vote of 56.8 percent, resulting in part from the fact that the Social Democrats, in opposition the previous June, were now in power and strongly supporting a "yes" vote, thus turning around many of their voters. This vote cleared the way for John Major to steer the treaty through the House of Commons, which he did with some shaky moments. When, in July, Major made ratification of the treaty as approved in Maastricht a vote of confidence, the anti-Maastricht Conservatives voted with him rather than bring the government down. Their votes barely offset those of the Labour Party, whose supporters of the treaty voted against the treaty as a vote of nonconfidence in the government, making it clear that they were not voting against the treaty as such.[18] This was probably the closest a British Prime Minister has come in the twentieth century to being defeated on a motion of confidence when his or her party enjoyed a clear majority in the House of Commons. Had it happened, it would have been the result of the defection of members of his own Conservative parliamentary party, the party which, under Edward Heath, had brought Britain into the EC in the first place. Although Maastricht was now fully ratified, how it would work in practice would be influenced considerably by the minimalist interpretation upon which the British and Danish governments insisted in return for their efforts to bring about ratification.

THE INSTITUTIONAL FRAMEWORK ESTABLISHED BY THE MAASTRICHT TREATY

The Maastricht treaty rewrote the Rome treaty (as amended by the SEA) to create the new European Union. It indicates what the then 12 member states agreed to abide by in the future, including former commitments and others over and above what the original six agreed to at Rome, as later amended. The 12 members expected any new entrants to the EU to commit themselves to these old and new undertakings as well. The name was changed to the European Union because the EC pillar was joined to two new pillars: the CFSP pillar, which brings the former EPC into the Rome treaty framework; and the JHA pillar, which adds new functions in the realm of internal security to the Rome treaty and SEA functions. Compared to the EC pillar, the CFSP and JHA pillars have a more intergovernmental structure of decision making and implementation, wherein the Commission, the EP, and the ECJ play reduced roles.[19] The treaty, however, summarizes the institutional characteristics of the EU to indicate continuity with the three "communities" that were established in the 1950s:

> ### Article C
> The Union shall be served by a single institutional framework which shall ensure the consistency and the continuity of the activities carried out in order to attain the objectives while reflecting and building upon the *acquis communautaire* [which means the legal powers the EC had already acquired]. The Union shall in particular ensure the consistency of its external activities as a whole in the context of its external relations, security, economic, and development policies. The Council and the Commission shall be responsible for ensuring such consistency. They shall ensure the implementation of these policies, each in accordance with its respective powers.[20]

In addition, the next article significantly refers to the heads of state and government and their agenda-setting role:

> ### Article D
> The European Council shall provide the Union with the necessary impetus for its development and shall define the general political guidelines thereof.[21]

Although this is worded very generally, Article D establishes that the European Council is the body, meeting "at least twice per year,"[22] that will take new initiatives, setting what we have called the extraordinary agenda for the new EU just as it had been doing for the now imbedded EC.

Citizens of the member countries now become, in a limited sense at least, citizens of the EU. The most important right of EU citizens is to live and work in any of the member countries, without restrictions that do not apply to citizens of those countries. They also have certain political rights. In any of the member countries where an EU citizen of another member country resides, he or she may vote in local elections or become a candidate for and serve in local elective office and may be a candidate for the EP.[23] Regarding the EC pillar, the principle of subsidiarity is stated and reinforced by the declaration emerging from the December 1992 Edinburgh Summit in a new article inserted into the Rome treaty:

Article 3b

In areas which do not fall within its exclusive competence, the Community shall take action, in accordance with the principle of subsidiarity, only if and in so far as the objectives of the proposed action cannot be sufficiently achieved by the Member States and can therefore, by reason of the scale or effects of the proposed action, be better achieved by the Community. Any action by the Community shall not go beyond what is necessary to achieve the objectives of this Treaty.[24]

In a fashion similar to the unspecified powers reserved to the states in the Tenth Amendment to the U.S. Constitution, the detailed meaning of subsidiarity will have to await subsequent decisions of the ECJ and of the courts of member states when future challenges are posed to the exercise of powers, at times by the EU-governing bodies, at times by those of the member states. Although subsidiarity is regarded by intergovernmentalists like British Prime Minister John Major as reinforcing the prerogatives of the member states, it could as easily become the means by which regional and local governments in hitherto centralized states (e.g., Britain and France) gain in power; or conversely, it could justify an acquisition of greater capacity on the part of the EU to steer the diplomatic affairs of the member states, on the grounds that "the objectives of the proposed action [in foreign and security matters] cannot be sufficiently achieved by the Member States and can therefore, by reason of the scale or effects of the proposed action, be better achieved by the Community."

The EP gains power in certain policy areas by virtue of a new procedure called *codecision*. Under this procedure, if a legislative act adopted by the Council of Ministers is amended by the EP, the Council may adopt any such amendments by QMV, except in the case of amendments on which the Commission has rendered a negative opinion, in which case the Council may pass them only if unanimity is obtained. If the Council fails to adopt an EP amendment, or if the EP rejects the original Council bill in its entirety, a conciliation committee is established, consisting of members of both the Council and the EP. This committee, in which the Commission also participates, will attempt to arrive at a version of the bill that is acceptable to both the EP and the Council. If so, the EP may adopt it by a simple majority (majority of the votes cast) and the Council by QMV. If either body fails to do so, the bill fails[25] (see Figure 6.2, chapter 6).

Thus, the EP is given the power to reject legislation the Council has adopted. Under the *cooperation* procedure instituted under the SEA for internal market legislation, the Council retained the capacity to adopt legislation rejected by the EP, although to do so it required unanimity. Under codecision, it cannot override an EP veto. But the kinds of legislation to which the new codecision procedure applies are restricted. Included are "measures on the single market, education, culture, health and consumer protection, as well as programmes for the environment, research and trans-European networks."[26] This list also means extension of the range of matters for which QMV applies in Council of Ministers votes, which will be in all of the above policy areas except for culture and research, where unanimity still applies.[27] The EP's legislative powers remain restricted in politically sensitive domains such as agricultural and industrial policies, but the parliamentary body gains by the treaty further powers (1) to approve international agreements reached by the EU if they touch on budgetary matters or areas where the EP has a legislative veto; (2) to approve the membership of the Commission, including its president, at the beginning of its new term; and (3) to deny admission of new countries to EU membership. With these new powers, the capacity of the EP to exert influence over the contents of both the ordinary and the extraordinary agendas will grow[28] (see chapter 6 for further discussion of these processes).

The powers of the ECJ to interpret EC legislation expand as the legislative powers expand. However, the ECJ was not explicitly given a role to play concerning the third pillar, JHA, although it is provided that conventions in this field, if drawn up on the initiative of a member state or the Commission and adopted by the Council with a two-thirds majority, "may stipulate that the Court of Justice shall have jurisdiction to interpret their provisions and to rule on any disputes regarding their application."[29] Concerning the areas in which the ECJ does have jurisdiction, if the Commission finds that a member state has failed to comply with a prior judgement of the Court, it can recommend that a fine be paid, and the ECJ may impose it if it so chooses. This represents an additional leverage over the process of implementing EU law, if the Commission and the ECJ act together.[30] Another new institutional development is the creation of a Committee of the Regions, consisting of members appointed by the Council on the proposal of member governments. The Committee's powers are advisory only, but its creation gives recognition to the growing voice of regions, especially the German states (Länder), which in turn reflects the growing recognition that EU policies have varying impacts upon different areas of any given member country.[31]

The EC pillar[32] outlined in the treaty represents a considerable expansion of the domain of EU power beyond that found in the Rome treaty and the SEA. Although there are uncertainties over how the subsidiarity principle will be applied, the policy areas involving extensions of the EP's legislative power include several additions to the list of areas subject to EU legislation: education, research, culture, public health, consumer protection, and trans-European infrastructure networks. New legislative areas for the EU where the new EP powers do not apply are labor market and industrial policy. In three additional areas—regional development, social assistance, and environmental policies—EU functions that existed prior to the treaty's ratification have been considerably expanded without a corresponding increase in EP powers. It can be seen generally that where the EU is becoming active in economic policy issues of explosive domestic political potential, directly involving the future of jobs and families' incomes, the member states have not wanted to lose control of the EU legislative process to the upstart parliamentary body (see chapter 9 for further discussion of these policy realms).

Social policy is another area in which EU powers have been expanded. As defined in EU parlance, social policy refers primarily to conditions of work, rights of employment, and processes of labor-management relations. A protocol to the treaty registers the fact that 11 of the member states, with the exclusion of the UK, separately contracted to coordinate their social policies through legislation that follows the original Rome treaty procedures, with some measures subject to QMV in the Council of Ministers and others requiring unanimity. "They may make laws by qualified majority on working conditions, on consultation of workers, on equal employment rights of men and women and on those excluded from the labour market."[33] Unanimity applies to matters of social security, termination of contract, collective defense of worker interests (trade union status), and consultation of workers by management (called *codetermination* after the German system).[34]

The most important policy development of the EC pillar was, of course, the inclusion of EMU, which is discussed at greater length in chapter 7. The principal institutional development involved in EMU will be the creation in the second stage of a European Central Bank (ECB) if certain economic and monetary conditions are met. In another special protocol to the treaty, Britain was conceded the right to opt out of these developments if it so wishes. The ECB is responsible to the economic and finance ministers of the member states, who meet as the Council of Ministers when they deal with these subjects. This body, known as ECOFIN, is also responsible for monitoring members' fiscal policies, and can recommend action to be taken to reduce excessive budget deficits. These are not legislative powers, and the broadened supervisory powers of ECOFIN represent an extension of intergovernmentalism. But the creation of the ECB is not, strictly speaking, a reinforcement of intergovernmentalism, as the bank must be independent of political controls, just as must be the members' central banks, whose governors sit on the council of the ECB.[35]

The second pillar, foreign and security policy coordination (CFSP), will be the province of the foreign ministers, meeting as the Council of Ministers between summit meetings, where the heads may make foreign policy decisions on their own. General foreign policy decisions, whether made by the heads or by the foreign ministers, require unanimous approval; but more detailed implementative decisions by the foreign ministers can be taken by QMV. On defense matters, the Western European Union (WEU) may implement CFSP decisions. Linked to NATO as well as to the EU, the WEU contains ten EU members, while five EU members are not members of WEU: Austria, Denmark, Finland, Ireland, and Sweden. The unanimity rule continues to apply to WEU decisions[36] (see chapter 11 for further discussion of the CFSP).

JHA cooperation, the third pillar, will involve efforts of interior ministers (called the home secretary in Britain) to join forces in dealing with problems of asylum, immigration, and other cross-border law enforcement matters, such as those involving fugitive criminals, terrorism, and drugs. In all of these areas, national laws are enforced within national borders, and it will be up to the interior ministers to reach agreement on conventions defining new rules and procedures. Such conventions may be adopted by two-thirds vote in the Council of Ministers, unless the conventions themselves provide otherwise. Functions may be shifted from JHA to the EC pillar, if the Council votes unanimously to do so[37] (see chapter 11 for further discussion of JHA).

FROM OPTIMISM BACK TO PESSIMISM

In the months that followed ratification of the Maastricht treaty in October 1993, the EU members were preoccupied with two matters that were of an essentially political nature: the expansion of the Union to include four new member countries—Austria, Finland, Norway, and Sweden—and the choice of a new Commission president to succeed Jacques Delors, whose 10 years in office were to be concluded at the end of 1994. In both cases, unanimity among the members was required to achieve a positive result, and in both cases the EP was in a position, as a result of the Maastricht treaty, to reject a decision made by the Council. These political issues in the EU were likewise political issues in the member countries.

The expected enlargement of the Union's membership on January 1, 1995, from 12 to 16, would add four relatively small and relatively rich northern members, meaning a change in the Council voting balance between small and large members and between richer northern and poorer southern members. As both a larger and a poorer southern member, Spain was reluctant to see an expansion which would take away the ability of the three "olive belt" members— Italy, Portugal and Spain—to block qualified majorities, because the enlargement would increase the number of votes necessary for blocking from 23 to 27. This change would mean that two large members and one smaller member would not have enough votes if faced by a solid majority of the other 13 members. Spain sought to keep the blocking majority at 23, which would mean raising the necessary votes for a qualified majority from 70 percent to 75 percent of the total votes.[38] For good measure, Spain also insisted on access of its trawlers to Norwegian fishing waters, thus raising the hackles of a segment of the Norwegian electorate whose solid vote against Norwegian entry to the EC had been a major factor in the defeat of that issue in the 1971 referendum (see chapter 10 for further discussion of the issues negotiated).

Under both Margaret Thatcher and John Major, the British government had opposed deepening of the Community through EMU and Political Union, arguing that widening should occur before deepening. Now, with widening of the Union on the agenda, Prime Minister Major sided with Spain's demand for a freezing of the blocking minority at 23 votes so that Britain could retain the ability to prevent further deepening with the help of one large member and one small one, or several small ones. Major's insistence was clearly a result of his weak domestic political position in early 1994. His own personal popularity and his party's rating had both slipped drastically after the September 1992 monetary crisis, when Britain pulled out of the ERM, leaving the government's economic policy strategy in disarray.[39] Lacking the personal authority of his predecessor, Major was at the mercy of the vociferous Euro-sceptic right wing of his party. Despite his government's desire to see the new entrants take their places, he had little choice but to adopt a strong stance on this symbolic issue.[40]

But Spain and Britain found themselves decidedly in the minority on the issue of voting percentages. While the specific issues outstanding between the EU and the four prospective entrants were settled by mid-March, including the issue of fishing rights in Norwegian waters, the dispute over voting remained. Chancellor Kohl became more outspoken in his refusal to compromise on the issue, while Jacques Delors searched for a face-saving compromise. Spain eventually came around to the majority position, leaving Major isolated. Meanwhile, the Socialist and Christian Democratic parties in the EP indicated that they would not vote for accepting the new members if Britain were to have its way on the voting issue. Moreover, there was growing concern that voters in the Nordic countries, if not in Austria, would turn against membership if the squabble continued. Referenda on entering the EU were to be held in Austria in June and in the three northern countries in the fall.[41] Under considerable cross-pressure, Major accepted the compromise in late March, and negotiations with the four prospective entrants were favorably completed.[42]

Major's Euro-sceptic colleages were not pleased with the compromise, by which it was agreed that, although the number of votes needed to block a majority would rise from 23 to 27 with four new members, if between 23 and 26 votes were cast in the Council against a measure requiring a qualified majority, there would be a cooling off period of unspecified length for a compromise to be sought. The Conservative Party doubters claimed that this was only a fig leaf to cover Major's failure to change the voting percentages.[43] On the other side, some Socialists in the EP claimed that Major had won a victory, although Delors's denial of this interpretation seemed to satisfy most MEPs. Sufficient assurances were given that the EP accepted the enlargement in a vote in early May, with Socialists and Christian Democrats strongly in support and only a handful of mainly right-wing MEPs in opposition.[44]

Elections to the EP were held in the 12 member countries on June 9 and 12 (see chapter 6). These produced negative results for a number of sitting governments, including that of John Major. But Chancellor Kohl received a higher percentage of the vote in Germany than expected. He claimed a victory and renewed his promise to provide positive leadership to get the EU back on track when it came his country's turn to hold the Council presidency in the second half of 1994. The most positive outcome for Euro-enthusiasts was the result of the Austrian referendum on EC membership, which was held the same Sunday as most of the EP polls. Against predictions that the vote would be very close, the Austrians gave two-thirds of their votes to the "yes" side. The Austrian vote was interpreted as a good sign for success in the fall referenda for the three Nordic candidates for membership, in all of which the polls were running very close.[45] As it turned out, Finnish voters ratified the treaty on October 16, 1994, with 57 percent in favor, as did Swedish voters by a narrower margin (52 percent) on November 13; but ratification failed in Norway on November 28, when 52 percent voted against it.

In all three Nordic countries, the governing parties supported ratification, but all three governments had difficulties convincing their own supporters to vote for it. In Finland, farmers were concerned about the loss of subsidies that are higher in Finland than they are under CAP for EU farmers. But a majority of Finnish voters saw membership in the EU as a security hedge against the uncertain political changes going on in neighboring Russia.[46] The farming population is a smaller component of the Swedish electorate but to their opposition were added urban votes, concerned both with the lower environmental standards and less generous welfare systems prevailing in most EU countries. These concerns, plus workers' fear of job losses, made the vote quite close in Sweden.[47] In Norway, the more generalized belief that Norway's special advantages in oil and fishing would be interfered with by membership in the EU added to the specific concerns of farmers and fishing communities to defeat Norwegian accession. The size of the negative vote and the reasons for it were very similar to what they were the previous time the Norwegian voters had rejected membership, in 1972.[48]

In 1996, the members are committed under the Maastricht treaty to reexamine the EU scope and institutions in light of the expansion already realized and the later foreseeable expansion into Central and Eastern Europe. With July 1994 marking the beginning of Germany's turn at the Council presidency, Chancellor Kohl was promising to begin the preparations for the intergovernmental conference. But before Germany could take over, the Greek presidency held its summit meeting in Corfu in late June. At Corfu, Prime Minister Major refused to support the election of the French and German candidate for the next Commission president, Belgian Prime Minister Jean-Luc Dehaene. Kohl emerged from the meeting announcing that the German presidency would schedule an extraordinary summit a month later to resolve the issue of the Delors succession. Because there were no clear reasons why Dehaene would not have been as acceptable to Major as any of the other possible candidates, none of whom looked like another Jacques Delors, it seemed clear that Major's opposition was motivated primarily by the desire to appease his Euro-sceptics in the Conservative parliamentary party by not giving in to French and German wishes.[49]

In the July 15 special summit at Brussels, the heads reached agreement on a compromise candidate, the Luxembourg Prime Minister Jacques Santer.[50] But the dispute may have had its repercussions 3 months later, in October 1994, when Santer, in assigning responsibilities to members of his new Commission, took away the responsibility for EU trade and economic assistance negotiations with Eastern Europe from returning external trade Commissioner, Sir Leon Brittan, a former British cabinet colleague of John Major. Major publicly protested Santer's treatment of the senior British Commissioner. Santer's motive may have been to dispel the impression, possibly held by the German chancellor, that the new Commission president owed his appointment to the British prime minister, although Santer's own explanation was that he wanted to separate responsibilities for the largely political questions involving EU relations with Eastern Europe from the largely economic questions regarding trade relations with other industrialized countries that remained Leon Brittan's principal concern.[51] The earlier disagreement over Dehaene between Major and Kohl and Major's reaction to Santer's treatment of Leon Brittan suggest that Commission appointments are highly significant to national political leaders as tests of their own and their governments' relative strengths.

Chancellor Kohl had to survive a close election in October 1994 before he could devote full attention to the agenda for the German presidency. In the next 2 months, he bent his efforts toward getting a commitment at the December summit in Essen to the steps that would need to be taken in order to expand the EU eastward into east-central and Eastern Europe. Six countries in east-central Europe had association agreements with the EU that extended the CU to them: Poland, the Czech Republic, Slovakia, Hungary, Bulgaria, and Romania. The prospect of absorbing some or all of these poorer countries into the EU was a daunting one. It was beginning to dominate discussions concerning the work of the IGC that would be set up in 1996 to reexamine the Maastricht treaty. The issues that would face that conference included how to alter the institutional framework to give more expression to the values of (1) democracy, (2) subsidiarity, (3) openness, and (4) decisional efficiency. There would be serious debates over whether to extend the powers of the EP (urged by Germany to reduce the democratic deficit); whether to transfer more power from the national to the supranational level or back in the other direction (a contest between Britain and some of the smaller countries over the meaning of subsidiarity); whether Council of Ministers meetings should be recorded, as in national legislative bodies (likely to make governmental leaders not used to such openness very nervous); and whether there should be reductions in the number of Commissioners and in the number of countries taking a regular turn at the Council presidency (steps proposed in the name of efficiency that would be likely to oppose large members to small members). And of course the vexing issue of unanimity versus QMV would have to be dealt with once again. These were all likely to be contentious issues, dividing governments from one another in different ways, but for that reason raising the possibility of solutions being reached through bargaining trade-offs.

Added to these complexities is the uncertainty whether enough member countries will meet the standards of the Maastricht treaty required for membership in the EMU. High public deficits in the Mediterranean countries—Italy, Spain, Portugal, and Greece—make their eligibility for EMU problematic. Public scepticism toward the idea of a single currency runs high in Britain and Germany, and probably in other countries as well, given the conservativism of most people about what they carry in their wallets and pocketbooks.[52] The prospect of expansion around the year 2000 to a number of newly democratized and newly capitalist eastern countries makes an already complicated set of questions a virtual nightmare.[53] Eastward expansion in its own right makes many people in regions of the existing EU that enjoy CAP subsidies or regional development funding fearful that these benefits will have to be cut back to have enough for the benefits to which the new members will be entitled by the same criteria. Governments of the countries bordering the Mediterranean have resisted the idea of expansion to include countries that are even poorer and less indus-trialized, such as Romania and Bulgaria, that will place them at the "bottom of the league" economically.

In the late summer of 1994, French Prime Minister Edouard Balladur ten-tatively broached the idea of varying degrees of EU membership, including an inner core of countries that could meet the EMU criteria by the late 1990s, presumably Germany, France, and the smaller northern countries; a middle rank of those that could not or would not fully join the EMU, but would take part in most of the domestic and foreign policies of the EU, which would include Britain and the Mediterranean countries; and then the outer circle of east-central and maybe Eastern European countries. Similar ideas were broached almost simul-taneously by officials of Chancellor Kohl's Christian Democratic Party. The unexpected way in which they were advanced helped to give them a hostile reception from the governments of countries not included in the inner core, especially the larger ones: Britain, Italy, and Spain. But in fact, the idea was not so far-fetched, considering that EU programs like the ERM, the Social Charter, and WEU already had varying memberships, with prospects of even more variation with the entry of Austria and the Nordic countries.[54] Though their governments pulled back from the suggestion in the face of criticism, the French and the Germans had managed to focus attention on some of the dilemmas facing the EU in the years ahead.

While avoiding mention of "inner cores" or "outer circles," Chancellor Kohl made sure the question of eastward expansion headed the agenda for the Essen Summit of December 1994.[55] Although no firm commitments were made at Essen, it was agreed that the question of EU expansion would be taken up again after the 1996 review of the Maastricht treaty had taken place and its recommenda-tions acted upon. It was clear that any of the east-central European countries that could meet economic standards (presumably not those for immediate membership in EMU) would be seriously considered, leading to speculation that Hungary and the Czech Republic, at least, might gain entry to the EU by 2000. To satisfy the objections of the Mediterranean members, whose chief spokesman was the French prime minister, the European Council placed two Mediterranean applicants for membership, Cyprus and Malta, in the same status as Hungary, the Czech Republic, Poland, Slovakia, Bulgaria, and Romania, as countries "next in line" after 1996. Likewise, Mediterranean regions would have their funding increased along with the eastern applicants in the coming years, and additional assistance would be given to countries in North Africa that had close links with France, Italy, and Spain, and were the countries of origin of large numbers of immigrants in those countries. Special emphasis was placed on Algeria, whose government was under heavy pressure from Islamic fundamentalists and was already receiving considerable aid from the French government, which was anxious not to see a deterioration of relations with its former colony (see chapter 10 for further discussion of the tug of war between south and east for the attention of the EU).

CONCLUSION

In this chapter, we have related how the two main elements of the eventual Maastricht treaty—EMU and Political Union—were placed on the extraordinary agenda, through the coordinated efforts of Commission President Delors, German Chancellor Kohl, and French President Mitterrand, with British Prime Minister Thatcher opposing most of the way, until her political demise in November 1990. Her successor, John Major, followed a more conciliatory approach, while trying to balance competing factions of his party at home. The treaty was agreed to at Maastricht in December 1991, was delivered a setback in the Danish and French referenda of mid-1992, then, under Major's auspices at Edinburgh in December 1992, was adjusted to reinforce the principles of subsidiarity and openness. This adjustment helped ratification succeed in Denmark and Britain, so that the treaty could come into effect before the end of 1993.

But Prime Minister Major had barely survived the British general election of June 1992 and was soon visited with a devastating blow by the monetary crisis of September 1992 that forced him to take the pound out of the ERM. By early 1993, faced with opponents inside his party as well as outside, he had become less constructive and conciliatory on EU issues and very nearly upset progress on expansion in March 1994. Then he did force a postponement of the election of a new Commission president in June. By the end of 1994, attention of EU leaders was turning to the agenda for the near future, to the 1996 IGC on treaty revision and to the questions of whether and when to admit new members from east-central Europe and the Mediterranean area. In the meantime, as will be seen in the next chapter, opposition to the agenda left by Maastricht was rising in a number of countries, most notably France.

ENDNOTES

1. Juliet Lodge has suggested that the agenda-setting role of the EP has been growing since the institutional changes of the SEA, but she is clearly referring to influence over agenda setting, not the power actually to set the agenda. Juliet Lodge, "Ten Years of an Elected European Parliament," in Lodge, ed., *The 1989 Election of the European Parliament* (New York: St. Martin's, 1990), pp. 30–31.

2. Margaret Thatcher, *The Downing Street Years* (New York: Harper Collins, 1993), pp. 740–758.

3. Ibid., p. 752. Cf. Geoffrey Howe, "The Triumph and Tragedy of the Thatcher Years," *Financial Times,* October 23–24, 1993, section 2, p. 7. Creating an IGC has become the principal means by which the European Council puts negotiation of a major treaty revising package such as the SEA or the TEU on the extraordinary agenda.

See Mary Troy Johnston, *The European Council: Gatekeeper of the European Community* (Boulder: Westview, 1994), p. xiii.

4. Neill Nugent, "The Deepening and Widening of the European Community: Recent Evolution, Maastricht, and Beyond," *Journal of Common Market Studies* 30 (September 1992): 313.

5. Thatcher, *The Downing Street Years,* pp. 688-726.

6. Howe, "The Triumph and Tragedy," p. 7.

7. Philip Norton, "The Conservative Party From Thatcher to Major," in Anthony King, et al., *Britain at the Polls* (Chatham, N.J.: Chatham House, 1993), pp. 29-59.

8. Thatcher, *The Downing Street Years,* pp. 796-798.

9. Peter Ludlow, "The Politics and Policies of the European Community in 1989," in Ludlow, ed., *The Annual Review of European Community Affairs 1990* (London: Brassey's, for the Centre for European Policy Studies, 1991), p. xlvi.

10. Thatcher, *The Downing Street Years,* pp. 812-815.

11. Subsidiarity is the principle that only those powers should be exercised at the EU level that cannot be as effectively exercised at the national or subnational level.

12. Peter Ludlow, "Reshaping Europe: The Origins of the Intergovernmental Conferences and the Emergence of a New European Political Architecture," in Ludlow, Jorgen Mortensen, and Jacques Pelkmans, eds., *The Annual Review of European Community Affairs* (London: Brassey's, for the Centre for European Policy Studies, 1992), pp. 400-406. A similar incrementalist approach was presented to the EP in March 1990 by rapporteur David Martin, British Labour Party MEP, but there was division within the EP between those following Martin's strategy and others, mainly Christian Democrats, seeking a more far-reaching leap to Euro-federalism (ibid., pp. 401-402). However, Richard Corbett argues that the Martin report influenced the shape the Belgian memorandum took, and therefore the shape of the subsequent IGC discussions. Richard Corbett, "The Intergovernmental Conference on Political Union," *Journal of Common Market Studies* 30 (September 1992): 274.

13. Corbett, "Intergovernmental Conference."

14. Ludlow, "Reshaping Europe," pp. 414-415.

15. A useful summary of the events covered in this section is found in Richard Corbett, "Governance and Institutional Developments," *Journal of Common Market Studies* 31 (August 1993): 27-50.

16. Walter Goldstein, "Europe after Maastricht," *Foreign Affairs* 71 (Winter 1992/93): 117-132.

17. David Baker, Andrew Gamble, and Steve Ludlam, "Whips or Scorpions? The Maastricht Vote and the Conservative Party," *Parliamentary Affairs* 46 (April 1993): 151-166.

18. *The Economist,* July 31, 1993: 19-21.

19. *The Economist,* October 17, 1993: 60.

20. Council and Commission of the European Communities, *Treaty on European Union* (Luxembourg: Office for Official Publications of the European Communities, 1992), p. 8. The treaty also officially changes the name *European Communities* to the *European Community,* although the EC now is only one of three pillars of the new EU (ibid., p. 11).

21. Ibid., p. 8.

22. Ibid.

23. Ibid., pp. 15-16.

24. Ibid., pp. 13-14.

25. Ibid., p. 77.

26. *The Economist,* October 17, 1992, p. 60. "Trans-European networks" refers to "transport, telecommunications and energy infrastructures." *Treaty on European Union,* p. 51.
27. *Treaty on European Union,* pp. 49 and 51.
28. Lodge, "EC Policymaking," p. 32.
29. *Treaty on European Union,* p. 133.
30. Ibid., p. 69.
31. Ibid., p. 82.
32. Although the discussion in this paragraph refers to the provisions of the treaty applying to the EC pillar, the initials EU are used so that it will be clear we are referring to the post-Maastricht powers of the European Union.
33. *The Economist,* October 17, 1992, p. 61.
34. *Treaty on European Union,* p. 198.
35. *The Economist,* October 17, 1992, p. 61.
36. *Treaty on European Union,* pp. 123-129.
37. Ibid., pp. 131-135.
38. *The Economist,* March 12, 1994, pp. 53-54. Under the rules applying to 12 members, with varying numbers of votes at their disposal, depending on the country's size, the total number of votes was 76, and the requisite number for a qualified majority was 54, which could not be attained if 23 or more votes were lined up on the negative side of a motion. With 16 members, the total would be 90, and the qualified majority 64, so that 27 negative votes would be needed to prevent a qualified majority.
39. Patrick Dunleavy, "Introduction: Stability, Crisis or Decline?" in Dunleavy, et al., eds., *Developments in British Politics* 4 (New York: St. Martin's, 1993), pp. 8-9.
40. *The Economist,* March 19, 1994, p. 64.
41. Ibid., March 26, 1994, pp. 17-18.
42. *Financial Times,* March 28, 1994, p. 1; ibid., March 29, 1994, p. 1.
43. Ibid., March 30, 1994, p. 1.
44. Ibid., May 5, 1994, pp. 1, 18.
45. *The Economist,* June 18, 1994, pp. 55-57.
46. *Financial Times,* October 11, 1994, p. 16.
47. Ibid., November 8, 1994, p. 2; November 15, 1994, p. 17.
48. Ibid., November 30, 1994, p. 2.
49. Ibid., June 27, 1994, p. 1
50. Ibid., July 16, 1994, p. 1.
51. Ibid., October 31, 1994, p. 2.
52. Ibid., December 5, 1994, p. 2.
53. Ibid., September 27, 1994, p. 3.
54. Ibid., September 3, 1994, p. 3; September 5, 1994, p. 3.
55. Ibid., December 12, 1994, pp. 1-2.

chapter 6

Agendas and Agenda Setting in the European Union

In previous chapters, we have referred to the ordinary and the extraordinary agendas of the EU, and to the processes of agenda setting. This chapter examines the institutions of the EU in terms of the processes by which agenda-setting decisions are reached on the ordinary and extraordinary agendas. We have distinguished the two agendas from one another in terms of the plan of action set by the Rome treaty and its modifications (the ordinary agenda) and the agenda for the modifications of the treaty itself (the extraordinary agenda). Some of the treaty modifications have been brought together in the two large packages of amendments, the SEA and the TEU (the Maastricht treaty). Others have been less formal and taken on an ad hoc basis, such as the establishment in the 1970s of European Political Cooperation (EPC, chapter 3) and of the EMS (chapter 4). We discussed agenda setting for the two main amendment packages in chapter 4 (SEA) and chapter 5 (Maastricht treaty), where we placed emphasis on the role of the heads of state and government gathered in the European Council and the president of the Commission as principal actors in the process of setting the extraordinary agenda.

In this chapter, we look first at the ordinary agenda and its processes of agenda setting and choosing between alternatives. We stress the roles of the Commission, the Council of Ministers, and the EP, which are the principal actors involved in the ordinary legislative process. Then we turn to the less formalized process of extraordinary agenda setting and consider the various types of situations and influences that affect the deliberations of the European Council. In addition to the role of the European Council, that of the ECJ as the final interpreter of the Treaty of Rome and its formal modifications will be discussed in the context of the extraordinary agenda.

In the third part of the chapter we introduce what should be considered still a third EU agenda: the public agenda. This is a much broader and less easily delimited concept than the other types of agenda with which we have been dealing. It is also a concept that could not until recently have been considered descriptive of something that exists in practice, as opposed to something that is merely theoretical. Until very recently, there was no EU public agenda because there really was no EU public. It was during the ratification of the Maastricht treaty, 1992–1993, that the emergence of such a public began to be seen. Prior to 1992, issues relating to European integration were only very rarely debated in the national political arenas of all or most member countries at the same time. When, in 1975, a debate was going on in Britain over whether to get out of the EC or to stay in, a debate was not going on at the same time in France or West Germany over whether to dissolve the EC, which would have been the consequence if either of these countries had dropped its membership. But in 1992, debates were going on simultaneously in Denmark, Ireland, France, and Britain over whether the Maastricht treaty should be ratified. Some of the same questions were on the agenda for four national publics, and not just for their four sets of political leaders.

In the last section of the chapter, we consider to what extent the issues facing the EU in the aftermath of the Maastricht treaty, issues that will involve a potentially very significant expansion of its membership and a major restructuring of its institutions and reorientation of their powers, are further bringing about a public agenda for the EU. In the section dealing with the public agenda, we first review the most recent elections to the EP, held in June 1994, to see if common EU-focused issues were on the agenda of election campaigns in the then 12 countries. Then we look at the recent politics of the three most important member states—Germany, France, and Britain—to see whether common issues are being fought out between the political parties in national-level campaigns during recent elections or in anticipation of elections in the near future.

THE ORDINARY AGENDA

When we examine the decision-making process on legislation authorized by the Rome treaty, the SEA, and the Maastricht treaty (the first pillar), the strong role of the Commission becomes quite apparent.[1] For most matters with which the Council of Ministers deals, and certainly for all legislative matters, the ministers are dependent upon the Commission to initiate proposals, or in other words, to draft the bills. Legislation proposed to the Council of Ministers falls into two categories: (1) regulations and decisions, and (2) directives. Regulations and decisions are applicable directly to member states and to individuals within them, and they take effect immediately within member states, obliging governments to enforce them, but without requiring further legislation on their part. *Regulations* tend to be of more general application than *decisions,* but the distinction is not hard and fast. *Directives* are binding upon member states in the sense of obliging them to bring about the necessary legal instruments (laws or executive acts) to give them force within their boundaries.[2]

It is thus the Commission that sets the legislative agenda for the Council of Ministers. The Commission generates its own proposals as a result of its interpretation of what has been mandated by the treaties; or it may respond to pressures from interest groups, from the EP, from a member government individually, or from member governments speaking collectively in the Council. The appropriate Directorate General (DG)[3] of the Commission consults with other units of the Commission. In consultation with COREPER, it takes in the views of governmental and nongovernmental experts, including interest group representatives, in the policy area in which the legislation would take effect. Then the DG drafts the proposal. The decision to go ahead is taken by the College of 20 commissioners, and the proposal is sent to the Council of Ministers, which passes it on to the Economic and Social Committee (ESC) and to the EP.

The legislative role of the EP is outlined below. Its importance has grown since the 1960s, while that of the other body consulted on legislation has remained quite limited. The ESC consists of 189 members appointed by the Council of Ministers on the proposal of the national governments. They are individuals considered representative of important economic interests, especially employers, workers, farmers, and various professional categories. In fact, many are leaders of important interest groups at the national level, and, as such, their influence on EU legislation comes in at various points in the legislative process, making the collective views of the ESC somewhat redundant. However, when it speaks with one voice on issues, such as social legislation, in which the interests might be expected to diverge, it can be influential. Whether the Council must solicit their views depends on classifications of legislative measures set forth in the Rome treaty and the SEA, but consultation with the EP is mandatory on all legislative matters. The ESC also may issue its opinions on policy matters not involving immediate legislation, such as trade relations with various regions of the world.[4] Although sometimes its published opinions may provide EU watchers with insights into issues being debated within inner circles of the Union, they cannot be taken as the official positions of the organization.

Within the Council of Ministers, legislative proposals are sent first to working groups of national civil servants, whose meetings are attended by representatives of the Commission. Members of a working group from each country consult with their government superiors and invite representatives of national interest groups or of their national parliaments to address the full working group if opposition to the proposal or some part of it is discovered at the national level. Objections raised at this stage will be communicated to COREPER, which in turn will ask the Commission to modify the proposal to remove or reduce the objections, which the Commission may or may not do. COREPER then attempts to reach agreement among the member states on outstanding issues. The Commission might decide to withdraw the proposal should the differences in members' positions appear unresolvable. Otherwise COREPER will send it back to the Council of Ministers, whether or not disagreements remain. The ministers will meet along with a Commission representative, making it possible for concessions to be made, not only by individual governments, but by the Commission itself.[5] Sometimes the Commission will present new alternatives for issues that remain unresolved among the ministers.[6]

According to Lindberg and Scheingold, in the 1960s the Commission's role in attempting to achieve consensus at each stage was an important one. At least before the empty chair crisis, the desire prevailed among all governments to go beyond the lowest common denominator of agreement and to achieve package agreements leaving each member better off than it would have been without the legislation. France violated the delicately fashioned norms of the Community in the mid-1960s with "threats, the making of extreme demands, a general disregard for the interests of her partners, and an unwillingness to make meaningful concessions."[7] When the "Community spirit" prevailed, the unanimity requirement did not pose an insurmountable obstacle. With the Commission's continued efforts to find accord, negotiations would continue "practically around the clock and for a week or more until it [was] possible to agree to some combination of heterogeneous items all [could] accept as more or less equitable."[8] In the absence of that spirit, and following the Luxembourg compromise, decisions could not be reached whenever one of the members dug an entrenched position for itself. As explained in chapter 3, such an action reduced the effectiveness of the Commission as agenda setter and as "coalition builder,"[9] because it undermined the confidence of ministers in the Commission's leadership and of the Commission in the ministers' ability to rise above the lowest common denominator.

Recovery of Decision-making Capability

The ability of the EC institutions to set and process the ordinary agenda did not disappear in the late 1960s. As noted in chapter 3, the CU and the CAP were put in place before 1970, and direct elections to the EP were finally instituted in 1979. The big news items of the 1970s for the most part involved actions on the extraordinary agenda: EPC, British entry, creation of the European Council, and EMS. But more quietly, as a study by Thomas Smoot and Piet Verschuren reveals, in 1975 the Council of Ministers considered 329 proposals from the Commission and adopted 75 percent within 2 years, averaging 150 days from the time they were sent to the Council by the Commission.[10] Arguably, the Commission would have proposed more if it could have expected a higher success rate, and many of the measures adopted were of minor significance, but both the success rate and the average length of time in processing are surprising in light of the conventional wisdom about the inefficiency and ineffectiveness of EC policy making during the period.[11]

Smoot and Verschuren show that the annual volume of Commission proposals rose steadily from 1975, reaching 456 in 1979 with a 77.4 percent success rate, and 522 in 1984 with an 84.3 percent success rate, while the lag time for processing dropped over the decade after 1975 from 150 to 108 days in 1984. Although the SEA, which extended the range of voting by qualified majority, was not adopted until 1986, in that year, 617 proposals were made with a success rate of 87.4 percent.[12] It seems apparent that the psychological atmosphere prevailing in both the Commission and the Council of Ministers had again become favorable to the agenda-setting and coalition-building roles of the Commission and to the ministers approaching the negotiating process as a positive-sum rather than a zero-sum game. The rising number of proposals reflects the growing range of detailed policy areas to which EC competence was extending, but it also shows greater confidence on the part of the Commission that proposals it had previously withheld would now be adopted. The growing success rate of the proposals reflects the greater willingness of states to yield on matters that once would have received an implicit veto, often because of interest group opposition at the national level. The negative overhang of the Luxembourg compromise was being replaced by the positive expectation that agreement would be reached and vetoes would be avoided.[13]

When QMV applies in the Council of Ministers, France, Germany, Italy, and Britain have ten votes apiece; Spain has eight; Belgium, Greece, the Netherlands, and Portugal, five; Austria and Sweden, four; Denmark, Finland, and Ireland, three; and Luxembourg, two. This totals 87 votes, of which 61, or 71.3 percent, constitutes a majority, and 26 votes will suffice to block the measure on which the Council is voting.[14] In 1986, according to Neill Nugent, over 100 decisions were taken by QMV, mostly in settled Treaty of Rome areas, such as the budget, agriculture, and trade. The SEA added new subjects to the ordinary agenda to complete the Single Market. Most of these were made subject to qualified majority voting under the SEA, and the number of such votes per year in the Council then rose further.[15] One reason for the extension of majority voting was the concern that, with the expansion of the Community to 12 members, achieving unanimity in the Council was likely to become an unwieldy process. On the grounds of sheer decision-making efficiency, majority voting seemed necessary. But Nugent observes that unanimity is still sought in controversial matters: Votes are delayed or not held in order not to isolate a member in disagreement.[16] Paradoxically, the unanimity principle sometimes makes it easier for certain decisions to be reached, because when majority voting applies abstentions count as negative votes. When unanimity is required, abstentions are simply not counted. As a result, ministers may use abstentions when unanimity is required if they wish to permit a positive result while not having to tell critics at home that they voted for it.[17]

The Gradual Rise of the European Parliament

The role of the EP in the legislative process remained quite limited until the SEA extended its legislative powers. Despite the direct elections of MEPs from 1979, before the SEA, the EP was consulted by the Council of Ministers and the

Commission during the legislative process, but neither body had to adhere to its opinions.

In the formulation of the EC annual budget, however, the EP gained in power at an earlier date. A treaty amendment of 1970 gave it the power to propose changes in EC spending of a noncompulsory nature, including the various forms of social and regional assistance that were of considerable interest to MEPs, but not including the majority of the budget, agricultural spending, which even the Commission and the Council of Ministers could not bring under effective control. Following a treaty amendment of 1975, the EP also gained the power to reject the annual budget outright, in which case the three principal Rome treaty bodies would have to negotiate an agreed upon budget, with the EP being in a good position to get the Council to approve expenditure increases, at least when the Commission supported the Parliament. The Council votes by qualified majority on budget issues, which are not made subject to the Luxembourg compromise; and it is faced with a timetable of rigid deadlines. These features give the Parliament an opportunity to seek allies among the member states in order to gain concessions from those, such as France and Britain, which usually oppose an extension of EP powers at the expense of the member states. For example, the Italian government shares the EP's desire to increase regional spending, and there is strong support in several of the national parliaments for an increase in EP powers, which governments such as those of Belgium and Germany must take into account.[18]

Today the EP is a body of 626 members, elected every 5 years by the voters of the 15 countries. The members divide into eight parliamentary groups, distinguishable in ideological terms as Christian Democrats, Socialists, Greens, and so on, each grouping together members of similar ideological persuasion across the country delegations (see the following discussion). The EP divides into 18 substantively specialized committees, that examine legislation and conduct fact-finding inquiries.

With the coming into effect of the SEA in July 1987, there existed two different types of procedure for EC legislation, the *consultation* procedure, which is a continuation of the procedure existing before the SEA, and the *cooperation* procedure, which added to the capacity of the EP to influence the outcome of legislation. Under the consultation procedure, the EP's role is to give a proposal a *single reading* after it has been received by the Council of Ministers from the Commission. The proposal is considered by a committee of the EP, which reports back to the full body. The EP may vote amendments, which it sends to the Commission. If the Commission accepts them, it will considerably enhance the ability of the EP to influence the final version of the legislation. A Commission-supported measure can be finally adopted by the Council by qualified majority, whereas EP amendments that the Commission rejects can be adopted by the Council only by unanimity, which is unlikely. After the Commission has acted on its amendments, the EP issues an opinion which becomes part of what the Council considers in its deliberations on the measure.[19]

According to a 1980 ruling of the ECJ, the Council must wait until the EP has expressed its opinion before enacting the legislation.[20]

The cooperation procedure introduced by the SEA applied to much of the legislation designed to create the Single Market by the end of 1992. It is more complicated than the consultation procedure, but in essence it gives the EP a *second reading* of the piece of legislation after the Council has adopted its common position. Again, the Commission plays a crucial role in being able to influence the fate of EP amendments at the second as well as at the first reading. The EP may reject the bill outright on second reading, if a majority of all its members votes to do so, in which case the measure can only become EC law if the Council votes unanimously to override the EP veto (see Figure 6.1). In the first 2 years, the procedure was in effect, the Parliament only once rejected a common position of the Council, but 66 percent of its first reading amendments were accepted by the Commission, and 48 percent were then approved by the Council.[21]

The Maastricht treaty provides for a third procedure, *codecision*. This replaces consultation for some, but not all types of legislation where consultation applied, and it is applied in some, but not all, of the new areas of EU competence under the treaty (see chapter 5). Unlike the consultation procedure, failure of the EP and the Council to reach agreement at the second reading will touch off a new step, the formation of a conciliation committee, including representatives of the Council, the EP, and the Commission, who attempt to work out an agreed position. If the committee cannot reach agreement on a common version, meaning that either the Council or the EP sticks to its position, the proposal dies. It is the Commission's job to find common ground between the Council and the EP. If a commonly agreed upon version is produced, it still could be defeated when it is returned to the Council, which needs a QMV to pass it, and to the EP, which could defeat the final version if a simple majority is not found for it. In essence, with codecision, the EP becomes a coequal legislative body, but only in those domains of policy making where the procedure applies (see Figure 6.2).

Implementation

Most EU legislation is implemented by actions taken at the national level. The Commission oversees this implementation and calls it to the attention of the offending government when it discovers either a failure to act or action which is contrary to the EU legislative intent. Continued failure of a state to comply with the Commission's wishes may lead the latter to refer the case to the ECJ. Several member states show higher rates of noncompliance than do others, Italy being the most notorious footdragger.[22] However, if the ECJ finds that a state has failed to comply with EC law, the failure will usually be rectified.[23]

The Commission also has administrative responsibilities of its own, as in the case of efforts to detect monopolistic and market-sharing violations of EC

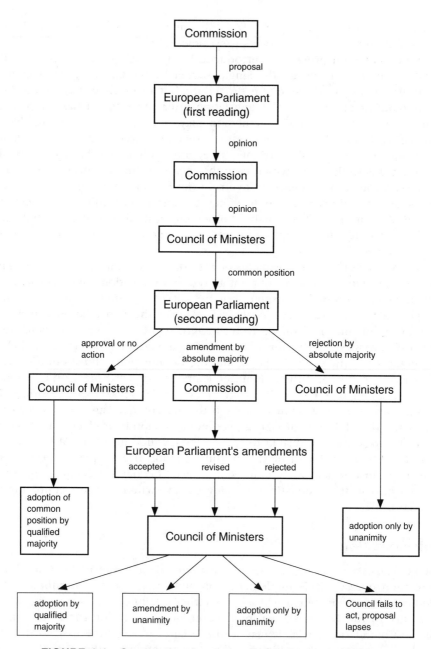

FIGURE 6.1 Cooperation procedure in the European Union

SOURCE: Adapted and refined from Frank McDonald and Stephen Dearden, *European Economic Integration* (New York: Longman, 1992), p. xxix; Neill Nugent, *The Government and Politics of the European Community* (Durham: Duke University Press, 1991), p. 292; and Juliet Lodge, "EC Policymaking: Institutional Dynamics," in Lodge, ed., *The European Community and the Challenge of the Future* (New York: St. Martin's, 1993), p. 29.

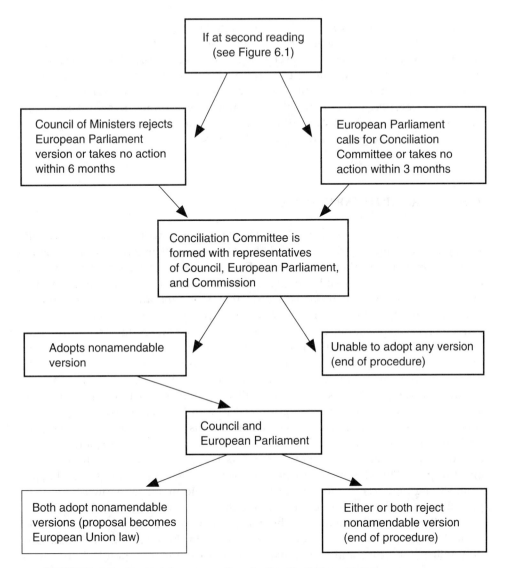

FIGURE 6.2   Codecision procedure in the European Union

SOURCE: Adapted from Juliet Lodge, "EC Policymaking: Institutional Dynamics," in J. Lodge, ed., *The European Community and the Challenge of the Future,* 2nd edition (New York: St. Martin's, 1993), p. 30. Copyright © Lodge, Juliet. Reprinted with permission of St. Martin's Press, Incorporated.

competition legislation, or in the case of agricultural, regional, and social funds, the spending of which it administers. These supervisory and direct administrative functions of the Commission mostly involve technically complex policy areas, and the phenomena to be dealt with far exceed the capacity of the relatively small Commission bureaucracy. Decisions as to which cases to pursue or which needs to satisfy within the industrialized member countries, each with its own vast bureaucracy, must inevitably be highly selective.[24] In turn, this need for selectivity may contribute to a certain negative image of the Commission, which is often accused of bureaucratic interference with national economies, even when it is taking action designed to open the market against state or private sector interference. It has certainly contributed to a public image of the Commission as a powerful regulatory body that can make examples of transgressors of EU law that had previously enjoyed benevolent state protection.[25]

THE EXTRAORDINARY AGENDA

The neofunctionalists expected that the EC agenda would expand gradually through recognition by the members that the accomplishment of tasks assigned by the Rome treaty would be impeded unless the EC took on auxiliary tasks that would make it possible to perform the assigned ones. National interest groups and government officials geared to an *incremental-economic* view of agenda building would facilitate and even press for this extension of the Community's responsibilities. As long as the member states agreed, there would be no need for amendments to the treaty. But France happened to be governed by a leader whose style and priorities were "dramatic-political" rather than "incremental-economic."[26] As discussed in chapter 3, Charles de Gaulle's agenda for the EC was political, befitting his realist view of international relations, and any economic advantages accruing to France from EC membership had to serve political ends. The Rome treaty was acceptable as far as it explicitly went, but de Gaulle did not want it to be stretched in such a way as to expand the EC's economic policy-making competence unless France could control the direction and the pace. The Commission's powers were curbed in 1965–1966 to keep it from sliding new items onto the agenda that would increase its own powers by providing different sets of economic benefits to each of the members.

Lindberg and Scheingold saw the heroic leader as a temporary phenomenon. Conceivably a less heroic concept would prevail in the French government after de Gaulle's departure, and France would come to see that its political ends were not incompatible with further accretion of the Commission's powers and the scope of EC responsibilities in the socioeconomic spheres.[27] In fact, the experience of the past quarter century since they wrote attests that the sphere of EC socioeconomic activity has increased immensely, and along with it the powers of the Commission and even the EP. More uncertainly, the political capabilities of the EC-12 have grown. In the early 1970s, with the United States bogged down in Vietnam and with monetary crises and energy crises demonstrating a loss of U.S. hegemony vis-à-vis its European partners, de Gaulle's vision for a political union of Europe became more plausible for France's EC partners, especially because the departure of de Gaulle from power also meant the disappearance of his grand design for French leadership in Europe.

As Robert Keohane has pointed out, "In world politics, power is always important. Any functional explanation, which deals with the value of a given process or pattern of interaction, must be embedded in an understanding of the political structure, especially the distribution of power among actors."[28] De Gaulle's perception of a decline in U.S. hegemony preceded that of his European partners, some of whom, such as West Germany under Ludwig Erhard, were unwilling to acknowledge it. But in the early 1970s, they began to turn to his vision for a "Union of European states" for the purpose of enhancing their collective capacity to play an effective role in the world.[29] The quest for greater cohesion was enhanced considerably by the creation of a Gaullist mechanism for setting and processing an extraordinary agenda. The mechanism, the European Council, removes the former dependence of the Council of Ministers upon the Commission for initiative taking beyond the EC's ordinary agenda, by allowing individual governments, acting through their most authoritative officers, their heads, to introduce extraordinary agenda items that can be sent to other intergovernmental bodies for processing. The capacity of the heads to do so existed before the establishment of the European Council, as seen in the case of the Hague Summit of 1969 (see chapter 3). The success of that summit in establishing an extraordinary agenda for the EC demonstrated the usefulness of institutionalizing the summits so that the extraordinary agenda could be more conveniently accessed by the heads. With the establishment of the European Council, the process of extraordinary agenda setting was brought into the open. Proceeding as it does with a great deal of fanfare attending the regular summit meetings, it is more reminiscent of de Gaulle's style of using the media to "make history"[30] than of Jean Monnet's preference for quiet work behind the scenes to gain elite support for what appear to be modest steps forward.[31]

The European Council

According to Simon Bulmer and Wolfgang Wessels,[32] there were two very general reasons institutionalized summit meetings came into being in the 1970s. First, the "institutional inertia" of the EC itself, especially the deadlocks occurring in the Council of Ministers, made it necessary for the heads to step in with the authority to achieve breakthroughs. As shown in chapter 3, newly elected French President Giscard d'Estaing proposed the institutionalization of summit meetings in 1974. The French president and the German chancellor were in the best positions to take leadership in this direction, because of the strong institutionalized offices at the disposal of these two leaders, with highly qualified officials in Paris assisting the French president and prime minister and the federal chancellor's office in Bonn assisting the German chancellor.[33] The heads began meeting in part to take pressure off their foreign ministers, who were doing double duty in the foreign policy realm and as coordinators and arbiters between different ministerial colleagues.[34] Second, the capacity of the member states to cope with their own growing policy agendas was diminishing because of an expanding welfare state in hard economic times and the rapid economic and political changes occurring in the world. The authority of the supreme political leaders of the member states was required to allow for decisive actions to be taken, especially when the only decisive action would have to be joint action by states unable to go it alone.[35]

From one point of view, the European Council is simply the most comprehensive and powerful of the various councils that evolved through the division of the responsibilities of the Council of Ministers between the General Affairs Council, comprising the foreign ministers of the member states, and the various functionally specialized Councils that emerged in the 1960s, 1970s, and 1980s. In 1989, there were 89 council meetings, of which only three were meetings of the European Council. An institutional link between the Councils is the Council Secretariat, headed by a secretary general, which keeps records of meetings and otherwise works with COREPER and with the Commission in attempting to achieve agreement in Council meetings.[36] The General Affairs Council, assisted by the Secretariat, has a role to play in reconciling conflicts between the Councils (e.g., between the Finance Council and the Agricultural Council), but from 1975 on, the leadership role that the foreign ministers attempted to play vis-à-vis their ministerial counterparts has been subordinated to that of the heads in the European Council.[37] Among the foreign ministers, the one whose country holds the presidency of the Council for the current 6 months continues to play an important coordinating and agenda-setting role.[38]

The SEA was the first EC constitutional source to give any legal recognition to the European Council, which it did in a two-sentence reference to its composition.[39] But by that time, the European Council had assumed a leadership role for the EC that exceeded that of the Commission and transcended that of the General Affairs Council. According to Peter Ludlow, "The conclusions of European Council meetings are, together with the Treaties, the most authoritative guide to the EC's evolving agenda. They usually include a list of tasks to be carried out by the Commission and/or the Council, as well as a definition of principles in the policy areas discussed at the Council in question."[40] As a body of such transcendent importance, it should properly be treated separately from the Council of Ministers wearing their various hats, in order better to show how the body of political superiors and the body of their lesser government colleagues relate to one another.

When originally established by the Paris Summit of 1974, the European Council was to meet three times per year. Usually two of the three meetings were located in cities of the countries holding the presidency of the Council of Ministers, which rotates every 6 months in alphabetical order based on the official names of the states in their own languages. The third meeting was usually held in Brussels. The SEA reduced the number of annual meetings from three to two, one held at the end of each of the year's two 6-month presidencies in a city of the country having that status. However, the press of business has been such that in some years a third and even a fourth (extraordinary) European Council meeting has been held. Thus, in 1990, as the eventual Maastricht treaty proposals were being developed, there were four summits: Dublin I and II and Rome I and II.[41]

Formal sessions of the European Council are restricted to two representatives from each member state: the head of state (France) or government, and the foreign minister (sometimes the prime minister in the French case). Also attending are the president of the Commission and one other Commissioner. Interpreters are, of course, present, as well as a very restricted number of national and European civil servants, the latter from the Council and Commission Secretariats.[42]

The European Council's agenda items come from various sources, as Neill Nugent has outlined, not all of them as extraordinary items for the EU decision-making process.[43] (1) At all summit meetings, the heads will discuss the state of the EU economy. This discussion may result in a very general statement of purpose on the part of the member states to work harder to improve economic conditions, and in that sense it may add some urgency to actions on the separate agendas of the member governments. Or it may result in specific instructions to the Council of Ministers to act on a matter that has been languishing on the ordinary agenda, as for example in providing a fund to train unemployed youth. (2) There may be matters on the ordinary agenda over which the Council of Ministers is deadlocked, resolution of which requires an appeal to the summit. Nugent gives the examples of budgetary and CAP deadlocks that cropped up frequently in the 1980s and could only be resolved by the heads. In the 1980s, the observation was commonly made that resolving deadlocks produced at the lower level was the primary function the heads performed.[44] This observation was even true in cases where QMV was to apply. If the minister of a particular country objected strongly enough on a matter of urgency, rather than voting on the matter, the ministers might well refer it to the summit; indeed, an extra-ordinary summit might be held. Of course, the fact that a particular matter comes within the purview of the European Council does not mean that the heads themselves will be able to reach agreement. The Luxembourg compromise still can be called upon this level, even though QMV is now in widespread use at the Council of Ministers' level.

Other sources listed by Nugent bring items to the European Council's agenda that are more likely to be extraordinary agenda items for the heads themselves or to produce extraordinary agenda-setting decisions by the heads. (3) International crises, such as the Gulf War, the civil war in Bosnia, or the threat of economic and political instability in post-Communist Russia, become extra-ordinary agenda items for the summit, because they are major preoccupations of the heads themselves, and sometimes because they defy the boundary line between the Maastricht first pillar responsibilities of the EC and the second pillar of foreign and security policies. The heads are likely in such situations to instruct their foreign ministers in the General Affairs Council to agree upon measures to be taken. They may also delegate responsibility or signal their general intent to the Commission, enabling the latter to take steps on its own. The heads do this simply by virtue of their authority as governmental leaders to act in emergency situations without requiring advance approval by their national parliaments and without having to amend the treaties to do so. At the following summit meeting, the heads will then review the action taken and mandate further action by the other bodies as they deem necessary.

There are three institutional sources of summit agenda items that may well be for the extraordinary agenda. (4) The most frequent initiator is the Commission, which is represented in European Council meetings and can make recommendations to the heads regarding matters which it considers to be within its sphere of responsibility. Among the most important examples of extraordinary agenda items initiated by the Commission are EMU and the Social Charter, initiated by Jacques Delors in 1988 and 1989 respectively. Others have had important Commission input at the initiating stage. As seen in chapter 4, Commission President Roy Jenkins played an important role alongside President Giscard d'Estaing and Chancellor Schmidt in putting the EMS on the agenda in 1977. Note that in cases where the Commission has played an initiating role, the European Council controls its own agenda and will decide what subsequent action will be taken on such items.[45]

(5) Other extraordinary agenda-setting initiatives have come from the country holding the Council presidency, for example, France's push in early 1984 for the European Council to take concrete steps to advance the goal of European union, which resulted in the decision at the June Fontainebleau Summit to commission an intergovernmental committee to study proposals for political union and make recommendations. Finally (6) the European Council itself sets its own extraordinary agenda by creating special intergovernmental bodies, like the one created at the Fontainebleau Summit, to report its findings at a later meeting.

The centrality of the European Council concerning the EU's extraordinary agenda does not rule out the capacity of the normal Rome treaty institutions to take on new responsibilities in the wake of fast-moving events, such as those which have occurred in Europe since 1989. These have especially involved the Commission and the Council of Ministers, both having to take action during the time when the European Council is not in session, dealing especially with the economic problems of the post-Communist states of Central and Eastern Europe.[46] The role of the Commission has been to conduct trade and assistance negotiations with these states and to propose action to be taken by either the foreign ministers or the heads, depending on who is meeting next. The foreign ministers, meeting as either the General Affairs Council or the Foreign Ministers Committee of EPC, have stepped into the breach at crucial times and taken on board new issues that had not been anticipated at the previous meeting of the European Council. This development suggests an outer limit to the capacity of the European Council as an extraordinary agenda setter. However, it also suggests that the existence of the European Council as a body that will meet later to approve or modify the actions taken by the other bodies in between its meetings has lessened the danger of inaction on the part of those bodies in the face of unanticipated situations that demand immediate responses.

Judicial Extension of European Union Competence

The Treaty of Rome, in Article 235, contains a provision reminiscent of the "necessary and proper" clause of the U.S. Constitution: "If any action by the Community appears necessary to achieve, in the functioning of the Common

Market, one of the aims of the Community in cases where this Treaty has not provided for the requisite powers of action, the Council, acting by means of an unanimous vote on a proposal of the Commission and after the Assembly has been consulted, shall enact the appropriate provision."[47] This provision has enabled the Council of Ministers, on the Commission's initiative and when the Council could attain unanimity, to enter into fields of activity not strictly outlined in the Rome treaty, that is, to pursue an extraordinary agenda. Principal examples have been in the domain of environmental policy, for example, a 1980 directive "on the protection of ground water against pollution caused by certain dangerous substances," justified under Article 235 as necessary to improve the "quality of life." This directive was based on references at the beginning of the treaty to the objective of raising living standards in the member countries.[48] The ECJ has permitted such extensions of the treaty as long as the Council has voted unanimously in favor of them. This development accords with the reasons we have assigned for the creation of the European Council: As it became more difficult for the Council of Ministers to achieve unanimity for new departures based only in general terms on the Treaty of Rome, additions to the extraordinary agenda could be made only by recourse to the higher authority of the heads of government. With the unanimous approval of the heads, they could then be acted upon by the Council of Ministers.

But the role of the ECJ in facilitating a loosening of interpretation of the Rome treaty should not be underestimated. Anne-Marie Burley and Walter Mattli have persuasively argued that neofunctionalism is alive and well, although it is to be found operating in purer form in Luxembourg, where the ECJ sits, than at Commission headquarters in Brussels.[49] In Luxembourg, "technical-economic" logic is couched in legalistic terms, but the effect is similar to what Ernst Haas had predicted: Community powers would expand through a gradual process of treaty interpretation by EU institutions under the pressure of economic interests seeking to gain advantages at the EU level that are denied them at the national. Business and farmers organizations, as well as national and multinational companies, put pressure on the Commission and the national governments, but they also employ lawyers specializing in Community law. These legal specialists present briefs to the ECJ, offering legal arguments for expanding EU authority.[50]

The judges in Luxembourg have responded by finding authority in the Rome treaty, as in Article 235, for expanded powers. They have also declared actions by member governments—and the failure to take action—as treaty violations in that they encroach on or detract from the authority of the original EC institutions as granted by or implied in the Rome treaty. By its decisions since the 1960s, the Court has created an atmosphere that is favorable to the transfer of power from the national to the EU level. But it must wait for the more political organs to place new initiatives on the extraordinary agenda, after which, in response to cases arising in the national courts and brought to it for opinions, it may give its stamp of interpretative approval to the conversion of such items from extra-treaty to treaty-ordained status.

Since the adoption of the SEA, there have been calls for the ECJ to assume a more aloofly juridical, less political stance.[51] Indeed, the Maastricht treaty has clipped the ECJ's wings by excluding it from having jurisdiction in new policy domains into which the EU will enter, most significantly the area of justice and home affairs.[52] The more overtly political organs of the Union have taken greater control of the extraordinary agenda since the mid-1980s, making it less necessary for the ECJ to prod them in the direction of new initiatives. But the Court still has "the power to pursue its own agenda."[53] If, in the future, leadership elsewhere in the Union is dormant, it may again provide the format for new initiatives, as it did in a 1979 ruling which pointed the way for the eventual Project 1992 to be implemented by ordinary legislation through the mutual recognition principle.

THE EMERGENCE OF THE PUBLIC AGENDA

In the 1990s, it has become apparent that the EU is no longer the exclusive property of political elites to shape as they wish whenever there is consensus among them. In the past the public was consulted from time to time in referenda, usually on the question of whether to join the EC after governmental leaders had worked out the terms. But elite calculations that the public would support their initiatives proved correct[54]—until the referenda on the Maastricht treaty. The fact that the treaty was rejected by Danish voters the first time around, and almost rejected by French voters showed that voter approval could neither be taken for granted nor easily manipulated. It is true that there were political parties or sections of political parties that opposed ratification, and the voters divided in their responses to appeals from both sides. But the fact that voters did respond to anti-Maastricht appeals shows that putting EU issues into the public domain can be a successful strategy for opponents of further empowerment of EU institutions. Even when the voters are not consulted directly in referenda, debates between or within the parties in national parliamentary bodies over EU issues threaten to become a part of the public agenda of issues that are debated in campaigns for national elective offices.

There is, of course, a directly elected body that is part of the institutional arrangements of the EU, the EP. As has been shown, the EP plays a minor role at best in setting EU agendas. Its involvement in processing the ordinary agenda is growing, and it has used its growing capacities judiciously while seeking to gain the confidence of the Commission and the Council. But the fact that the EP is still the least powerful of these three bodies is a source of disappointment to those who are critical of the alleged elitism and technocratic aloofness of the Commission and the frequent cases of timidity on the part of the Council, including the European Council at times when the heads seem to have lost their common drive. It is also at the heart of criticisms about a "democratic deficit."[55]

The European Parliament Election of June 1994

The democratic deficit relates not only to the weakness of the only directly elected EU body, but also to the lack of awareness of and concern for the EU and what it does on the part of ordinary citizens of the member countries, who are now citizens of the EU. Awareness of what the EU does is greater among certain publics than among others. Businessmen and farmers are affected by the EU in more tangible ways than are persons employed in other economic sectors. Those who regularly read newspapers and magazines with extensive coverage of EU activities are likely to be persons with a direct stake in the outcomes of those activities. They are also likely to be members of organizations with access to appropriate government agencies and institutions of the EU, especially the Commission.[56] But at the time of the first direct elections to the EP in June 1979, public indifference to the then EC was a source of concern for those hoping that direct elections would make Community governance more democratic. In June 1979, the turnout rate across the nine countries for the first direct elections was 62 percent, not unrespectable by U.S. standards, but well below the 75 percent to 90 percent levels usually recorded in national elections in EU countries. Four months later a Euro-barometer poll revealed that "only two out of three respondents recalled having heard anything about the European Parliament, and only 44% were able to identify what it was that they had heard."[57] We have charted the recent accretions of power by the EP. The question remains, has the EP moved any closer to the voters than when it first became a directly elected body? We will use the fourth direct elections to the EP, held in June 1994, as a testing ground for answering this question.[58]

The Setting.   Toward the end of its 5-year term, the EP that had been elected in June 1989 consisted of 518 MEPs divided among eight cross-national groups, as well as 21 nonattached MEPs, or independents belonging to none of the groups. The eight groups correspond to the ideological classifications of political parties in the member countries (see Figures 6.3 and 6.4 for the group memberships in Parliament elected in 1989). In the 1989–1994 EP, the two largest groups were the European Socialist Party group (PES), consisting of 197 MEPs, and the European People's Party group (EPP), consisting of 162 MEPs. Both of these groups differed from smaller groups in that they contained MEPs from all 12 countries. In the Socialist group, the largest national components were the 46 British Labour MEPs, the 31 German Social Democrats, the 27 Spanish Socialists, and the 22 French Socialists. The 46 Labour MEPs were the largest single bloc in the EP of fellow partisans from a given country. Having become more committed to European integration in the 1980s, the Labour MEPs could comfortably share with their continental Socialist colleagues a common program that emphasized extending EU powers through social programs and measures to overcome unemployment.

The EPP group consisted of Christian Democrats from countries with large Catholic populations and their EP allies, who included the 33 British Conservative MEPs. The largest Christian Democratic contingents were the 32 German CDU/CSU MEPs and the 27 Italian Christian Democratic MEPs. Christian Democrats have been at the very core of the European integration movement from the very beginning. The 1989 EP elections had resulted in the EPP losing its status as the largest group to the Socialists. Alliance with the British Conservatives and

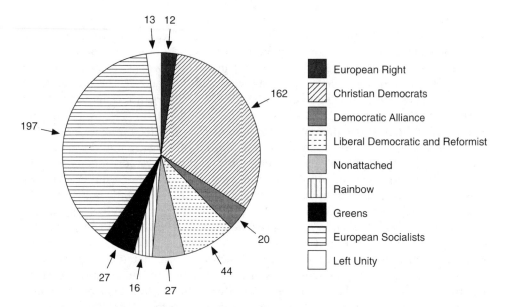

FIGURE 6.3 1989 European Parliament (Distribution of groups early in the parliament)

FIGURE 6.4 1994 European Parliament

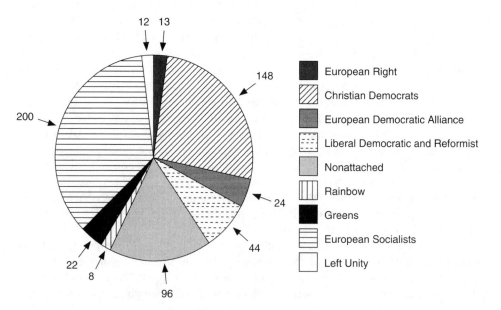

assorted other groups augmented the EPP during 1989–1994 from 121 to 162 adherents, but this was at the price of diluting the strong prointegration orientation of the Christian Democrats. Although a majority of British Conservative MEPs were pro-Maastricht in their sympathies, they had to accommodate their stances in the EP to the more Euro-sceptic views of their national party leaders, Prime Ministers Thatcher and Major.[59]

Other groups in the EP were much smaller than the PES and the EPP. The Liberal Democratic and Reformist group (LDR) comprised 44 MEPs from national nonsocialist and non-Catholic parties of the center and center-right. The largest of these was part of the French UDF contingent, led in the EP election campaign by former French President Giscard d'Estaing, and consisting of ten members. All components of the LDR group were prointegrationist in their sympathies. In order of size, the remaining groups were the Greens (27 MEPs); the European Democratic Alliance (EDA), which was primarily the French Gaullist delegation and totaled 20 MEPs; the Rainbow group, a second, more ideologically diverse group of Greens (16 MEPs); the Left Unity (LU) group of Communists and ex-Communists (13 MEPs); and the European Right (ER) group of MEPs belonging to far right parties in France, Germany, and Belgium (12 MEPs).

During the course of the 1989–1994 EP, there were dramatic changes that occurred in the politics of all four of the largest member countries. We have discussed two of these developments in the preceding chapter, the unification of Germany and the fall of Margaret Thatcher as British prime minister. Two other changes were the defeat of the French Socialist government by the parties of the center-right in the March 1993 legislative election and the almost complete overturn of the established parties in Italy in 1993 and 1994. We will briefly note the significance of these developments for the 1994 EP elections in the three most important member states: Germany, Britain, and France.

German unification in October 1990 was followed by parliamentary elections in December, which the governing CDU/CSU–FDP coalition headed by Helmut Kohl and Hans-Dietrich Genscher won rather easily. Incorporation into the FRG of five former East German states did not alter the political party balance significantly, but it did add to Bonn's economic responsibilities with repercussions for the ERM (see chapter 7). Support for European integration in German public opinion declined with rising hostility to the idea of replacing the DM with a single EU currency. However, the most direct implication of German unification for the 1994 EP elections was an increase in the number of Germany's parliamentary seats from 81 to 99. Lesser increases were given to France, Britain, and Italy (from 81 to 87 seats each); to Spain (from 60 to 64); to the Netherlands (from 25 to 31); and to Belgium, Greece, and Portugal (from 24 to 25). The least populous countries retained the number of seats they had held previously: Denmark (16), Ireland (15), and Luxembourg (6).

As we have seen, the replacement of Margaret Thatcher by John Major in November 1990 helped pave the way for Britain to agree, albeit with reservations, to the Maastricht treaty. But since the 1992 ERM crisis, Euro-scepticism had risen in the parliamentary Conservative Party, and Major's stance in EU deliberations had hardened. As the 1994 EP election campaign began, Major staked out a position on EU that was more resistant to further change than that of the Labour Party. But Labour preferred to concentrate on domestic issues in the EP campaign, and it soft-pedalled its differences with the Conservatives over EU, including its support, along with other European Socialists, of the Delors Social Charter.

The new French government that took office following the March 1993 elections was headed by a Gaullist, Edouard Balladur, a former political chief of staff to President Pompidou and close adviser of Gaullist leader and former Prime Minister Jacques Chirac. Balladur's early popularity as prime minister undermined the certainty that Chirac, who had run for president in 1981 and 1988, would again be the strongest Gaullist candidate in the 1995 presidential election. Given the unlikelihood that François Mitterrand, now in his late 70s, would stand again as a presidential candidate, the most likely Socialist candidate for president was former Prime Minister Michel Rocard, whom the Socialists chose to lead their list for the EP elections. But there was also speculation concerning the fact that Jacques Delors would be available by the time of the presidential election, since his term as EU Commission president was concluding at the end of 1994. Although Delors's credentials as a Europhile could not be bettered, Rocard had strong Euro-credentials as well, and Delors let it be known that he would not become a candidate with Rocard in the race. Meanwhile, on the French right the September 1992 Maastricht referendum campaign in France had given Chirac an opportunity to stake out a Euro-sceptic position that had not appeared when he was prime minister coinhabiting power with Mitterrand in the Euro-euphoric years of 1986–1988. Once in office, Prime Minister Balladur cooperated with Mitterrand in attempting to maintain France's leadership role in the EU in tandem with Germany. As the EP elections approached, breakaway lists were formed on the Left by Bernard Tapie, an industrialist-politician with presidential ambitions, to challenge the official Socialist list headed by Rocard, and on the Right, by Phillipe de Villiers, who had been a leader of the anti-Maastricht campaign in the 1992 referendum. Villiers's anti-EU campaign was supplemented in more virulent form by the far right National Front, led by Jean-Marie Le Pen. It was clear that Europe had once again become an important issue in French politics, where it had lain dormant since Mitterrand's moves in 1983 and 1984 that had paved the way for the SEA (see chapter 4). As in Britain, Europe was a more divisive issue for the Right than for the Left, where the principal opposition came from the Communist Party, a diminishing and (by the 1990s) marginalized force in French politics.

Campaign and Outcome. With the exception of France and Denmark, the Maastricht treaty and the future of the EU was not at issue in the campaign. The referendum battles in France and Denmark had politicized the EU to the extent that voter turnout rates for EP elections in both countries were up by 5 to 6 percent from 1989, while the overall turnout rate for the EC-12 of 56.4 percent was down from 58.5 percent in 1989 and was the lowest turnout of the four EP elections held since 1979. Anti-Maastricht lists captured 25.5

percent of the Danish vote and 25.3 percent of the French. Elsewhere, anti-EU sentiment was marginalized (as in Belgium and Germany), muted (as in Italy), or allowed to go unchallenged (as in Britain). In all 12 countries, the main issue was "who can best govern this country?" Governing parties lost support in most countries relative to their 1989 percentages, with the most serious losses coupled with opposition gains being those in Denmark, Spain, the Netherlands, and Britain. On the other hand, Chancellor Kohl could claim a victory over the opposition Social Democrats in Germany, and new Italian prime minister Silvio Berlusconi reproduced his rout of the former governing parties 2 months earlier. Even in Denmark and France, the anti-Maastricht vote may have been more a general repudiation of all parties that had been in government in recent years and had, in the voters' eyes, demonstrated an inability to solve the country's problems. As for the Conservatives in Britain and the Socialists in Spain, each had been in power long enough to be the single focal point of hostility. By contrast, in Germany the recent economic upturn helped Kohl achieve a victory in place of the defeat that the polls had predicted in the preceding weeks.

The new EP elected in June 1994 has 567 MEPs (see Figure 6.4). Again, the two leading groups are the Socialists, up from 198 to 200, and the EPP (Christian Democrats and allies), down from 162 to 148. The British Labour contingent rose from 46 to 62 seats, remaining the single largest national party bloc. This gain helped to offset the loss of 6 seats by the French Socialists and 5 by the Spanish Socialists, plus the near removal of the Italian Socialists, down from 12 seats to 2. The most severe EPP losses were sustained by the Italian Christian Democrats, who lost 16 seats, and the British Conservatives, who lost 14. In partial compensation for these losses, Helmut Kohl's CDU/CSU gained 24 seats, largely because of the increased number of German seats available. The third largest category in the new EP were 96 nonaligned MEPs, which included 55 of Italy's 86, reflecting the near total collapse of the old Italian party system. Of the smaller groups in the EP, only two appeared to have gained seats: the Gaullist-dominated EDA (four seat gain) and the European Right group (one seat gain).

It should be clear from the foregoing that, even in countries where many voters have strong views about EU issues, the opportunities to express them in EP elections are few. In most countries, most of the parties support the Maastricht treaty and the EU as it is today. Wherever a party has taken a stance against the treaty or against certain parts of it, many of the voters who agree with the party on this issue may be supporters of other parties on domestic issues. Only in France were large members of Euro-sceptic voters able, if they were supporters of the socialists or the center-right parties, to vote for a list of their fellow partisans who were making Europe a campaign issue. As a result, it is significant that the turnout of the French was greater in 1994 than in 1989. Elsewhere, even where Europe had the potential as an issue to activate voters, as it might have in Britain, the parties concentrated on issues of domestic governance, and turnout stayed the same or dropped.

EU supporters might worry that the opportunity the elections gave French and Danish opponents to stage a replay of the 1992 Maastricht referendum campaigns was a negative development, and the fact that the EU was not at issue elsewhere was just as well. But this would be to display nostalgia for a time when voters ignored Europe altogether and were content to treat the EP elections as just another test of strength between national parties to see which of them were in the best position to win national power in the next general election. Maastricht has raised the stakes that voters have in the EU. Many voters are pleased with the new powers that have been or are soon to be transferred to the Union. But many others who were basically indifferent to the old EC have become alarmed about where the new EU is headed. In 1992 and 1993, the referenda in Denmark, Ireland, and France, the fights within the Conservative party in Britain, and perhaps the case before the Federal Constitutional Court in Germany raised voter awareness and concern in those countries. From the standpoint of removing the EU's democratic deficit, it may not be such a bad thing from the Euro-enthusiast standpoint if this heightened public concern spreads to the remaining countries and is augmented by the already heightened voter awareness in new member countries (Austria, Finland, and Sweden). Whatever size and shape the EU takes in the future, it cannot even dimly resemble a single democratic polity unless the issues that divide the member governments when they meet in Council are issues which also divide (or unite) the voters as well as the political parties in each of the member countries. The June 1994 EP elections showed some signs that this might become the case in the future.

The European Union Agenda and Domestic Politics: Germany, France, and Britain

Political leaders are well placed to determine what issues will reach the public agendas within their own countries. But, especially as national elections loom, they must compete with leaders of opposition political parties, and sometimes with others within their own government or governing coalition, for control of the public agenda. The frequency with which EU-related issues have become stakes in the domestic political contests of member countries appears to have been growing.

A case in point is EMU. When the stages of EMU were being worked out by the Delors Committee in the late 1980s and by the IGC which led to the Maastricht treaty provisions regarding EMU in 1991, public attention was minimal, even in Britain, where Margaret Thatcher's battles over EMU with fellow heads of government and even with her own ministers were more of a spectator sport for the public than anything most people felt it necessary to make part of their personal likes and dislikes. But once a tentative date was set for the introduction of a common currency, this changed, especially for publics in those countries with a long-standing tradition of regarding their currency as a symbol of national greatness. The idea of having to replace their DMs, their francs, or their pounds with something called the "ECU" was not something German, French, or British citizens could accept with equanimity. In a poll conducted in

November 1994, interviews were held with nearly 2,500 German and 2,000 British citizens.[60] They were asked: "Is your country's membership of the European Union a good or bad thing?" Twenty-six percent of the British respondents said it was a "bad thing," against only nine percent of the Germans. But the number of Germans saying it was a "good thing" had declined from 57 percent in September 1992 to 46 percent in November 1994, while the British decline was from 44 percent to 37 percent. It has long been true that Britons are among the least enthusiastic of Euro-citizens, but the gap between them and the Germans may be closing. The single currency may be one of the reasons. Majorities of both British (64 percent) and Germans (65 percent) supported holding a referendum on whether the EU should introduce a single currency. Only 33 percent of the British said they would vote for a single currency, with 56 percent opposed and 11 percent undecided. German figures were a mere 24 percent in favor, 53 percent opposed, and twice as high a proportion of undecideds: 23 percent.

The government of Helmut Kohl supports EMU to the fullest extent, while that of John Major has withheld any commitment to a single currency. There was no major German political party or leader who challenged Kohl's position on the issue in the October 1994 Bundestag elections. The principal voice questioning EMU is Bundesbank President Hans Tietmeyer, who is concerned that monetary controls will be weaker with a single currency, unless EMU membership is confined to those countries meeting criteria that are even more rigid than those set forth in the Maastricht treaty.[61] This position may be one reason Kohl's CDU joined French Prime Minister Balladur in suggesting a multispeed EU, with different classes of membership (see chapter 5). With the election over and Kohl holding a very narrow majority of seats in the Bundestag (which reelected him Chancellor by one vote), the chancellor must find a way of convincing Germans that their money will remain sound under EMU. It is an issue that is waiting on the threshold of the German public agenda.

Chancellor Kohl's commitment to the full implementation of EMU, as well as his apparent interest in the idea of confining its full implementation, at least initially, to an inner circle, is consistent with his commitment to making substantial progress in the direction of a "federal Europe" during the 1996 review of the Maastricht treaty.[62] The elements of federalism found in the Basic Law of the FRG serve as a model for Kohl's party, the CDU, suggesting what at least a minority of member states of the EU might accomplish together in the future. In this model, the states retain considerable administrative responsibility for programs determined jointly by the federal and the state governments, with an important role played by the upper house of the Federal Parliament, the Bundesrat, or Federal Council, in which the states are able to defend their interests against too heavy-handed a federal government. The full vision would be realized gradually, but enhanced powers for the EP and the Commission could, the CDU hopes, be agreed upon in the 1996 review.[63]

These dreams of a future European federation do not sit well with either of the Kohl government's two largest partners, the governments of France and

Britain. After Balladur's initial proposal for a multispeed EU, the French foreign minister, Alain Juppé, specified that this should not be taken to mean an exclusive inner circle. Like British Prime Minister John Major, the French government envisaged different sets of core countries playing a full role in different policy areas.[64] Thus, although Britain would not join with the others in carrying social policy to the fullest extent, it would play one of the leading roles in developing common foreign and security policies. On this, France seemed to be siding with the British against the Germans. Further alternative scenarios for post-1996 came from the French government in late 1994, signaling a potential rift in the Franco-German partnership, which has provided the engine that drives successful EU reforms. Prime Minister Edouard Balladur, in an article in the newspaper *Le Monde* on November 30, 1994, set forth views about EU reform that, again, appeared much closer to those of John Major than to those of Helmut Kohl.[65] The positions taken were not necessarily in accord with the views of President Mitterrand, but presidential illness and the fact that his term would be coming to an end in May 1995 had made the president look increasingly like a lame duck. Chancellor Kohl would soon have to try to work out a new partnership with Mitterrand's successor.

The presidential election campaign was already heating up in November 1994, 5 months early. Former Prime Minister Jacques Chirac, the leader of the Gaullist party to which Prime Minister Balladur also belonged, declared his candidacy, as did Jean-Marie Le Pen, the far right opponent of immigration of North Africans into France.[66] Le Pen has always been critical of European integration in general and of the Maastricht treaty on the grounds that it is likely to mean EU interference with the ability of the French government to restrict immigration. Perhaps hoping to head off inroads into his more nationalistic constituency, Chirac weighed in with a call for a referendum on France's membership in EMU, if that should imply acceptance of a single currency.[67] The narrowness of the 1992 French referendum ratifying the Maastricht treaty had made it clear to Chirac that there was a body of voters who were opposed to any further moves toward a federal Europe, and that it would be best to position himself close enough to them that they would not be susceptible to Le Pen's more extreme anti-EU appeals. However, in January 1995, another right-of-center candidate, Pierre de Villiers, who had been a leader of the antiratification campaign in 1992, but was more respectably conservative than Le Pen, announced his candidacy.[68] Villiers appeared likely to compete with Chirac for the votes of Euro-sceptics who normally vote for the moderate-right parties.

Chirac's move had put Balladur, an undeclared candidate for the presidency, in a difficult position. To his left, the most likely Socialist candidate appeared to be European Commission President Jacques Delors himself. Balladur had reason to hope that he would receive moderate Euro-enthusiast right-of-center support from the party of former President Giscard d'Estaing, the UDF, which was joined with the RPR in the governing coalition. But Delors would cut into this support while holding most of the Socialist vote. Polls in late November showed that Delors had taken over the lead from Balladur in voter preferences among the likely candidates.[69] Therefore, Balladur's November 30 *Le Monde* article can be viewed as an attempt to stake out a position that was not Euro-sceptic like Chirac's, but at the same time not Euro-enthusiast like that of Delors. This involved Balladur taking the position that the 1996 review should not point to a federal Europe, but that positive steps could be taken to make EU decision making both more efficient and more open. He had words of criticism for efforts to make the Delors Commission a "federal executive," and criticized the ECJ for decisions that had extended EU powers. But a companion article by Balladur's European affairs minister, Alain Lamassoure, elaborated by indicating that the Council of Ministers should be more open in its decision making, and that the codecision powers of the EP, granted in some policy areas by the Maastricht treaty, should be extended.[70] Thus, Balladur was keeping his options open in both directions on European issues.

In December 1994, Jacques Delors announced that he would not seek the presidency, partly because of his age—almost 70—and also because he would have to face a right-of-center majority in the National Assembly. As a result, unless and until the voters would elect a center-left majority in the Assembly, he would have to suffer the indignities of cohabitation with a right-of-center prime minister, which Mitterrand had twice been forced to endure. With no experience of electoral politics, he evidently did not feel willing to throw his energies into what might be a futile effort.[71] It is also conceivable that the maneuverings between Chirac and Balladur had raised the spectre of an election in which the EU would be the major issue—a repeat of the 1992 Maastricht referendum campaign, in which strong French nationalistic feelings, abhorrent to a true European, had manifested themselves. If Delors himself were not in the race, the temptation Chirac or Balladur might have to play the anti-EU card might be reduced, and the EU might be just another issue, not *the* issue in the presidential election campaign. In fact, European issues did not play a major role in the contest between Chirac, Balladur, and Socialist candidate Lionel Jospin. Balladur, Le Pen, Villiers, and others were eliminated on the first ballot, and Chirac won the second ballot run-off against Jospin on May 7, 1995.

In British politics, the main debate over Europe goes on within the governing Conservative Party. The degree of firmness that the British government led by Prime Minister Major exhibits in EU deliberations is an object of close scrutiny by right-wing Conservative MPs who doubt that he is as firm in EU negotiations as Margaret Thatcher was. Although Euro-scepticism is not the only badge of distinction that enables Conservative MPs to be identified as right-wingers, the EU is the one area of concern that is most likely to get the prime minister in trouble with them. A case in point was the conflict in late 1994 over an obligation Major had incurred at the Edinburgh Summit 2 years earlier to increase Britain's contribution to the EU budget, as part of a package of mutual concessions that enabled Major to make the Maastricht treaty more compatible for home consumption (see chapter 5). When 20 or so Euro-sceptic MPs signaled their intention to vote against the increase, Major took this as a repudiation of a solemn pledge he had made on behalf of his government. At the opening of the new parliamentary session on November 16, 1994, he announced that the vote would be considered a matter of confidence, meaning that, if the increased contribution were defeated, he would ask the Queen to dissolve Parliament and declare new elections, $2\frac{1}{2}$ years before they were due to be held.[72] Although this was the prime minister's right under British constitutional traditions, the Euro-sceptics claimed that he was going out of his way to widen divisions within the party. When it came to the vote, eight right-wing MPs abstained. Their abstention was not enough to defeat the measure, but Major added to the animosity of his right wing by "withdrawing the whip" from the abstainers, meaning that they were temporarily excluded from parliamentary party functions, although they continued to be Conservative Party members.[73] Technically, Major no longer had a majority in the House of Commons of full-fledged Conservative MPs. He was punished a week later when Euro-sceptic Conservatives joined with the opposition parties to defeat a part of the annual budget that would raise the level of the VAT, a step which likewise stemmed from British commitments to the EU.[74] But this had not been made a matter of confidence in the government, so Major had to live with the defeat, by no means his first on EU-related matters.

The opposition Labour Party under its new leader Tony Blair was meanwhile moving in a more Euro-enthusiastic direction. In January, he indicated solid Labour Party commitment to EMU, a common foreign and security policy, and institutional reform to make the EU more democratic.[75] This move put the opposition party clearly to the Euro-enthusiastic side of the Major government. Assuming that these lines hold until the next election, which might not be until after the 1996 EU review, the EU could become an interparty campaign issue for the first time in Britain. In the past, the battle has taken place within each of the two major parties. But if Labour solidarity holds, then only the Conservative Party will be divided, and Major's only hope for a united party front in the election will be to make concessions to Euro-sceptic sentiments by resisting further EU reforms.

Political infighting is putting EU issues on the British public agenda, but whether the voters will move out of the spectator ranks remains to be seen. The Conservative Euro-sceptics argue that public opinion is on their side, given the grumbling about "Brussels" they hear from their constituents. But, as of November 1994, the Labour Party held a seemingly unapproachable 30 percent lead over the Conservatives in the public opinion polls.[76] On December 16, the Conservatives lost a parliamentary seat in a by-election held to fill a vacancy created by the death of one of their MPs. The 29 percent swing in the constituency vote from the Conservatives to Labour compared to the 1992 general election was the biggest swing away from the governing party since 1933.[77] The Conservatives' downward slide in the polls had begun 2 years earlier, when voters were shaken by the monetary crisis of October 1992, which had resulted in Major pulling Britain out of the ERM. Even though the economy was in better condition in late 1994, for the first time since the pre-Thatcher years, voters seemed to believe that the Labour Party would be better able than the Conservatives to manage the economy.[78] Although the Major government was not panicking with the general election still 30 months away, it could be predicted that it will increasingly play the EU card in an effort to portray the Labour Party as being poorly positioned on EU issues (i.e., too Euro-enthusiastic) from the standpoint of the average voter.

CONCLUSION

At the end of 1994, the institutions of the EU were, more than in most periods, in a transitional stage. Some of the new structures, powers, and rules set forth in the Maastricht treaty were just being put into place, while others were scheduled for later emplacement. Four countries had been accepted for member-ship, but voters in only three—Austria, Finland, and Sweden—voted to ratify membership, enabling those countries to join on January 1, 1995. Voters in Norway elected to stay outside. In 1996, an IGC would be convened to consider further modifications of the structures, powers, and rules in anticipation of further new entrants. Just how far the staged formation of EMU would go by the end of the century was anyone's guess.

In this chapter, we have discussed the structures, powers, and rules as they stood in mid-1994 in terms of their bearing on the ways in which the ordinary and extraordinary EU agendas are set and processed. Ordinary agenda setting is primarily the job of the Commission, while processing the agenda involves an interaction between the Council of Ministers and the EP, with the Commission playing a mediating role that often is used in practice to augment the influence of the EP. Three different procedures are used, as specified by the Treaty of Rome, the SEA, and the Maastricht TEU. In order of the ascending importance of the EP, the procedures are (1) consultation, which gives the EP a voice; (2) coopera-tion, which gives it a conditional blocking power; and (3) codecision, which gives it an ultimate veto. The capacity of one or a few member governments to block a legislative measure in the Council of Ministers has been diminished further by each treaty. Over time we may expect the frequency of the use of codecision to increase relative to the other procedures and the success of both formal and informal blocking minorities in the Council to diminish.

We have emphasized the distinction between the ordinary and the extra-ordinary agenda to show that the hard bargaining between states attempting to balance the costs and benefits of yielding elements of their sovereignty to a supranational body usually goes on at the summit level at the time the heads of state and government are determining whether to commit themselves to some action that will alter the balance of power within the EU or between the Union and the member states. Once the commitment is made, the detailed alternatives are worked out by less exalted bodies. The complicated rules pertaining to consultation, coordination, and codecision do not apply at this level; indeed, the changes in the mode of processing the ordinary agenda have occurred on the basis of bargains reached by the European Council. With the expected further expansions of the Union going on early in the next century, and the need to make institutional adjustments to them, and with the unresolved fundamental issues regarding EMU, the CAP, the Social Charter, and the CFSP (to name only the most obvious), there seems little reason to expect that the European Council will be able to relax sufficiently to allow the original Rome treaty institutions to get on with their work without having to anticipate what will happen at the next summit or during the next presidency. In chapters 7–11, we examine the outstanding EU policy issues more closely.

Extraordinary agenda decisions can be thought of as basic constitutional decisions that are made in the formative stages of institution building. Such decisions are also made for the EU by the ECJ in opinions that are of constitutional significance, and require adjustments on the part of member governments and other EU organs, not unlike the decisions that are reached jointly by the heads of government. The ECJ's decisions have less immediate impact than those of the European Council, but over a longer term they constrain other actors to behave according to rules on which general agreement has come to prevail. There are signs that, with the Maastricht treaty, some of the most fundamental constitutional issues regarding the old EC, or first pillar, set of arrangements have been resolved (e.g., unanimity versus QMV on legislation in the Council), but new juridical issues will arise regarding the principle of subsidiarity and the second and third pillars of the EU. It remains to be seen whether gradually the ECJ will come to play a role in interpreting the new structures, powers, and rules set forth in the Maastricht treaty, just as it has those of the parent Treaty of Rome.

The Maastricht treaty is silent on the question of how democratic the EU institutions ought to be. The burden of making them responsive to voters is in the hands of the directly elected EP, and it depends heavily upon the EP elections held every 5 years in the member countries. The outcomes of bargains reached among the heads at the summit are visible to the voters if they are paying attention, but the concessions that have been made by their government may be more harmful to certain categories of voters in a country (e.g., workers in industries threatened by an opening of trade) than the gains achieved in the compromise are beneficial. Voters who lose may not be aware of what or how they have lost unless the media, interest groups, or political parties can focus their attention upon the losses. But the issues are often so complicated that only elites can debate them with other elites. The lack of attention to European issues in most of the countries in the 1994 EP election campaign suggests that the EU remains a largely elite-driven set of political institutions. Not much democracy has yet filtered into Brussels from the national capitals where the ire of the voters can be and is felt. Elections in all of the EC countries are held frequently at national, regional, and local levels, and the EP election every 5 years is just another of them. Except in Denmark and France, the leaders of the established national parties as yet have no reason to believe that what they do on the European stage will have anywhere near as much impact on the outcome of the EP electoral test of strength as what voters believe the government is or is not doing to manage the economy or to alleviate other societal problems that are seen by most voters as problems specific to their own country.

But in the 1990s, EU issues have been appearing more frequently on national public agendas. In Britain EU issues divide majority and opposition parties from one another as well as threaten the capacity of the John Major government to continue governing. The issue of whether Britain should give up its pound for a common EMU currency is coming to the surface of public attention, and it could come to a head in the next general election. The issue of EMU is gaining increasing public attention in Germany as well, despite the long-standing consensus in support of European integration that has existed in that country, and it could in time put the government of Helmut Kohl, with its federalist ambitions for the EU, at odds with a majority of the German citizenry, depending upon whether opposition parties decide to exploit the EMU issue. In France, the future of the EU was a factor in the early stages of the lengthy campaign for the election of a new president in April–June 1995. And in Denmark, which experienced two referenda on ratification of the Maastricht treaty, as well as in Sweden, where there was a closely fought referendum over entry into the Union, EU issues are very much on the public agenda. A true European public opinion has not yet emerged. It is still fragmented into its 15 different national components, but in some of these components, a healthy public attention to important issues on the EU agenda is developing.

ENDNOTES

1. Leon N. Lindberg and Stuart A. Scheingold, *Europe's Would-Be Polity: Patterns of Change in the European Community* (Englewood Cliffs, N.J.: Prentice-Hall, 1970), pp. 87–95. This earlier work contains what is still in many respects an accurate description of how the ordinary agenda is set and processed.
2. Neill Nugent, *The Government and Politics of the European Community*, 2nd ed. (Durham, N.C.: Duke University Press, 1991), pp. 168–172.
3. The Commission is organized into 23 Directorates General (like the departments of a national government's executive-administrative structure). These are headed by 20 commissioners, some of whom have responsibility for more than one DG.
4. Nugent, *The Government and Politics of the European Community*, pp. 210–217.
5. Ibid., pp. 283–290.
6. See examples given in Jan M. M. Van den Bos, "The Policy Issues Analyzed," in Bruce Bueno de Mesquita and Frans N. Stokman, eds., *European Community Decision Making: Models, Applications, and Comparisons* (New Haven and London: Yale University Press, 1994), pp. 34–49.
7. Lindberg and Scheingold, *Europe's Would-Be Polity*, p. 97.
8. Ibid.
9. Ibid., p. 93.
10. Thomas Sloot and Piet Verschuren, "Decision-Making Speed in the European Community," *Journal of Common Market Studies* 29 (September 1990): 77.
11. Helen Wallace, "The Council and the Commission after the Single European Act," in Leon Hurwitz and Christian Lequesne, eds., *The State of the European Community:*

Policies, Institutions and Debates in the Transition Years (Boulder: Lynne Rienner), p. 25.

12. Smoot and Verschuren, "Decision-Making Speed," pp. 77–83.

13. Wallace, "The Council and the Commission," p. 25; Peter Ludlow, "Introduction: The Politics and Policies of the EC in 1989," in Ludlow, ed., *The Annual Review of European Community Affairs 1990* (London: Brassey's, for Centre for the European Policy Studies, Brussels, 1991), p. xxv; W. Nicoll, "The Luxembourg Compromise," *Journal of Common Market Studies* 23 (September 1984): 35–43.

14. *The Economist,* October 22, 1994, p. 20.

15. Nugent, *The Government and Politics of the European Community,* p. 123.

16. Ibid., p. 124.

17. Nicoll, "The Luxembourg Compromise," pp. 36–37.

18. Helen Wallace, *Budgetary Politics: The Finances of the European Communities* (London: George Allen & Unwin, 1980), pp. 77–89.

19. Nugent, *The Government and Politics of the European Community,* pp. 284–290.

20. Ibid., p. 131.

21. Ibid., pp. 291–298.

22. Ibid., pp. 298–303.

23. Anne-Marie Burley and Walter Mattli, "Europe Before the Court: A Political Theory of Legal Integration," *International Organization* 47 (Winter 1993): 67–68.

24. Nugent, *The Government and Politics of the European Community,* pp. 77–93.

25. Commission administrative decisions are subject to prior review by management committees of national-level civil servants, which can block draft Commission decisions regarding the CAP, and regulatory committees, with similar compositions, which can refer a Commission draft harmonization measure to the Council of Ministers, which in turn might block or allow the measure. Ibid., pp. 84–86.

26. Lindberg and Scheingold, *Europe's Would-Be Polity,* p. 81. Lindberg and Scheingold are using terms coined by Ernst B. Haas in "The 'Uniting of Europe' and the Uniting of Latin America," *Journal of Common Market Studies* 5 (June 1967): 328–329. The dramatic-political style coincides with a preoccupation with diplomacy and national security matters rather than with the technical and economic matters favored by neofunctionalists.

27. Lindberg and Scheingold, *Europe's Would-Be Polity,* pp. 81–82.

28. Robert O. Keohane, *After Hegemony: Cooperation and Discord in the World Political Economy* (Princeton, N.J.: Princeton University Press, 1984), p. 206.

29. Jan Werts, *The European Council* (Amsterdam: North Holland, 1992), pp. 32–69.

30. Susan Hayward, "French Politicians and Political Communication," in Alistair Cole, ed., *French Political Parties in Transition* (Aldershot: Dartmouth, 1990), p. 25.

31. Francois Duchene, "Jean Monnet's Methods," in Douglas Brinkley and Clifford Hackett, eds., *Jean Monnet: The Path to European Unity* (New York: St. Martin's, 1991), pp. 193–196. It is noteworthy that Monnet himself came in the early 1970s to recommend the creation of a European Council, which he called a "provisional European government." Werts, *The European Council,* pp. 64–67.

32. Simon Bulmer and Wolfgang Wessels, *The European Council: Decision-Making in European Politics* (Basingstoke and London: Macmillan, 1987), pp. 17–27.

33. Ibid., p. 23.

34. Ibid., p. 20.

35. Ibid., pp. 21–27.

36. Peter Ludlow, "The European Commission," in Robert O. Keohane and Stanley Hoffmann, eds., *The New European Community: Decisionmaking and Institutional Change* (Boulder: Westview, 1991), p. 115.
37. Ludlow, "Introduction," pp. xvi–xviii.
38. Emil Joseph Kirchner, *Decision-making in the European Community: The Council Presidency and European Integration* (Manchester, England, and New York: Manchester University Press, 1992).
39. Nugent, *The Government and Politics of the European Community*, p. 195.
40. Ludlow, "Introduction," p. xvi.
41. Nugent, *The Government and Politics of the European Community*, p. 198; Juliet Lodge, "EC Policymaking: Institutional Considerations," in Lodge, ed., *The European Community and the Challenge of the Future* (New York: St. Martin's, 1989), p. 49.
42. Nugent, *The Government and Politics of the European Community*, p. 195.
43. Ibid., p. 197.
44. Bulmer and Wessels, *The European Council*, p. 101.
45. The heads may, of course, consider that the Commission is stepping over its bounds in taking the initiative, but they are in a position to act upon the recommendation whether they consider the bounds to be overstepped or not. Here we may see intergovernmentally assisted stepover, if not incremental supranational spillover.
46. Anna Murphy and Peter Ludlow, "The Community's External Relations," in Ludlow, ed., *The Annual Review of European Community Affairs 1990*, pp. 205–217.
47. Howard Bliss, ed., *The Political Development of the European Community: A Documentary Collection* (Waltham, Mass.: Blaisdell Publishing, 1970), p. 65.
48. J.A. Usher, "The Scope of Community Competence: Its Recognition and Enforcement," *Journal of Common Market Studies* 24 (December 1985): 121.
49. Burley and Mattli, "Europe Before the Court," pp. 41–76.
50. Ibid., pp. 58–59.
51. Ibid., p. 71.
52. Ibid., pp. 73–74.
53. Ibid., p. 74.
54. The exception before 1992 was the 1972 rejection of membership in the EC by Norwegian voters.
55. See Shirley Williams, "Sovereignty and Accountability in the European Community," in Keohane and Hoffmann, eds., *The New European Community*, pp. 155–176.
56. Russell J. Dalton and Richard C. Eichenberg, "A People's Europe: Citizen Support for the 1992 Project and Beyond," in Dale L. Smith and James Lee Ray, eds., *The 1992 Project and the Future of Integration in Europe* (Armonk, N.Y., and London: M.E. Sharpe, 1993), pp. 73–91.
57. Martin Slater, "Political Elites, Popular Indifference and Community Building," *Journal of Common Market Studies* 21 (September/December 1982): 76.
58. Material in this section regarding the composition of the 1989–1994 EP draws upon Juliet Lodge, "1989: Edging towards 'Genuine' Euro-elections?" in Lodge, ed., *The 1989 Election of the European Parliament* (New York: St. Martin's, 1990), pp. 210–235; and Juliet Lodge, "EC Policymaking: Institutional Dynamics," in Lodge, ed., *The European Community and the Challenge of the Future* (New York: St. Martin's, 1993), pp. 23–25. For events leading up to the June 1994 election, see *The Economist,* issues of May and June 1994; and *Financial Times,* issues of May and June 1994. Percentages and seats overall and by country are found in

The Economist, June 18, 1994, pp. 56–57; and *Financial Time*s, June 14, 1994, pp. 7–11.

59. Martin Westlake, *Britain's Emerging Euro-Elite? The British in the Directly-Elected European Parliament, 1979–1992* (Aldershot, U.K.: Dartmouth, 1994), p. x.
60. See the report in *Financial Times,* December 5, 1994, p. 2.
61. Ibid., September 7, 1994, p. 2; November 23, 1994, p. 3.
62. Ibid., November 9, 1994.
63. Ibid., September 1, 1994, p. 1.
64. *The Economist,* November 26, 1994, p. 56. Juppé became the new French prime minister in May 1995.
65. Ibid., December 3, 1994, p. 62.
66. *Financial Times,* November 5, 1994, p. 2.
67. Ibid., November 7, 1994, p. 2.
68. Ibid., January 10, 1995, p. 2.
69. *The Economist,* December 10, 1994, p. 48.
70. *Financial Times,* November 30, 1994, p. 2.
71. *The Economist,* December 17, 1994, pp. 51–52.
72. Ibid., November 19, 1994, pp. 65–66.
73. *Financial Times,* November 30, 1994.
74. *The Economist,* December 10, 1994, p. 57.
75. *Financial Times,* January 11, 1995, p. 1.
76. *The Economist,* December 24, 1994, p. 76.
77. Ibid.
78. Ibid.

chapter 7

The Snake, the EMS, and the EMU

With this chapter, we turn our attention to various policies of the EU as the member countries attempt to deepen economic integration among themselves. After an overview of the regional and systemic developments that gave rise to coordination of exchange rate policy between the EC countries, we analyze the "snake-in-the-tunnel" and the failure of the members to achieve a zone of monetary stability in Europe. We then examine the EMS and the EMU, finally discussing the impact of the Maastricht treaty on EMU and assessing the conditions set by this document on achieving such union.

After the creation of the CU and until the adoption of the EMS in 1978, the members of the EC experienced serious economic difficulties that threatened the future of economic integration. Whereas many scholars argue that this was a period of disintegration, we believe that this conclusion is misplaced (see chapter 4). If disintegration was the order of this period, then how can one account for the creation of the EMS that highlighted a process of trial and learning in exchange rate policy? Moreover, the Regional Fund came into effect in 1975. As we will explain in chapter 9, this fund is crucial for the development of the underprivileged regions of the EC. Finally, the Community expanded to nine countries after Britain, Denmark, and Ireland became members in 1973.

The economic difficulties experienced by the EC resulted from important changes in the international economic order. The collapse of the Bretton Woods monetary system was the first serious shock to the EC that put to test these countries' seriousness in achieving economic integration. During the 1960s, there were important developments that weakened this monetary system. The weakening of the U.S. dollar strained the stability of European currencies: the West German government revalued the DM in 1961 and 1969, and the French government devalued the franc in 1969. These measures attempted to stabilize the U.S.

dollar in international markets. However, these attempts failed to eliminate exchange rate instability in the system and persuaded the EC leaders that alternative policy options had to be considered for the Community. The policy recommendation came at the Hague Summit of 1969, where the EC heads of state and governments accepted Willy Brandt's call for an economic and monetary union (EMU). Subsequently, the Werner Plan of 1970[1] laid down the basic idea for this monetary union, but, unfortunately, its introduction coincided with the collapse of Bretton Woods and the rise of the "everyone-for-himself" period of the floating exchange rates.

According to Miltiades Chacholiades, "two or more countries form an *economic union* when they form a common market and, in addition, proceed to unify their fiscal, monetary, and socioeconomic policies. An economic union is the most complete form of economic integration."[2] A common market, by itself, involves establishment of a customs union between two or more countries and free movement of all factors of production among the member states. The United States represents the most successful economic and monetary union.

Europeans' interest in EMU stemmed from their fear that continued revaluation of their national currencies vis-à-vis the dollar would threaten the stability of exchange rates, and thus intra-EC trade, that had existed in the Community since 1957. The CU and the maintenance of the CAP required that stability, therefore, unstable exchange rates threatened the survival of the Community.

TRIAL AND ERROR IN EXCHANGE RATE POLICIES: THE ROAD TO EMS, 1971–1979

When the Bretton Woods system collapsed, the United States wanted the revaluation of the DM and the Japanese yen against the dollar. This would have had the same effect on the U.S. trade deficit as an approximately 10 percent devaluation of the dollar, the difference being that its impact would have been on those economies that contributed the most to the American trade deficit. The subsequent Smithsonian Agreement of 1971, where the industrialized democracies' leaders attempted to coordinate their monetary policies, failed to bring stability to this situation. More crucial from the European point of view, this agreement and the subsequent reaction of the EC members to the collapse of Bretton Woods demonstrated how uncoordinated the European response was to the apparent crisis.

In accord with the Smithsonian Agreement, the U.S. government devalued the dollar by 10 percent. Furthermore, the agreement permitted widening of fluctuations between key currencies from ±2 percent to ±4.5 percent. That is, the agreement implied a 9 percent range of fluctuations between each two EC currencies. Although this arrangement looked like a viable compromise for maintaining some degree of exchange rate stability between EC currencies and the U.S. dollar, the increased range of the intra-EC bilateral fluctuation was too large for the functioning of the CU. Intra-EC trade faced immense obstacles from unstable prices caused by exchange rate fluctuation. The EC responded to this pressure by establishing the snake-in-the-tunnel and reduced the excursion allowed by the Smithsonian Agreement by half. The limit for fluctuations between EU currencies was to be only 4.5 percent. Before accession to EC membership, Britain, Ireland, and Denmark agreed to join the snake. The par value of each EC currency vis-à-vis the dollar represented the center of the tunnel. According to the agreed upon formulation, a variation of ±2.25 percent on either side of the dollar exchange rate determined the walls of the tunnel. Effectively, this arrangement established a joint float (snake) of the EC currencies that stayed within the walls of the tunnel formed by the maximum fluctuations around the dollar.

Despite initial enthusiasm about the snake, this arrangement lasted for only a short period, from April 1972 to March 1973. In June 1972, the British pound left the snake and began to free-float. Ireland and Denmark followed soon after, though Denmark later rejoined the snake. In February 1973, the Italian government took the lira out of the tunnel. Finally, in March 1973, the EC central banks ended their support of the margins vis-à-vis the dollar, and the snake left the tunnel to free-float. To make matters worse, the United States devalued the dollar by another 10 percent in 1973. The subsequent "floating snake" of the EU lasted until 1979 but only included West Germany and four members (Belgium, the Netherlands, Luxembourg, and Denmark), which maintained their currencies close to the DM.

Problems faced by the Europeans worsened as the U.S. administration continued to pressure America's trade partners to undertake enormous economic responsibilities. For example, President Carter's "Locomotive Theory" called for West Germany and Japan to assume major responsibilities in reviving the world economy.[3] According to this theory, countries with balance of payments surpluses (Japan and West Germany) were to follow expansionary policies that would serve as engines of growth for the rest of the world. German Chancellor Helmut Schmidt, who was already at odds with the American president over Western defense policy, opposed this theory and began to search for alternative policies for West Germany and its EC partners. Schmidt worried about the implications of U.S. policies for the future of economic stability in Europe. First, the worsening of America's balance of payment deficit could cause the value of the dollar to fall against the DM, allowing more funds to flow to the DM zone, which would result in the overvaluation of the latter, thus putting pressure on West Germany's exports. Second, the depreciation of the dollar resulted in the DM becoming a de facto international reserve currency as investors looked for alternative reserves to the dollar. The result would then be increased upward pressures on German interest rates, probably beyond the limits set by the Bundesbank. Furthermore, as the United States continued to experience large balance of payments deficits, the dollar crisis of 1978 emerged: the dollar fell by 10 percent between October 1977 and February 1978 and by another 10 percent by Fall 1978.[4] These were background conditions that influenced the decision to create a European monetary system.

Another dimension of this monetary problem was that the traditional Keynesian macroeconomic policies did not seem to work following the 1973 oil crisis. The countries with the worst inflation, France and Italy, also experienced the highest unemployment rates. In addition, they also had the poorest economic growth rates. According to Stephen George, "the tradeoff between inflation and growth did not appear to be working, and accelerating inflation threatened economic collapse."[5] Under these circumstances, it became clear to the EC leaders that they had to protect EC currencies against fluctuations in the value of the U.S. dollar. Furthermore, there was a general dissatisfaction with the floating exchange rates among EC officials because exchange rates had been highly volatile during the mid-1970s as a result of overspeculations in the currency markets. In addition, the European leaders believed that fixed rates had a beneficial effect upon intra-EC trade.[6]

The answer to these problems seemed to lie in the formulation of a new exchange rate system for the EC currencies. However, the EC leaders had to make sure the mistakes of the snake-in-the-tunnel would not be repeated. They had learned that the previous system failed because of the asymmetry of the exchange rate mechanism and the failure of the exchange market intervention rules to provide the necessary credibility to the margins allowed for currency fluctuations.[7] Under the snake, the central banks agreed to provide each other unlimited financing for intervention in currency markets. This new facility was the Very Short-Term Financing Facility administered by the European Monetary Cooperation Fund. Furthermore, the claims and liabilities between the central banks had to be settled within a period of a month. Not only was this period very short, but there were insufficient funds available under the Very Short-Term Financing Facility for intervention by several central banks. As a result, the system did not operate efficiently, and it contributed to the breakup of the snake.[8]

The system that emerged was a compromise around a Belgian proposal that combined the German plan with the French, Italian, and British alternative. The West Germans wanted to continue the arrangement of bilateral parities found under the snake, where each currency would be tied to every other currency in the system. Furthermore, to ease the pressure on currencies, the Germans called for wider margins than the old ±2.25 percent of the snake for exchange rate fluctuations and argued that the central banks should intervene to restore the agreed upon parities. In the alternative parity grid plan, the French, the British, and the Italians asked that instead of bilateral parities, all currency values be determined in relation to an alternative basket currency system based on the weighted averages of all EC currencies known as the European Currency Unit (ECU). They argued that the German proposal was an unfair system because it provided an unnecessary burden upon countries with the weaker currencies. Finally, a compromise was reached around a Belgian proposal which combined the two systems and was a substantial improvement over the old snake system. It included four main components: (1) a basket currency, the ECU; (2) the ERM; (3) credit provisions among the participating central banks; and (4) the pooling of reserve assets among the members.[9]

The ECU is the renamed and restructured European Unit of Account (EUA, introduced in 1975). It is a basket currency that serves four functions: (1) the denominator for the ERM; (2) the basis for a divergence indicator; (3) the denominator for operations in both the intervention and credit mechanism; and (4) a reserve instrument and a means of settlement between monetary authorities in the Community.[10] Basket currencies, like the ECU and the IMF's Special Drawing Rights (SDR), are stable reserve currencies that counteract exchange rate volatility.

The ERM called for participating countries to maintain their exchange rates within bilateral limits of ±2.25 percent. More precisely, the upper par of the band was 2.275 percent above the central parity, while the lower par of the band was 2.225 percent of the central parity. Italy negotiated a wider margin of ±6 percent because of its weak national currency. As Michael Artis and Mark Taylor explain, "According to these provisions, when a currency triggered its divergence indicator threshold (calculated as the ECU value of a 75 percent departure of its bilateral rates against all the other countries), a presumption was created that the country concerned should take corrective action."[11]

To enable member countries to meet this obligation, the EC created a large credit fund, known as the European Monetary Cooperation Fund, and the member states contributed 20 percent of their gold and dollar holdings to this fund in exchange for ECUs. The facilities involved in the intervention mechanisms were the Very Short-Term Financing Facility, the Short-Term Monetary Support, and the Medium-Term Financing Assistance. The latter two indicated significant improvements over the system that existed under the snake.

The EMS seemed to work rather well throughout the 1980s, and it looked as though the EC finally managed to create a zone of monetary stability. During these years, the EC currencies became less variable against one another as well as against the U.S. dollar and the Japanese yen (see Table 7.1). At the same time, the ERM countries experienced a steady decline in inflation.[12] Thus, the European leaders believed that they found the answer to the currency problems of the EC in the new EMS. With this apparent success, they again moved to consider monetary union among the EC states.

THE EMU AGAIN

The concept of economic and monetary union is not new. The Werner Plan of 1970 had promoted it. Furthermore, while the SEA did not call for an EMU, it did recall in one of its preambles that in 1972 the European Council "approved the objective of progressively creating an EMU."[13] With the relative success of the EMS in bringing about a zone of monetary stability in Europe during the mid-1980s, the EC moved to reexamine the feasibility of an EMU at the Hanover Summit in 1988. At this meeting, the European Council agreed to set up a committee of central bankers and technical experts under the leadership of the European Commission president, Jacques Delors, to prepare a report by the June

TABLE 7.1 Bilateral nominal exchange rates against ERM currencies, 1974–1990 (variability is the weight sum of standard deviations of monthly percent changes)

Currency	Before EMS, 1974–1978	Recession, 1979–1983	SEA period, 1984–1986	After SEA, 1987–1990	Average after EMS, 1979–1990
Belgium, Luxembourg franc	1.2	1.3	0.6	0.4	0.9
Danish crown	1.4	1.0	0.5	0.5	0.8
German DM	1.5	1.0	0.5	0.5	0.8
Greek drachma	1.8	2.3	2.5	0.7	2.1
Portuguese escudo	3.0	2.1	0.8	1.1	1.8
French franc	1.9	1.1	0.7	0.5	0.7
Irish punt	2.0	0.7	1.2	0.5	1.0
Italian lira	2.2	1.0	0.9	0.6	0.8
Dutch guildeer	1.0	0.8	0.6	0.3	0.5
Spanish peseta	2.8	2.0	1.1	0.5	1.7
UK pound	2.2	2.6	2.4	1.9	2.4
EC mean	1.7	0.7	0.5	0.4	0.4
US dollar	2.2	2.5	2.9	2.7	2.7
Japanese yen	2.3	2.7	2.0	1.9	2.5

SOURCE: Data obtained from the IMF, *International Financial Statistics* (Washington, DC: IMF, quarterly publications).

1989 Madrid Summit on the steps to be taken to achieve EMU. The resulting report, known as the Delors Plan, proposed a three-stage plan to build the EMU:[14]

Stage 1

Economic: Completion of the internal market (Project 1992), strengthened competition policy, full implementation of the reform of the Structural Funds, enhanced coordination and surveillance of economic policies, and budgetary adjustments in high debt, high deficit countries.

Monetary: Capital market liberalization, enhanced monetary and exchange rate policy coordination, realignments possible but infrequent, all EC currencies in the narrow bands of the ERM, and extended use of the ECU.

Stage 2

Economic: Evaluation and adaptation of Stage 1 policies, and review of national macroeconomic adjustments.

Monetary: Establishment of the ESCB, called a *Eurofed* in the report, and a possible narrowing of the EMS exchange rate bands.

Stage 3

Economic: Definitive budgetary coordination among the member states, and a possible strengthening of the structural and regional policies.

Monetary: ESCB or a similar institution in charge of monetary policy, and irrevocably fixed exchange rates that would pave the way to replace national currencies with a single currency, the ECU, administered by the European Monetary Cooperation Fund.

The Delors Plan was much more explicit about the EMU, its institutions, and the necessary deadlines than any previous plan on the subject. Stage 1 was to commence in July 1990 and was linked to the completion of the Single Market. Stage 2 was to start on January 1, 1994, and Stage 3 would be completed by the end of the century. As John Pinder explains:

> The Community's money would be managed by a European System of Central Banks with a policy-making Council comprising the central bank governors and the members of the ESCB Board that would be responsible for overseeing the execution of the Council's policy. The Council would, like the Bundesbank, be independent from instructions of governments. It would be committed to the overall objective of price stability but, subject to that priority, bound to support the EC's general economic policy. Operations to implement the Council's policy would be undertaken by the central banks of the member states; and the Council would have to account for its activities to the European Council and the European Parliament.[15]

The European Council accepted the plan at the Madrid Summit in June 1989, but the decision was not unanimous. A major objection to the plan came from the British government. Prime Minister Margaret Thatcher made it very clear that she was not pleased with the plan's objective and methods even though she accepted the general goal of establishing a single market (Stage 1). At the following Milan Summit, Thatcher outlined the conditions for putting the pound sterling into the ERM: the British inflation rate must be on a falling trend toward convergence with the other member states' rates; there must be tangible progress toward the achievement of the Single Market; and other members must have dismantled their controls on the movement of capital.[16] Following this move, the British government announced that it would propose its alternative to the Delors Plan. The British plan, which the new chancellor of the exchequer John Major revealed to other members in November 1989, called for a parallel currency to the national currencies. The parallel currency would be used for trade, bank deposits, and issue of Eurobonds (which was already in substantial use). Against this background, the European Council decided at its Strasbourg Summit in December 1989 to set up an IGC to consider the EMU in Rome in December 1990. The only objection came from Margaret Thatcher, who argued that the EMU would undermine British monetary sovereignty.

The idea of a parallel currency received little support from the other member countries. Furthermore, the Delors Plan discussed and rejected it on the grounds that it might be inflationary. Also, the British government ignored a basic economic fact that economies strongly prefer to use one currency for almost all transactions. For example, in Israel, most Latin American countries, and the east-central European states, people did not abandon national currencies and use dollars until inflation got out of hand; that is, parallel use of national currency and dollars did not occur until hyperinflation seriously hurt the pocketbooks of the people.

The final agreement on EMU came during the Maastricht Summit in December 1991. The resulting Maastricht treaty, based on a revised Treaty of Rome, establishes a European union (the EU) consisting of the old union (EC), EMU, and two additions: (1) a common foreign and security policy (FSP), and (2) cooperation between the 12 governments in justice and police matters (JHA, see chapter 5). However, the Maastricht treaty includes several deadlines that raise serious concerns about the implementation of EMU:

1. A European Monetary Institute (EMI) is to be set up in 1994 to co-ordinate monetary policies, oversee preparations for the transfer to the ECU and create the right conditions for the final stage. Frankfurt was chosen to be the site for the EMI in 1993. National governments will still retain monetary sovereignty, but their central banks must be independent by the end of this stage. The institute will become the European Central Bank shortly before the final stage of EMU begins.
2. This will be in 1997 if the European Council decides, by qualified majority vote, that a majority of EU members meet five criteria: inflation within 1.5 percent and interest rates within 2 percent of the three best performing states; a budget deficit of less than 60 percent of GDP; and no devaluation within the exchange-rate mechanism for the past two years. Otherwise EMU will start in 1999 with as many members as can make the grade.[17]

As a concession to the UK, the other members agreed to allow her the right to opt out of EMU. Moreover, any member that stays outside the currency union will not be allowed to vote on EU monetary policy. Those inside the EMU will lock their exchange rates irrevocably and later replace their respective national currencies with the ECU. The ECB will determine interest rates in accordance with its commitment to price stability. In determining interest rates, the ECB is also required to support the EU's economic policies and objectives such as sustainable economic growth, social welfare, and high employment.

The ECB will have a policy-making council composed of national central bank governors and an executive board. This council will be an independent body similar to that of the U.S. Federal Reserve Board. The president of the ECB Council will report to the EU finance ministers and the EP. The meeting of the ECB Council president and the Council of Finance Ministers is referred to as

ECOFIN. ECOFIN's functions include determining ECU exchange rates in consultation with the ECB and issuing broad guidelines for the EU's economic policy. Moreover, ECOFIN will have the authority to recommend changes to any member states' economic policies if these policies are considered to be inconsistent with the broad goals of EMU. Although the general framework of the treaty on EMU envisions a more complete economic integration for the members of the EU, not everyone is in agreement about the path and methods of the plan. Nevertheless, in accordance with the Maastricht provisions, the EMI located in Frankfurt, became operational in January 1994.

Interests and Motives For and Against European Monetary Union

The acceptance of the EMU as part of the Maastricht treaty by the EC member states owes much to French persistence at the time. The French wanted to have a greater say in monetary policy making than they had under the EMS. This was a calculated move to weaken the Bundesbank's dominant position over monetary policy and to strengthen the EC institutions as a constraint upon German power.[18] However, the Germans did not oppose EMU either. On the contrary, the German government has been one of the greatest supporters of this idea. So why were the French so eager to push for EMU at the IGC? One explanation could be that Mitterrand wanted to lock the Germans into the Union before German unification could give them any idea of opting out of Europe. More generally, as Wayne Sandholtz explains, "many leaders, including key Germans, desired to bind Germany irrevocably to the EU, and monetary union was a crucial means of doing so. In short, foreign policy ideas seem to provide the best explanation for German support for EMU."[19] Sandholtz also provides other political reasons for the enthusiasm for EMU.

The first is the spillover effect from the Single Market. The success of the EC in achieving the necessary requirements of Project 1992 persuaded the Commission that there was a functional linkage between the Single Market and EMU. The Single Market was a major step toward a complete economic union where greater economic benefits could be realized.[20] The other explanation relates to the idea of an independent monetary authority, the Eurofed, or ECB. This independent institution would provide credibility to monetary policy, guarantee member states low inflation, and assure price stability. As Sandholtz states, "National politicians could not cause inflation for political purposes [and] EMU would tie the hands even of future governments. For governments that found it difficult domestically to achieve monetary discipline, EMU offered the chance to have it implemented from without."[21]

The EMU plan also received considerable support from the business sector. Corporate leaders created an Association for the Monetary Union of Europe in 1992. The president of this institution was the president of Philips Corporation and its vice-president was the chairman of Fiat of Italy. The main factor for this private sector support was the fact that big business in Europe had become thoroughly transnationalized. Therefore, complete economic integration with full monetary union promised increased benefits to big business. Even under the Single Market, the multiplicity of currencies imposes transaction costs and information costs. The transaction costs are estimated to be around 15 billion ECUs.

There are other benefits of EMU. It would provide macroeconomic stability by sound, coordinated fiscal policies, price stability, and disappearance of noncooperative exchange rate policies.[22] In terms of its external effects, EMU, with a common currency, would strengthen the Union's position in the international economic system. It would provide an alternative hard currency to the U.S. dollar—especially in the portfolio market with increases in ECU-denominated assets. Moreover, as the Union's international power increases, it would be able to alter the present balance of power in the international monetary system against the dollar and the yen. Today, the EU is more likely to absorb rather than set international monetary conditions. Though it is doubtful that the dollar would lose much of its dominance, the EMU could give the EU more influence in the international monetary system.[23]

Critics of EMU, led by the British government, argue that the costs of monetary union outweigh its potential benefits. One influential critic, Nobel Prize–winning economist Martin Feldstein, argues that the creation of a single market does not require a single currency and that a single currency would result in the unnecessary loss of monetary autonomy.[24]

It is quite correct that sometimes the effects of exchange rates on trade are exaggerated. Yet, events in Europe, especially since the collapse of the ERM in September 1992, suggest that companies and states have sustained considerable costs from volatile exchange rates. This is particularly the case of intra-EU, trade-dependent economies. Since all the EU states trade with each other more than they do with non-EU countries, exchange rate stability is an important issue for them.

With regard to the loss of monetary autonomy, the critics are quite correct. EMU specifically calls for greater monetary union (loss of monetary policy autonomy for the individual states) with exchange rate stability in a highly integrated financial market. The fear is that the weaker economies would lose out when they are tied so closely to the German economy because they would end up following the strict monetary policies of the Bundesbank. Ironically, the Germans, particularly the former president of the Bundesbank Helmut Schlesinger, worried that Germany would import inflation from its partners. Finally, Margaret Thatcher seemed least willing, among the member state leaders, to share monetary sovereignty with the EU. However, in the present information age, with the internationalization of the financial and money markets and the technological revolution in telecommunications, economic agents are increasingly holding diverse currency portfolios. Even when countries control their money supply, as the UK tried in the 1980s, they are not able to control the long-run domestic inflation rate because only international monetary policies could ensure meaningful control of inflation over the long run.[25] Monetary sovereignty, to some extent, is at the mercy of international currency markets and the concept only applies to short-term policies of governments. Thus, monetary autonomy of member states in the EU is already limited.

Another attack on EMU centers around the use of exchange rate policy to respond to inflation rate differentials.[26] Monetary union would eliminate this policy option for the individual countries. Ordinarily, high inflation countries could devalue their national currencies to adjust to such problems. However, this would be irrelevant under EMU because with a single currency there will be a single inflation rate and, therefore, no inflation rate differential between the member countries. In connection, the EMU is also questioned on the ground that it might lead to stagnation in weaker economies with high inflation, such as Greece, Italy, Portugal, and Spain.[27] Whether this is indeed a valid argument depends on productivity, wage rates, and labor mobility.

Although the supporters and critics of EMU argued over the feasibility of such a union in the EU, they were stunned by the collapse of the ERM in September 1992. As speculators continued to test the willingness of the British government to defend the parity of the pound in the ERM, the pound sterling dropped out of its target zone on Black Wednesday, September 16, 1992, and began to free-float. Speculators then began to test one EC currency after another. In the end, the Italian lira also dropped out of the ERM, the other weak currencies (the escudo, peseta, and punt) faced major devaluations, and finally in August 1993, the EC finance ministers revised the target zone of the ERM to ±15 percent. The causes and effects of the ERM crisis raise serious concerns over the future of EMU.

What Went Wrong in the Exchange Rate Mechanism?

During the ERM crisis of September 1992, early explanations of its causes focused too much on German interest rates. However, with 20/20 hindsight, we now realize that there were various factors behind the currency crisis. As David Cameron points out, many factors contributed to the ERM crisis of September 1992: (1) The EMS became a quasi-fixed system that failed to carry out a currency realignment needed since 1987; that is, although the mechanism was supposed to adjust in response to changing pressures from the international currency markets, the EC failed to bring about the necessary realignment of the ERM currencies with the mechanism behaving as if it were a fixed system. (2) The rapid expansion of the currency markets caused instability. (3) The economic and monetary policies of the German government and the Bundesbank were at fault, as they tried to fight inflationary pressures in Germany caused by unification. (4) Political uncertainties resulted from the Danish rejection of the Maastricht treaty and the possible similar outcome in the French referendum of September 1992.[28]

Two additional factors also contributed to the ERM crisis. The first such factor was the British government's failure to control public spending at a time of economic recession in Britain, which increasingly exposed the pound to speculative attacks. The second factor was the role of the U.S. dollar in international markets. As shown in Table 7.2, during 1991–1992, the dollar fell and continued to fall. The Federal Reserve cut interest rates no fewer than eight times after 1990 to stimulate the U.S. economy. In response to these cuts, the dollar lost value against other major currencies. By September 1992, the dollar was 48 percent lower than its peak in February 1985 and 8 percent lower than in September 1991. In the early 1980s, the dollar reached as high as 3.47 DMs. In September 1992, it was 1.39 DMs—a total decline of 60 percent. The net result for the United States was increased competitiveness of American products in international markets. This weakness of the dollar placed the ERM under great pressure as investors and currency speculators switched from dollars to DMs. At the same time, investors and speculators were abandoning the pound sterling in favor of DMs. In view of these developments, we can ascertain whether the EMS was a success in creating a zone of monetary stability.

To appraise the actual performance and soundness of any international monetary system, economists use three tests: adjustment, liquidity, and confidence. Adjustment mechanisms involve monetary costs. Liquidity means the availability of an adequate supply of reserves to make the financing of adjustments possible. And confidence means absence of panicky shifts by the monetary authorities from one reserve asset to another. Another element of confidence is the reputation of the monetary system among economic agents.

The founders of the EMS thought that they eliminated the inherent problems of the snake (insufficient availability of funds for intervention, weak adjustment mechanism, and lack of confidence) from lessons learned during the 1970s. The

TABLE 7.2   Exchange-rate fluctuations against the U.S. dollar

Date	DM	Franc	Guilder	Lira	Pound
9-15-89	1.99	6.69	2.24	1,424	0.65
9-15-90	1.59	5.33	1.79	1,186	0.54
12-22-90	1.49	5.09	1.68	1,123	0.52
3-16-91	1.57	5.35	1.77	1,175	0.54
6-22-91	1.81	6.16	2.04	1,349	0.62
9-14-91	1.69	5.76	1.91	1,268	0.58
12-21-91	1.58	5.39	1.78	1,191	0.55
3-14-92	1.67	5.68	1.88	1,253	0.58
6-20-92	1.57	5.28	1.77	1,186	0.54
9-12-92	1.39	4.74	1.57	1,063	0.50
12-26-92	1.57	5.35	1.76	1,405	0.64
3-13-93	1.67	5.66	1.87	1,609	0.70
6-19-93	1.64	5.51	1.84	1,489	0.66
9-11-93	1.61	5.67	1.81	1,567	0.65
12-25-93	1.70	5.83	1.91	1,685	0.67

SOURCE: "Economic and Financial Indicators" *The Economist* (selected issues).

economic agents in the financial markets of the late 1980s and early 1990s, on the other hand, discovered that they had the power to crack the system by speculative attacks. At the end, one of the ERM's most important elements, the credibility of the central banks to honor exchange rate commitments, suffered serious damage. As a result, there is very little confidence in the system even though the monetary authorities have announced their willingness to defend any future exchange rate parities.

A great deal of fault lies with the monetary authorities in the EC during the late 1980s and early 1990s. As speculative pressures on the ERM gradually increased, officials refused to acknowledge the seriousness of the problem and to realign ERM currencies. One could say that the ERM had become too rigid as the member state governments treated the ERM like a fixed exchange rate system. According to *The Economist,* a revaluation of the DM against other ERM currencies was necessary following German unification to offset the inflationary pressures of the German budget deficits. Yet, the French dismissed this idea, and the Bundesbank was left with no option but to push German interest rates upward.[29] In a similar fashion, the British and French officials publicly asked for a lowering of German interest rates during the spring and summer of 1992, when they knew quite well that the idea was not acceptable to the Germans. They could have instead privately asked for revaluation of the DM against all other ERM currencies, which may have been more acceptable to the Germans.

The failure of EC monetary officials to recognize the urgency of currency realignments was further underscored in a special report of the *Financial Times.* In its review of the events and actions of finance ministers during 2 weeks prior to Black Wednesday, the *Financial Times* experts found that when pressures on currencies mounted and the finance ministers met in Bath on September 4 and 5, the leaders failed to address the issue of currency realignments, largely for political reasons.[30] According to the Dutch prime minister, Ruud Lubbers, "'realignment was not possible because England had its pride and France said that it couldn't be done because it was facing a difficult referendum and they couldn't discuss it; and the English said then that the Bundesbank should do something first, and so the discussion went.'"[31] Basically, the French finance minister, Michel Sapin, and his British counterpart, Chancellor Norman Lamont, succeeded in keeping realignment off the agenda. Lamont repeatedly pressured Schlesinger to cut German interest rates, which Schlesinger, as "'mere *primus inter pares* on the Bundesbank's decision-making council,'"[32] could not do on his own even if he wanted to. At the end of the meeting, the ministers decided to defend ERM rates, and the Germans only agreed not to further increase interest rates.[33]

In the days following the Bath meeting, the ERM continued to suffer under speculative attacks that led to its collapse. On September 12, 1992, the Italian government devalued the lira by 7 percent; on September 16, the pound sterling left the ERM followed by the lira on the next day; on November 22, 1992, the Portuguese escudo and Spanish peseta were devalued 6 percent each; on January 30, 1993 the Irish punt was devalued 10 percent; and on May 13, 1993, the escudo and peseta faced devaluation once again, by 6.5 percent and 8 percent respectively. Finally, the French franc, which had been shored up in September 1992, came under speculative attacks in July 1993. Economic recession, high unemployment, and interest rates that remained high to maintain the DM-franc ERM parity, convinced the speculators to test France's ability to match the Bundesbank's tight monetary policy.[34] Similar attacks on the Danish krone, the Belgian franc, the Portuguese escudo, and the Spanish peseta followed. The central banks tried to intervene to stabilize the ERM parities but their efforts failed, and on July 30, 1993, the EC Monetary Committee called an emergency meeting of the finance ministers and central bank governors. At this meeting, following the Bundesbank's decision not to cut its discount rate, EC finance ministers and central bank governors agreed to widen the fluctuation bands between ERM currencies to ±15 percent of their rates, effective August 2, 1993.[35] The only exception to this rule was a voluntary agreement between Germany and the Netherlands to retain the previous ±2.25 percent between the DM and guilder.

In conclusion, we can say that many factors led to the ERM crisis: Germany's problems in absorbing the East German economy prevented the Bundesbank from lowering its interest rates to help its EC partners; overvalued DMs put immense pressure on other currencies to maintain their par values vis-à-vis the DM within the ERM bands; the budget deficit continued in the UK; speculations arose about the future of the Maastricht Treaty; and the decline of the U.S. dollar had a destabilizing effect in currency markets. But what does all this mean for the overall soundness of the ERM and the future of EMU?

The Costs of Exchange Rate Instability

There is no doubt that the collapse of the ERM inflicted political and credibility damage on the EU. However, there have been some very serious economic costs as well. It is estimated that the Bank of England and other central banks spent 15-20 billion pounds sterling to defend the British currency during the days leading to Black Wednesday.[36] When the lira came under attack, the Bundesbank spent 90 billion DMs in support of currencies against their ERM margins, and this was on top of some 200 billion DMs that were previously expended on currency support.[37] The bulk of these sums went into the hands of the speculators.

The move to more flexible rates also did not ease economic recession in the EU. In fact, the 1992-1993 recession in Europe was the deepest since the recession of 1974-1975. Several factors contributed to this problem. During the 15 months following September 1992, the EC currencies fell against the U.S. dollar: DM, 22 percent; franc, 23 percent; guilder, 21 percent; lira, 58 percent; and the pound, 34 percent. However, this did not translate into increased overall exports by Germany because the DM also rose sharply against other EU currencies. Because intra-EC trade far outweighs extra-EC trade for the Community members, it is the ERM shifts that have greater consequence for export competitiveness. Unpublished figures from the Organization for Economic Cooperation and Development (OECD) showed that the volume of exports of manufactured goods from Germany fell by 11 percent during the first half of 1993, compared to a 1.9 percent increase during the same period a year before.[38] The French exports also showed a similar trend to Germany's. During the same period in 1993, "exports from France declined by 11.3 percent. By contrast, exports of Italy increased by 19 percent and the British trade deficit declined to 7.6 billion pounds from 13.4 billion pounds in the previous year particularly in trade with non-EU countries."[39] By this time, the pound and the lira were both outside the ERM. Exports of EC countries, except Germany and France, showed marked improvement because of improved exchange-rates vis-à-vis the dollar, DM, and franc, but the EC-wide economic recession worsened nevertheless.

The answer lies in the economic problems of Germany and to a lesser extent France. Benefits of devalued British, Spanish, and other EC currencies have been canceled by the negative economic impact of currency appreciation (with regard to EC currencies) in Germany. In addition, the costs of German unification contributed to roughly a 1.5 percent contraction of the German economy. Since an average 20 percent of total non-German exports in the EU are destined to Germany's market, this economic contraction has contributed to the overall export problems of other member states.

What Does the Future Hold for the EMU?

Despite these economic difficulties, the EU leaders seem determined to push ahead with EMU, though hardly anyone believes that they will keep to their time schedule. Politically, the EMU timetable looks highly unlikely, yet in economic terms, developments since Black Wednesday suggest that it might make economic sense. In addition, the EU countries seem determined to push ahead with the time schedule. In accordance with a provision in the Maastricht treaty, Article 109g, the composition of the ECU basket was frozen on November 1, 1993.[40] According to this decision, the ECU basket remains as defined on September 21, 1989, which is the last time it was adjusted.

Another important development is that since August 1993, the Belgian franc, the French franc, and the Danish krone have returned to their precrisis ±2.25 percent of their central rates against the DM.[41] Although this does not mean that the old narrow bands are officially back, market forces started working in this direction once the bands were widened. This development suggests that other noneconomic factors were also behind the speculative attack of 1992–1993, which was a test of the political will and credibility of monetary authorities. Nevertheless, one should not expect the EU central banks to quickly call for a return to narrow bands. The main reason for this is that the speculators will again test the central banks' willingness to defend the bands. Given the nature of economic recession in the EU, the central banks would not be able to sustain currency values.

Therefore, the future of EMU will depend on the delicate interplay between economic and political forces. Since all EU countries trade more with each other than they do with the rest of the world, exchange rate stability is extremely important to them. Creation of a zone of monetary stability in the EU has always been on the agenda of Community leaders, but this issue is more relevant today than ever before. The question, then, is how can they create this zone of monetary stability if the markets have destroyed the ERM?

The EMU in Europe cannot proceed unless a sufficient number of the EU member countries are ready to participate in it. The term *economic convergence* is used to cover two distinct, but not totally independent processes. The first process, more precisely referred to as *nominal convergence,* is concerned with the gradual convergence of the member countries in those areas that directly influence the transition to and the success of a monetary union. The Maastricht treaty, which covers actual (consumer price index) and expected inflation (long-term interest rates), budget deficits, the ratio of public debt to GDP, and exchange rate stability, relates to this process. The second process, known as *real convergence,* refers to the long-term process of convergence in living standards, usually approximated by the level of Gross Domestic Product (GDP) per head at purchasing power parities of the different regions of EU.[42]

As we explained before, the Maastricht treaty sets out five criteria relating to nominal convergence for transition to the third stage. In our previous discussion of the currency problems and developments since Black Wednesday, we showed that the markets have brought back a convergence of exchange rates in the ERM. Therefore, one could argue that this requirement of the Maastricht treaty seems, at least for now, to have been achieved. The question of convergence, then, relates to the other requirements. In the next section, we will review the progress that has been made by the EU toward meeting the other criteria (see Table 7.3).

Economic Convergence: Inflation, Budget Deficit, Current Account, and Unemployment

Consumer price inflation differentials have narrowed considerably among the ERM member countries during the early 1990s. Table 7.3 shows that the Netherlands, Belgium, and more recently France, Ireland, Luxembourg, and Denmark, achieved an inflation convergence with the German inflation rate. Among the other member states, the UK, Spain, Portugal, and Italy show movement toward convergence. The only exception is Greece. Therefore, unless major distortion occurs in the near future, the EU members seem to be moving toward satisfying one of the conditions set for EMU by the Maastricht treaty.

Convergence in the Maastricht treaty, however, is not limited to monetary convergence. It also applies to fiscal policies and, in particular, to budget deficit. As the figures in Table 7.3 show, in 1993, only four countries (Denmark, France, Ireland, and Luxembourg) had budget deficits that were about 3 percent or less of their respective GDP. As explained previously, this is a major requirement for convergence in the Maastricht treaty. The deterioration has been quite severe in the UK, where the deficit in 1993 increased by over 2 percentage points to 8.3 percent of GDP. In Germany, the budget deficit in 1993 increased to 3.9

TABLE 7.3 Main economic nominal convergence indicators

Country	Inflation (private consumption deflator)				Budget deficit (percent of GDP)				Current Account Balance (percent of GDP)				Unemployment (percent of civilian labor force)			
	1990	1991	1992	1993	1990	1991	1992	1993	1990	1991	1992	1993	1990	1991	1992	1993
Belgium	3.1	2.9	2.4	2.8	-5.7	-6.6	-6.9	-6.2	0.9	1.7	1.8	1.8	7.6	7.5	8.2	9.3
Denmark	2.1	2.4	2.1	1.6	-1.4	-2	-2.3	-2.7	0.5	1.3	3	3	8.1	8.9	9.5	9.5
Germany	2.7	3.9	3.9	3.6	-2	-3.6	-3.5	-3.9	3.5	1.2	0.9	-0.1	4.8	4.2	4.5	6
Greece	19.7	18.4	16	13.5	-18.6	-15.2	-13.4	-9.8	-6.1	-5.1	-3.3	-3	7.2	7.7	7.7	8.5
Spain	6.4	6.3	6	5.5	-4	-4.9	-4.6	-4.2	-3.7	-3.5	-3.7	-3.4	16.1	16.3	18	19.5
France	3.2	3.2	2.6	2.7	-1.4	-1.9	-2.8	-3.2	-0.8	-0.5	0.1	0.2	9	9.5	10.1	10.8
Ireland	1.7	3.2	2.9	2.2	-2.5	-2.1	-2.7	-3	1.3	6	6.7	6.6	14.5	16.2	17.8	19.2
Italy	5.9	6.8	5.3	5.8	-10.9	-10.2	-10.5	-10.2	-1.4	-1.9	-2.4	-2.4	9.9	10.2	10.2	10.6
Luxembourg	3.6	2.9	3.4	4.7	5	-0.8	-0.4	-1	34.2	27.9	19.9	18.7	1.7	1.6	1.9	2
Netherlands	2.3	3.3	3.1	2.7	-4.9	-2.5	-3.5	-3.5	4	3.9	3.6	3.6	7.5	7	6.7	7.6
Portugal	12.6	11.9	9.1	6.8	-5.5	-6.4	-5.6	-4.8	-2.5	-3.5	-2.1	-4.2	4.6	4.1	4.8	5.4
UK	5.3	7.2	5.1	5.1	-1.3	-2.8	-6.2	-8.3	-4.2	-1.8	-2.7	-3.5	7	9.1	10.8	12.3
EC/EU	4.5	5.3	4.5	4.4	-3.8	-4.4	-5.3	-5.7	-0.3	-0.5	-0.6	-0.9	7.5	8.1	8.7	9.7

SOURCE: *Eurostat* (selected issues, Luxembourg: Official Publications of the European Communities).

percent from 3.5 percent. The average German budget deficit as a percentage of GDP has been about 3.2 percent for the last 20 years. In summary, with only four members meeting the Maastricht treaty requirement on budget deficit, it is doubtful that convergence can be met among the rest of the EU countries in a timely fashion to proceed with EMU.

With regard to current accounts, Belgium, Denmark, France, Ireland, Luxembourg, and the Netherlands had surpluses in 1993. Germany, on the other hand, in 1993 had its first current account deficit in the last 20 years. With the exceptions of Luxembourg and the Netherlands, the current account surpluses of the European countries represented an overall improvement of their economies. Conversely, the UK, Spain, Italy, Greece, and Portugal continued to display significant current account deficits. However, it is important to note that both Greece and Spain show some improvement in their account deficits in 1993, compared to previous years. All in all, the picture for convergence in current account balance does not support the requirements of the Maastricht treaty. If the members insist on meeting the treaty deadlines, substantial improvements are needed in the areas of current account and budget deficits. The central bank governors support our observations. For example, Hans Tietmeyer, the Bundesbank president, warned that budget deficits stood at twice the necessary level for achieving EMU.[43]

Even though the Maastricht treaty does not require the EU countries to meet any specific criteria with respect to unemployment rates (achieving some degree of convergence in this area), the member governments are particularly concerned about it for their own political and economic futures. The figures show that both Spain and Ireland have unemployment rates well above 15 percent of their respective work forces. Similarly, France, Italy, and the UK have high unemployment rates (above 10 percent). The overall unemployment rate in the EU was about 10.5 percent in 1993, and it seems to be increasing. Currently, some 17 million people are unemployed in the Union and the number is expected to reach 20 million soon.[44] This figure compares quite unfavorably with that of the United States, which has an unemployment figure of about 5.5 percent. Such unemployment implies that economic gains made by the EC during the last 5 years of the 1980s, vanished in the first 3 years of the 1990s.[45]

CONCLUSION

In view of these observations, there are three options that the EU leaders could consider for the future of EMU. The first option is to continue with the present flexible ERM, somewhere around the ±10 percent band. The second option is to create a single currency as quickly as possible. And the last choice is to create some combination of the first two, in a way similar to the British parallel currency idea. The Maastricht timetable favors option two, but economic problems create obstacles. Option one is similarly ruled out by the Maastricht schedule. Option three, however, could be worked out. Those countries with the stronger economies could move towards monetary union and at the same time maintain a flexible ERM vis-à-vis the weaker economies until appropriate conditions are met for expanding the EMU. Already, France and Germany announced on November 2, 1993, that they have reached an agreement on the broad guidelines of plans to bring their economies together in the planned EMU by the end of 1999, though one should take this announcement with great caution.[46] The third option is a more incrementalist approach to EMU and would require revision of the Maastricht schedule. In any case, according to the central bank governors, the timetable for monetary union is simply too tight.[47] In addition, the idea is not without its historical merit: The ERM of the EMS also developed in an incrementalist fashion.

Finally, it became apparent on December 5, 1994, that the EU intended to push forward with EMU in one form or another. At the meeting of the EU finance ministers in Brussels, the officials made a cautious endorsement for the present wide bands of the ERM and signaled that there existed a remote possibility for achieving a single European currency in 1997. This decision received a significant boost on January 8, 1995, when Austria entered the ERM based on the ±15 margins.[48]

ENDNOTES

1. For a detailed discussion of the Werner Plan see John Pinder, *European Community: The Building of a Union* (Oxford: Oxford University Press, 1991), pp. 119-121.
2. Miltiades Chacholiades, *International Economics* (New York: McGraw-Hill, 1989), p. 225.
3. Stephen George, *Politics and Policy in the European Community* (London: Oxford University Press, 1991), p. 174; Pinder, *European Community*, pp. 119-24.
4. Pinder, *European Community*, p. 176.
5. George, *Politics and Policy in the European Community*, p. 176.
6. Dennis Swann, *The Economics of the Common Market* (London: Penguin Books, 1992), pp. 202-203.
7. Neil Thygesen, "The Emerging European Monetary System: A View From Germany," in R. Triffen, ed., *EMS: The Emerging European Monetary System* (Offprint from the Bulletin of the National Bank of Belgium, LIV, I, 1979).
8. Francesco Giavazzi and Alberto Giovannini, *Limiting Exchange Rate Flexibility: The European Monetary System* (Cambridge: MIT Press, 1989), p. 26.
9. For a detailed description of the EMS, see Michele Fratianni and Jürgen von Hagen, *The European Monetary System and European Monetary Union* (Boulder: Westview, 1992); Giavazzi and Giovannini, *Limiting Exchange Rate Flexibility*.
10. David M. Wood, Birol A. Yeşilada, and Beth Robedeau, "Windows of Opportunity When EC Agendas are Set and Why?" (Paper presented at the Third Biennial International Conference of the European Community Studies Association in Washington, D.C., May 27-29, 1993), p. 11. Following three realignments of exchange rates inside the ERM in November 1992, the new ECU central rates (in units of national currencies per ECU) were as follows: Belgian franc, 40.6304; Danish crown, 7.51410; DM, 1.96992; peseta, 143.386; French franc, 6.60683; Irish punt, 0.735334; Luxembourg

franc, 40.6304; Dutch guilder, 2.21958; escudo, 182.194; Italian lira, 1,690.76; sterling, 0.805748; and drachma, 254.254. These central rates establish a parity grid of bilateral exchange rates between the national currencies. See *Financial Times,* November 23, 1992, p. 2.

11. Michael J. Artis and Mark Taylor, "Exchange Rates, Interest Rates, Capital Controls and the European Monetary System: Assessing the Track Record," in Francesco Giavazzi, Stefano Micossi, and Marcus Miller, eds., *The European Monetary System* (Cambridge: Cambridge University Press, 1988), p. 187.

12. For a detailed analysis see Birol A. Yeşilada and David M. Wood, "Learning to Cope With Global Turbulence: The Role of EMS in European Integration" (Paper presented at the Annual Meeting of the Midwest Political Science Association, Chicago, Illinois, April 18-20, 1991).

13. Dennis Swann, *The Economics of the Common Market* (London: Penguin Books, 1992), p. 216.

14. The Delors Report as cited in the EC Commission, *Report on Economic and Monetary Union in the European Community* (Luxembourg: Office for Official Publications of the European Communities, 1988).

15. John Pinder, *European Community* (London: Oxford University Press, 1991), p. 137.

16. According to Stephen George, Sir Geoffrey Howe, the then foreign secretary, said that the Madrid conditions were only adopted by the prime minister after both he and the then chancellor of the exchequer, Nigel Lawson, threatened to resign unless they were adopted. See Stephen George, *Politics and Policy in the European Community,* 2nd ed. (London: Oxford University Press, 1991), p. 183.

17. "Maastricht at a Glance," *The Economist,* October 17, 1992, pp. 60-61.

18. Pinder, *European Community,* p. 139.

19. Wayne Sandholtz, "Choosing Union: Monetary Politics and Maastricht," *International Organization,* 47 (Winter 1993): 32-33.

20. Ibid., p. 20.

21. Ibid., p. 38.

22. EC, *European Economy: One Market, One Money,* No. 44 (October 1990), p. 50.

23. Pinder, *European Community,* p. 140.

24. Martin Feldstein, "The Case Against EMU," *The Economist,* June 13, 1992, pp. 19-22.

25. George Zis, "European Monetary Union: The Case for Complete Monetary Integration," in Frank McDonald and Stephen Dearden, eds., *European Economic Integration* (London and New York: Longman, 1992), p. 45.

26. Ibid., p. 45.

27. Ibid. See also Feldstein, "Europe's Monetary Union."

28. David Cameron, "British Exit, German Voice, French Loyalty: Defection, Domination, and Cooperation in the 1992-1993 ERM Crisis" (Paper presented at the Third International Conference of the European Studies Association, in Washington, D.C., May 27-29, 1993), p. 5.

29. "Shooting the Messengers," *The Economist,* August 7, 1993, p. 23.

30. "The monetary tragedy of errors that led to currency chaos," *Financial Times,* December 11, 1993, p. 2.

31. Ibid.

32. Ibid.

33. *The Sunday Times* London, September 6, 1992, sec. 3, p. 8.

34. *Eurecom,* 5.5 (September 1993): 1.

35. *Financial Times,* August 3, 1993.

36. Samuel Brittan, "Black Wednesday's Cost," *Financial Times,* November 30, 1992.
37. Ibid.
38. "Fluctuations in the Balance," *Financial Times,* December 15, 1993, p. 13.
39. Ibid.
40. *Eurecom* 5.10 (November 1993): 3.
41. "Nothing Like the Old Days," *The Economist,* December 25, 1993–January 7, 1994, p. 101.
42. European Commission, *Annual Report of European Community* (Brussels: 1993), p. 9.
43. "Tietmeyer rails at Emu Criteria," *Financial Times,* November 23, 1994, p. 3.
44. "EU Urged to Catch up with the World," *Financial Times,* December 8, 1993, p. 2.
45. See *Annual report of European Commission* (1993), p. 27.
46. "France, Germany plan for EMU," *Financial Times,* November 3, 1993, p. 16.
47. "Monetary Union Timetable too Tight, Say Banks," *Financial Times,* September 20, 1994, p. 1, 20.
48. "EU States Welcome Austria into the ERM," *Financial Times,* Janaury 9, 1995, p. 1. The Austrian Schilling (Sch) has a central rate of Sch 7.0355 to the DM and Sch 13.7167 to the ECU.

chapter **8**

Common Agricultural Policy

$\mathbf{T}$his chapter provides an overview of developments in the agricultural policy area in light of the CAP's future structure, operations, position in the EU's budget, and importance to the Union's external trade policies. As we noted in chapter 4, CAP promoted and reflected increased economic interdependence of the six original members of the EEC: Belgium, France, Italy, Luxembourg, the Netherlands, and West Germany. For example, while France needed markets for its agricultural products, West Germany was in need of food imports. Inclusion of Italy in this picture provided the otherwise unavailable goods in Europe's northern markets. West Germany, on the other hand, needed markets for its manufactured exports. Therefore, in a unique way, CAP ensured the steady supply of a variety of agricultural products for the EEC citizens. It is also important to realize that although CAP is an agricultural price support system, it also promoted the restructuring of the West European farms to establish fewer, larger, and more efficient farms.[1]

THE EVOLUTION OF COMMON AGRICULTURAL POLICY

From the signing of the Rome treaty until CAP came into effect in 1968, the EEC reached agreements on three important objectives. First, it eliminated national agricultural support systems. Second, it replaced the national systems with a Community-wide agricultural support system. And third, agricultural protection between EEC countries was eliminated, allowing common agricultural prices to take effect.[2] The Council of Ministers, following the proposals of the Commission, set annual agricultural support prices.

The evolution of CAP was a difficult process. On the one hand, every year the Council of Ministers held a series of marathon meetings during which they accepted package deals on EEC regulations for different products. For example, in December 1961, a marathon meeting resulted in common policies for grains, pig meat, eggs, poultry meat, fruit and vegetables, and wine. Also, the Council agreed on general principles regarding the financing of these policies.[3] Other marathon sessions in December 1963 and December 1964 resulted in regulations on milk and dairy products, beef and veal, rice, fats, and grain.[4]

The success in achieving common policies for the above categories of agricultural products, however, was not followed by an agreement over the financing of the EEC budget. The Commission had expected France to be interested in financing the budget because of her strong agricultural production, which the CAP was designed to help finance, but France had other plans. In 1965, the Commission proposed to finance expenditures on CAP from the customs duties on industrial products entering the EEC countries and the variable levies on agricultural imports, which were to be effective as soon as the CU became operational. The Commission also argued that it should receive these receipts directly, rather than waiting for the national parliaments' approval of the budget every year. Furthermore, the budget should also be approved by the EP. With the exception of France, all other member states supported this proposal. As a result, de Gaulle withdrew France from participation in all EEC business until further notice and created what became known as the empty chair crisis (see chapter 3). Under the Luxembourg compromise, the EEC shelved the issue of parliamentary control of the EEC budget. When they reintroduced CAP in mid-1967, its main source of finance came from contributions by the member states. This arrangement continued until after de Gaulle resigned as president of France.

The CAP adopted by the EEC is a unique system known as the variable levy (*prélèvement*). The basic idea is quite simple. First, the Council of Ministers determines in advance the desired internal price of each agricultural product. This is the support price, known as the target price (*prix indicatif*). It also estimates expected domestic production and consumption of these products. Then, the EU imposes a variable levy on non-EU farm products equal to the difference between the lowest world market price and the target price (in the EEC/EU). When there is a change in the world market price, the variable levy is adjusted accordingly. In effect, the variable levy shifts the burden of adjustment to variations in the EU consumption and production onto third-country providers, which discourages the other countries from subsidizing their exports. Other support policies in CAP include export subsidies, supplementary and fixed rate aid, and structural aid to the farmers. Export subsidies make up the difference between intra-EU prices and world market prices and enable the European farmers to compete in international markets. By the early 1980s, export subsidies accounted for about half of all CAP spending. The supplementary aid and the fixed rate aid, on the other hand, only apply to a handful of commodities where support prices remain low (e.g., durum wheat, olive oil, tobacco, and oilseeds). In these cases, the farmers receive direct payments in proportion to their output.

Finally, structural aid refers to payments toward farm modernization and improvement of productivity.

It is important to note that the EEC introduced the CAP payment programs during the world of fixed exchange rates. Since the collapse of the fixed exchange rate system in 1972, CAP financing has faced difficult problems, which forced the implementation of the use of *green money,* a set of special exchange rates which the Commission uses to convert common farm prices into national currencies through the mechanism known as the Monetary Compensatory Account (MCA).

Following the adoption of CAP, the Commission introduced a memorandum entitled "Agriculture 1980," which became known as the Mansholt Plan, named after Commissioner Sicco Mansholt, in December 1968.[5] This plan called for restructuring agriculture by encouraging small farmers to leave the land and giving financial assistance for the amalgamation of holdings. The incentives included grants, pensions to farmers over the age of 55, and assistance to younger farmers in finding new careers. However, there was one point of this plan that created problems with the French and West German farmers: the proposal to cut price levels so that inefficient farmers would be forced to leave agriculture.[6] The only supporter of the plan was Britain, which was in the process of applying for a membership in the Community at the time. However, the British government was not eager to make reform of CAP a condition for the UK's entry into the EC. The result of the growing opposition to the plan in France and West Germany was 3 years of discussion in the Council of Ministers. When the final decision came in April 1972, the EC revised the Mansholt Plan: It only provided for a modest financing of loans to the farmers, early retirement incentives, and assistance for information and training to increase efficiency. The budget for price support did increase every year, but its component for "guidance" remained rather small.

The empty chair crisis also resulted in the decline of the Commission's powers. First, the member states created COREPER, consisting of the representatives (ambassadors) of the six countries, to evaluate Commission proposals and settle most controversial matters before they reached the Council of Ministers. Second, the Management Committee procedure restricted the powers of the Commission. These committees came into being under the CAP but soon expanded to other areas of common EU policies. Here, the civil servants who come from the member countries oversee and approve actions of the Commission in implementation of respective common policies. More generally, the empty chair crisis made the Commission more dependent on support of the governments to determine the extraordinary agenda of the EU.[7]

THE COMMON AGRICULTURAL POLICY IN THE 1980s AND 1990s

During the 1980s, additional reforms of the CAP occurred. In 1984, the member countries agreed on a system of quotas for dairy products, supports for which had been very costly to the EC budget. During this time, CAP accounted for about 64 percent of the EC budget. The reforms also included phasing out the MCA by 1988 and controlling future expenditure on agricultural subsidies and other support mechanisms.[8] The dairy sector reforms were followed by a more serious attack on other sectors. In 1985, the Council of Ministers agreed on a general price package which restricted agricultural price increases to a figure below the Union's inflation rate. For example, during 1984-1985, agricultural prices (in national currencies) increased by 1.8 percent, while the inflation in 1985 was 5.8 percent. The ratio was less dramatic in 1986: 2.2 percent and 2.5 percent respectively. Nonetheless, this marked the first major decrease, in real terms, in agricultural prices.

The reforms then moved into the beef sector when the EC decided to modify beef support arrangements in 1986. Previously, the EC's intervention price in this sector acted as the floor price. The reforms changed this practice by specifying when support buying would take place. Accordingly, the Union would engage in support buying when (1) the average market price in the EC was 90 percent of the intervention price, and (2) the price in the target country was 87 percent of the intervention price.[9] All in all, this meant a 17 percent decline in price. Yet, despite these measures, the cost of the CAP increased by an average of 18 percent per year from 1985 to 1987. One new problem area was cereals, which witnessed a substantial increase in production because of new technological advances, coupled with a decline in world market prices.

The problem proved to be a major cause for concern. In 1986, Jacques Delors announced that the EC was running out of funds and expected an estimated budgetary shortfall of 4-5 billion ECUs in 1987. The expansion of the EC to include agricultural countries like Portugal and Spain further complicated this problem. Thus, additional sources of funding seemed to be in order, which not all members agreed upon. The goverments of the Netherlands and the UK demanded strong limitations on agricultural overproduction. The latter went so far as to indicate that it would not agree to more funds until this issue was seriously addressed. Following intense debates, the European Council accepted a series of measures, the Delors package, to reform the CAP, according to the following guidelines:

1. Budgetary discipline, which was to be realized through an agreed own-resources ceiling of 1.2 percent of EC-12 Gross National Product (GNP) and an expenditure ceiling of 27.5 billion ECUs for the European Agricultural Guidance and Guarantee Fund (EAGGF).[10]
2. Increase in agricultural expenditure was to be equal to or less than 74 percent of the EC's GNP growth rate. The Commission was to introduce a new early warning system to monitor monthly expenditures against their monthly profiles. The profiles were an aggregate of 3 prior spending years.[11]
3. Stabilizers, coupled with set-aside measures, would be used in agricultural control. It was agreed that from 1988-1989 to 1991-1992, 160 million tons were to be the threshold for cereals. Any production

beyond this limit would result in price cuts of 3 percent and continue until production fell within the allowed limit.[12]

Since then, other policies have been introduced to reform the CAP. These included diversifying farmers into rural tourism, promoting rural craft industries, and expanding set-aside (land) policies. Furthermore, in 1991, the Commission approved a report by its agricultural commissioner, Ray MacSharry, recommending a radical reform of the CAP. The plan, known as the MacSharry II Proposals, called for a significant reduction in support for cereals and for establishing much of a two-tier EC farm policy that would favor small and medium-size farms.[13] Fiona Butler provides an overview of these reforms accepted by the European Council during its Lisbon Summit in June 1992:

1. *Level of price cuts:*
   MacSharry II had proposed reductions in price support for cereals of 35 percent; 10 percent for milk, 15 percent for butter and 5 percent for skimmed milk powder; and 15 percent for beef. The sizable cut in cereals support prices was seen as important not merely to reduce surplus production but to reduce the costs to farmers of producing other products, given that animal foodstuffs are a major variable cost in farming activity. The Brussels Agriculture Council eventually agreed to a 29 percent cut in cereals support prices. The original recommendation of 15 percent cut for beef production was accepted, but ministers would only agree to a 5 percent cut in support for butter production.

2. *Related compensation payments for loss of income*
   Although the MacSharry II proposals were accepted (that is 'professional' producers with annual outputs of more than 92 tons of cereals, in order to benefit from compensatory payments, would set aside 15 percent of their cultivated land), disquiet was none the less expressed over the fact that both efficient and inefficient farmers would be subject to this requirement. In this context British negotiating was perhaps more concerned with protecting rural constituencies by extending the benefits of compensation payments rather than risking a major confrontation over inefficient farming units being asked to set aside more than 15 percent of their land.[14]

EXTERNAL IMPACT OF THE COMMON AGRICULTURAL POLICY

While the above reforms have significantly changed the EU's agricultural policy, the CAP has had a negative effect on world market prices by subsidizing exports and contributing to instability in the market. The negative side of the CAP was considered one of the major hurdles in the Uruguay Round of trade talks from September 1986 to December 1993. However, it is unfair to single out the EU as the only guilty party. According to Loukas Tsoukalis, agricultural support levels were 35 percent of output in the United States, 46 percent in Canada, 75 percent in Japan, and 49 percent in the EU[15] (see Table 8.1).

According to these figures, the EFTA countries, including the newest members of the EU (Austria, Finland, and Sweden), and Japan provided more transfers to agriculture, on a per capita basis, than the EU in 1991. As a result, the new members of the EU face the serious task of reducing their farm subsidies. However, this pressure does not mean that disagreements over agricultural subsidies will end soon. The EU, the United States, and Japan will continue to accuse each other of cheating, despite the recent agreement on the Uruguay Round negotiations.

External trade policy of the EU is significantly affected by the CAP as demonstrated by developments in the Uruguay Round trade negotiations. The Uruguay Round trade talks began in September 1986 in Punta del Este, Uruguay, as by far the most complex and ambitious talks on free trade since the founding of GATT in 1947. This round was the first time that the members of GATT addressed trade rules for agriculture, textiles, services, intellectual property rights, and foreign investment. Whereas it is not the purpose of this chapter to discuss all aspects of the Uruguay negotiations, we will examine the specifics of the agricultural talks because disagreements in this area between the EU and the United States threatened to derail the entire effort to achieve a successful completion of this Round (see Table 8.2 for the chronology talks, with the crucial times when the EU or France objected to proposals over time underlined).

As Table 8.2 shows, the negotiators did not have an easy time getting the parties to sign a trade agreement, failure of which threatened the very existence

TABLE 8.1 Transfers to agriculture, 1991

Country	Total ($billion)	Taxpayers ($ per head)	Consumers ($ per head)	Total ($ per head)
Austria	4.1	143	381	524
EU	142	168	241	409
Finland	5.9	460	677	1,137
Sweden	3.6	100	316	416
Norway	4.2	493	494	987
Switzerland	6.4	236	689	925
US	81	200	118	318
Australia	1.2	41	29	70
Japan	63.2	16	494	510

SOURCE: The Economist, "Survey of the European Community" (July 11, 1992), p. 22. © 1995 The Economist Newspaper Group, Inc. Reprinted with permission. F urther reproduction prohibited.

of the GATT. The breakthrough came in the November 1992 Blair House agreement between the United States and EU negotiators, which established the following conditions:

1. Subsidized farm exports to be cut by 21 percent in volume over 6 years. Value to be cut by 36 percent, with internal supports trimmed by 20 percent.
2. The EU land for oilseeds production limited to 5.128 million hectares.
3. Oilseeds for industrial use limited to 1 million tons.
4. Ten percent of EU oilseeds land to be set aside permanently.
5. Compensation allowed to farmers for taking land out of production.
6. A 6-year "peace clause" agreed on outstanding disputes, preventing either the United States or the EU from taking unilateral action against each other on trade.
7. Extension to EU of the agreement to curb exports of subsidized beef to Asian countries.[16]

The French government reacted angrily to the agreement and stated that the deal did not fare well with the EU's reform of the CAP, which France supported. It then called for reopening the agreement for more negotiations. The French position created a division within the EU and prompted John Major to threaten a British blocking of French initiatives on Europe. After long arguments between the different parties, the United States decided to make the following concessions to secure French acceptance of the Uruguay Round accords:

1. Exempt the EU's existing 25 million ton cereal stockpile from the Blair House agreement.
2. Switch the base year from which subsidized exports must be reined in from the 1986–1989 average, to 1992. Since the EU's subsidized cereal exports rose from 17 million tons to over 20 million tons in 1992, the change significantly reduced the impact of the Blair House accord and, over the 6-year life of the implementation of the agreement, allows the EU (primarily France) to export an additional 8 million tons of cereal.
3. Extend from 6 to 8 years the peace clause under which the United States could not challenge the EU's export subsidy regime.[17]

In response to the above U.S. concessions, the Europeans agreed to improve market access for American pork, grains, dairy products, and specialty goods (nuts, vegetables, almonds, and processed turkey). These allowances, however, did not mean much because they were not expected to significantly increase the sale of American goods in the EU markets since the demand is not expected to increase significantly. Thus, the EU agreed to other concessions for the US: tariffs on steel, wood, pulp, and paper would be cut to zero; semiconductor equipment would also see tariff reduction to zero, but the semiconductors

TABLE 8.2 The Uruguay Round trade talks

1985

November: Geneva. GATT members agree to establish a preparatory committee to draw up an agenda for the new round, but arguments persist over inclusion of services and the priority to be given to Third World interests. Paris signals worries on farm export subsidies.

1986

July: Geneva. Preparatory committee ends with two draft agendas, one compiled by OECD countries and the other by developing countries. Switzerland and Colombia produce a compromise "café au lait" draft finally vetoed by France over farm trade.

August: Cairns, Australia. Fourteen food-exporting countries set up a group to represent their interests.

September: Punta del Este, Uruguay. Uruguay Round starts. The US bulldozes services, intellectual property, and foreign investment restrictions onto agenda despite objections from developing countries led by India and Brazil. EC reluctantly agrees to inclusion of agriculture as part of global package.

1987

January: Formal negotiations begin in 15 subject areas.

July: US tables audacious plan to scrap all farm subsidies within 10 years. EC reacts with incredulity.

1988

December: Montreal. Midterm review. Agricultural discord prevents agreements on intellectual property, safeguards (emergency import protection), and textiles. Ministers agree to a negotiating framework for services, lower trade barriers for tropical products, improved disputes settlement, country policy reviews, and a one-third target for overall tariff cuts. But Argentina insists these be put on ice until the farm trade row is settled.

1989

April: Geneva. The US backs down on farm subsidies, with final agreement referring only to "substantial progressive reductions" in trade-distorting farm supports.

1990

January: Geneva. The US blocks majority preference for formula approach to tariff-cutting across the board, which would have forced bigger reductions in high tariffs such as the US textile duties. Negotiations obliged to bargain line by line, country by country.

July: Houston. Leaders of the seven largest industrialized countries pledged to complete the round by the end of the year. This pledge was later repeated in 1991 (London), 1992 (Munich), and 1993 (Tokyo), thus damaging the G-7's credibility.

December: Brussels. Ministerial meeting. Trade ministers of 107 countries fail to conclude the Uruguay Round. Discussions again founder over agriculture. Argentina and other Latin American countries walk out.

1991

May: Washington. Congress grants President Bush a 2-year extension of "fast-track" negotiating authority.

December: Arthur Dunkel, GATT director-general, attempts to force negotiators' hands by compiling a complete draft package of accords–the "draft final act." France denounces the agricultural text before it is published, and the EC later demands "substantial improvement" to the Dunkel draft.

1992

May: Brussels. EC members agree to plans for radical reform of the CAP, virtually to eliminate export subsidies and cut support prices.

158

November: Washington. <u>The US and the EC agree</u> to terms for reducing EC exports of subsidized farm goods. The Blair House accord paves the way for resumption of the negotiations but is <u>bitterly opposed by France</u>.

1993

January: Washington. President Clinton takes office.

June: Washington. The US Congress grants new fast-track negotiating authority requiring President Clinton to notify by December 15 his intention to sign a Uruguay Round accord and submission of the final deal to Congress by April 16, 1994.

July: Geneva. Peter Sutherland, former EC competition commissioner, takes over from Dunkel.

July: Tokyo. The G-7 countries agree on a detailed tariff-cutting package which, though the interpretation is later disputed, acts as a platform for country-by-country bargaining in the final months.

December: Geneva. Countries formally agree to submit the final Uruguay Round package to their governments for approval. The US negotiating authority expires.

SOURCE: *Financial Times*, December 16, 1993, p. 5.

themselves would retain protection, averaging 3 percent, and the tariff on nonferrous metals would also be reduced.[18]

These debates, coupled with protectionist and counterprotectionist threats, and the resulting concessions on both sides stimulated a series of more demands from the EU ranks. Other EU members proceeded to demand more concessions from the United States and the EU for certain sectors. Portugal asked for greater market access for its textiles in the United States and a promise from the EU to help restructure the Portuguese textile industry. Greece objected to U.S. protectionism in ocean shipping. France and Spain requested a tougher stance against the so-called Super 301 provision of the 1988 Omnibus Trade and Competitiveness Act of the United States. Furthermore, France asked for a guarantee that its farmers would not have to set aside any more land if the output forecasts of the reformed CAP push the exportable agricultural surplus beyond GATT limits on subsidized food exports. The main purpose of the reforms was to cut EU prices to world market levels so that it would be forced to export without subsidy. According to David Gardner, the French position meant that:

> Farmers would get direct compensation for the cuts which would cost the EU 2 billion ECUs for every 10 ECUs by which the world price target had been missed. A joint Franco-German text spelled all but the cost of this out, and in addition, offered German farmers guarantees their incomes would not be affected by any further revaluation of the D-mark, as well as letting East German farmers off part of the penalty for exceeding by 10 percent the area they are allowed to plant.[19]

At the end of all this debate, France succeeded in attaining the concessions it wanted from both the United States and the EU. The signing of the Uruguay Round, however, does not mean that EU-US trade relations are without future problems. The challenge for the European and American officials is how to resolve future disagreements without further straining EU-US relations.

THE COMMON AGRICULTURAL
POLICY AND THE FUTURE

It is conceivable that the recent reforms of the CAP under the MacSharry II proposals could result in an outcome similar to what the European leaders envisioned in 1968, namely, the development of a smaller and more productive agricultural sector where the EU could better sustain incomes and levels of production, thus eliminating a major budgetary burden. However, with the Single Market becoming more and more a reality and with new countries joining the Union, more frequent revisits to the CAP reforms will become necessary. Farming incomes, surplus production, lower food prices, and budgetary issues will continue to dominate the agenda of the CAP. Harmonization of agricultural policies of the EU-12 has been difficult enough. With the entry of the four EFTA countries into the Union, each one of these issues will require closer scrutiny. Furthermore, as the EU tackles its internal problems of agricultural production, reforms in this area will carry important implications for the Union's external trade policy (see chapter 10). Agriculture continues to represent an important policy area for the EU, as can be seen in Figures 8.1-8.3.

These charts clearly show agriculture's importance for Greece, Ireland, the Netherlands, Portugal, and Spain. In terms of exports, the list of countries also

FIGURE 8.1 Agricultural production as percent of gross domestic product (GDP), 1990

SOURCE: *Financial Times,* June 8, 1994, p. 2.

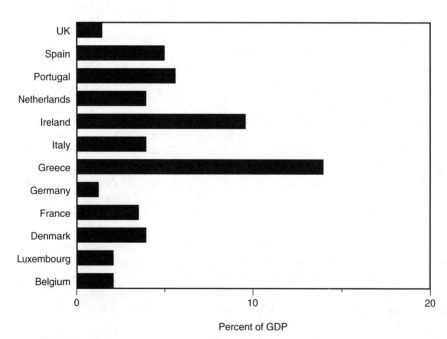

Percent of GDP

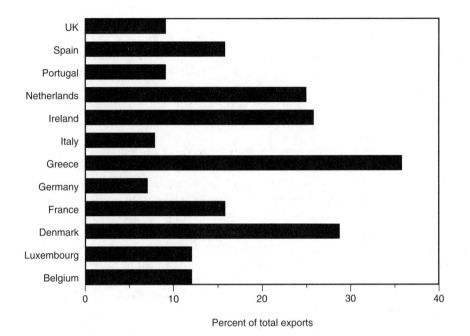

Percent of total exports

FIGURE 8.2 Agricultural exports as percent of total exports, 1992

SOURCE: *Financial Times,* June 8, 1994, p. 2.

FIGURE 8.3 Farm workers as percent of total work force

SOURCE: *Financial Times,* June 8, 1994, p. 2.

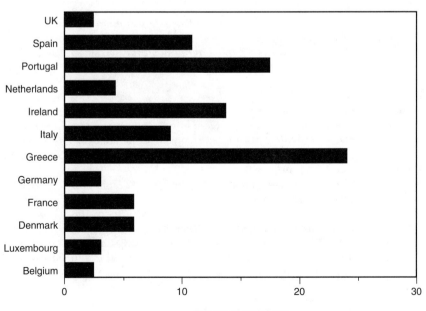

Percent of work force

includes Denmark and France. The addition of Austria, Finland, and Sweden to EU ranks further increases the significance of agriculture in EU policy agenda. As we noted earlier, the Single Market reforms called for elimination of MCA by the end of 1992. The reforms introduced in 1992, in the form of direct payments to farmers as compensation for cuts in price supports, made the subsidies more transparent. In 1994, CAP accounted for half of the EU budget, with a 36.5 billion ECU price tag. The additional reforms to end subsidies will enter into effect by the end of 1996.

Reforming CAP, however, will continue beyond the measures expressed in Project 1992. Recently, Sir Leon Brittan, the EU trade comissioner, called for a new debate on the future of CAP based on four academic reports from Britain, France, Germany, and Italy,[20] which examined CAP in light of the EU's decision to expand its membership to include east-central European countries in the first quarter of the next century.[21] The reports indicate that adopting CAP in its present form would seriously hurt consumers in east-central European countries while the farmers would benefit. Higher farm prices also mean increased output in these countries and, therefore, more surplus for the EU. In turn, these developments would undermine EU's commitment to abide by GATT agreements on agricultural subsidies. Moreover, the long-term cost of this expansion to CAP will be around 23–27 billion ECUs, or a 70 percent rise in the current farm subsidies. We return to this subject in chapter 10 when we discuss the expansion issue.

ENDNOTES

1. Stephen George, *Politics and Policy in the European Community,* 2nd ed. (Oxford: Oxford University Press, 1991), pp. 134–135.
2. Dennis Swann, *The Economics of the Common Market* (London: Penguin Books, 1991), p. 229.
3. Ibid.
4. Ibid.
5. Commission of the European Communities, "Memorandum on the Reform of Agriculture in the European Economic Community," *Bulletin of the European Communities: Supplement 1/69 Z* (Brussels: European Communities, 1969).
6. John Pinder, *European Community: The Building of a Union* (London: Oxford University Press, 1991), pp. 84–85.
7. Ibid., pp. 12–13; The Economist Newspaper Limited, *The EEC in Transition* (Cambridge: Cambridge University Press, 1983), pp. 2–3.
8. George, *Politics and Policy in the European Community,* p. 148.
9. Swann, *The Economics of the Common Market,* p. 247.
10. Fiona Butler, "The EC's Common Agricultural Policy (CAP)," in Juliet Lodge, ed., *The European Community and the Challenge of the Future,* 2nd ed. (New York: St. Martin's, 1993), p. 116.
11. Ibid.
12. Swann, *The Economics of the Common Market,* p. 248.

13. John Gibbons, "The Common Agricultural Policy," in Frank McDonald and Stephen Dearden, eds., *European Economic Integration* (London: Longman, 1992), p. 139.
14. Butler, "The EC's Common Agricultural Policy," pp. 121–122.
15. Loukas Tsoukalis, *The New European Economy* (Oxford: Oxford University Press, 1991), p. 260.
16. *Financial Times,* September 20, 1993, p. 3.
17. *Financial Times,* December 6, 1993, p. 3.
18. Ibid.
19. David Gardner, "EU issues a pledge it hopes never to redeem," *Financial Times,* December 13, 1993, p. 3.
20. "Brittan Seeks CAP Debate After Critical Reports," *Financial Times,* January 16, 1995, pp. 1–2.
21. The reports are by Allan Buckwell of Wye College, University of London, UK; Stefan Tangermann, University of Göttinger, Germany; Secondo Tarditi, University of Siena, Italy; and Louis Mahe, University of Rennes, France.

chapter 9

Regional, Social, and Industrial Policies

In this chapter, we turn our attention to other important internal policies of the EU that have significant implications for the future of integration. The social and regional policies relate closely to EMU. Since 1989, the EC took upon itself the duty of coordinating regional policy, and the Maastricht treaty addresses the social, regional, and industrial policies as interdependent policy concerns presupposing EMU. Regional policy should no longer be viewed as separate from the EU's social and industrial policies because in economic terms EMU will change the status of member countries within the former EU to that of regions within the Union. The relative effect of EMU on these regions will depend on their labor costs, competitiveness in trade, and investment flows. When exchange rates are no longer available for states to manipulate, wage level adjustments in the labor market become crucial in determining an economy's competitiveness. This, in turn, is highly dependent on what happens to the social policy of the Union. Finally, we evaluate the environmental policy of the EU as a policy package that carries important implications for the future of economic integration in the Union.

THE REGIONAL POLICY

One major accomplishment of the EU members during the difficult times of the 1970s was the establishment of the European Regional Development Fund (ERDF) in 1975. This fund originally provided compensation to the UK for the budgetary loss it suffered from participating in the CAP.[1] However, from the day the EEC was established, the Commission worked hard to develop a system by which it could tackle the challenges of the regional problems in the Community.

The Action Program of 1962, the Memorandum of Regional Problems in 1965,[2] and the Memorandum on Regional Policy in 1969 addressed the problem in detail. These proposals recommended the coordination of national policies and Community policies to overcome regional imbalances and the creation of the ERDF. Of the original members, only Italy, which had its own regional development problem, viewed these proposals favorably. The other two larger members of the EEC, France and West Germany, did not want to provide more funds for the EC budget or surrender more national regional policies to the Commission. The French were particularly disturbed by the sovereignty issue and the Germans were feeling the pressures of making large contributions to the CAP.[3] Nevertheless, the UK application for membership in the EU changed the views of these countries about the ERDF. A commitment to an attractive regional policy became linked with British entry into the Community. Two different factors explain the change in the French and German positions.

First, it was clear that the UK's membership would provide additional export markets for German exports. If the British stayed out of the Community, then Germany would have likely faced greater competition from the United States in the UK market. Second, the French also favored British membership, but for political reasons. According to Stephen George, "President Pompidou had made British entry one of the bases of his *rapprochement* with the center parties, and he had staked his personal prestige on the exercise."[4] Furthermore, Pompidou and the British prime minister, Edward Heath, had a working relationship. Thus, the shift in the French and German position on regional policy became clear at the Paris Summit of the European Council in 1972. At this meeting, the EC leaders announced that a high priority should be given to correcting regional imbalances in the EC, which could otherwise hinder the future development of EMU. Therefore, they agreed to establish the ERDF by the end of 1973.

However, several developments prevented the realization of this deadline. First, the oil crisis of 1973 pushed regional funding to a lower priority on the Community agenda. The British government did not want the EC to interfere in any way in future production and distribution of North Sea oil. The Germans, on the other hand, wanted to link this issue with the regional development fund. When the British refused to link the two issues, the Germans changed their position on the regional fund and pulled out of the negotiations.[5] Second, the new Labour government in the UK, which was divided on EC membership, refused to accept "offset payments towards CAP with receipts from the ERDF."[6] And third, the arrival to power of Helmut Schmidt and Valéry Giscard d'Estaing marked the beginning of the Franco-German alliance that would dominate the EU for the rest of the 1970s. The Franco-German alliance would oppose the British position on the ERDF as long as it required additional funds from these two countries. Yet, despite the gloomy picture, the Community leaders reached an agreement to set up the ERDF at the Paris Summit of December 1974. This development was a direct result of the Irish and Italian governments making it known that unless a compromise was reached on the ERDF, they would boycott the summit meeting.

The ERDF started with a small budget of 1,300 million EUAs, which was considerably lower than the Commission's proposal of 2,500 million EUAs (see Table 9.1 for a summary of ERDF appropriations from 1975 to 1988).

Since its establishment, the ERDF operated under four separate sets of rules: 1975–1979, 1980–1984, 1985–1988, and new rules that became effective after 1989 as result of the SEA. Initially, the allocation of funds was based on the quotas of the member states, subject to approval by the Council of Ministers. In 1979, the Council amended the structure of the ERDF to allow for a proportion of the fund to be disbursed on a strictly regional basis, separate from the national allocations. This was an important development because it allowed the consideration of region-specific problems without having to deal with national politics.[7] It is important to note that the net impact of the ERDF was greatly hampered by other EC policies, notably CAP. CAP was not based on regional needs. Rather, it provided assistance based on productivity and type of product, and did not take into account the regional distribution. Unlike ERDF, CAP, which had a much bigger budgetary allocation, allocated funds to regions less in need of them than others. Nevertheless, two significant developments in the 1980s resulted in a much improved ERDF. The first was the expansion of EC membership to include Greece (1981) and Portugal and Spain (1986). The second was the adoption of the SEA in 1986.

TABLE 9.1 European Regional Development Fund appropriations, 1975–1988 (millions of ECUs)

Year	Total	Annual Increase (%)	Share of EC Budget (%)
1975	257.6[1]	—	4.8
1976	394.3[1]	53.1	5.6
1977	378.5[1]	−4.0	4.9
1978	581.0	53.5	4.6
1979	945.0	62.7	6.1
1980	1,165.0	23.3	6.7
1981	1,540.0	32.2	7.3
1982	1,759.5	14.3	7.6
1983	2,010.0	14.2	7.6
1984	2,140.0	6.5	7.3
1985	2,289.9	7.0	7.5
1986	3,098.0	35.3	8.6
1987	3,311.0	6.9	9.1
1988	3,684.0	11.3	8.1

[1]These figures are converted from EUA to ECU at January 1978 rates.
SOURCE: *The Economics of the Common Market* by Dennis Swann (Penguin Books 1970, Sixth edition, 1988) Copyright © Dennis Swann, 1970, 1972, 1975, 1978, 1981, 1984, 1988. Reprinted with permission.

In addition, the three Mediterranean countries increased the pool of the countries with large underdeveloped regions: Greece, Ireland, southern Italy, Portugal, Spain, and the northern UK. Recent inclusion of East Germany also places pressures on the EU to seriously address regional issues.

The SEA and Project 1992 specifically targeted regional issues. The EC officials felt that redistribution of wealth from rich to poor areas was absolutely essential to achieve a harmonious economic integration. As a result, the member countries reached an agreement in 1988 to double the size of the structural funds before the completion of Project 1992. Moreover, they revised the mechanism for the distribution of funds by identifying the five main objectives of the Community and reforming the structural fund allocations to the member states. Each objective received its own respective fund.

Objective or region 1 funded the development of structurally backward regions, receiving funds through the ERDF, the European Social Fund (ESF), and the EAGGF. In this category, the allocation of funds to members, in billion ECUs, between 1989 and 1993 were as follows: Spain, 9.78; Italy, (southern provinces) 7.44; Portugal, 6.96; the UK (Northern Ireland), 0.88; Ireland, 3.67; and France (overseas departments), 0.88.[8] In these regions, per capita GNP in purchasing power standard was less than 75 percent of the EC average.

Objective or region 2 reconverted regions in industrial decline by funds received through the ERDF and ESF. The distribution of funds during 1989–1991 in billions of ECUs was as follows: Spain, 0.74; Italy, 0.26; the UK, 1.51; France, 0.70; Germany, 0.36; Belgium, 0.20; the Netherlands, 0.10; Denmark, 0.03; and Luxembourg, 0.02.[9] The UK was the obvious chief beneficiary under this program. However, since it is largely excluded from Objective 1, with the exception of Northern Ireland, the UK did not receive the larger amounts available through the structural funds.

Objectives or regions 3 and 4 received funding by the ESF and addressed the need to combat long-term unemployment and youth unemployment respectively. From 1990 to 1992 the allocations of funds for these purposes, in billions of ECUs, was as follows: Spain, 0.56; Italy, 0.59; the UK, 1.03; France, 0.87; Germany, 0.57; Belgium, 0.17; the Netherlands, 0.23; Denmark, 0.10; and Luxembourg, 0.01.[10] These objectives are not restricted by regions, but some newer priorities seem to show regional considerations.

Finally, Objective or region 5 has two parts: (a) the adjustment of agricultural structures (related to reform of CAP) and funded under the EAGGF, and (b) the development of rural areas funded by the ERDF, ESF, and the EAGGF. From 1989 to 1993, a sum of 2.64 billion ECUs reached member states under this objective. The distributions was as follows: Spain, 0.29; Italy, 0.39; the UK, 0.35; France, 0.96; Germany, 0.53; Belgium, 0.03; the Netherlands, 0.04; Denmark, 0.02; and Luxembourg, 0.03.[11]

Through these programs, the EU has been attempting to reduce regional differences and promote a more balanced growth under the SEA. In essence, the reforms elevated regional issues to the EU level and, therefore, require close coordination of efforts between Brussels and the national governments. Three mechanisms are necessary to accomplish coordination between the regional policies of the EU and member state governments: (1) competition policy regulations, (2) the new system of regional planning, and (3) Community initiatives and national operational programs.[12] There is no doubt that the future years will put more demands on the ERDF, especially since EU-wide economic recession is threatening to widen the gap between the regions. Harvey Armstrong proposes five urgent steps to jump start the ERDF to meet the challenges of the 1990s:

1. The ERDF must be greatly increased. Doubling the fund by 1993 will not be sufficient to allow the ERDF to begin reducing regional disparities. Without more the disparities may widen.
2. The extra finance should be partly at the expense of the agricultural price guarantee policy, itself still anti-regional.
3. The EU requires greater powers to try to force member states to use ERDF money in a truly "additional" manner.
4. The EU has been only partially successful in coordinating the ERDF and member states' regional policies. Simply relying on the new generation of programmes and on the CSFs [Community Support Framework] will not be sufficient to achieve the required extra coordination.
5. Improved evaluation of the effectiveness of ERDF operations is needed.[13]

These proposals are very important because under the EU, the ERDF should blend with the other social and industrial policies. The overriding concerns about regional policy can also be found in the Bundesbank president's suggestions for the Delors report on regional policy:

within the monetary union, balance-of-payments policy is replaced by regional policy, with the latter helping to finance inter-regional differences in current account imbalances through transfer payments. The differences in the level of economic development of individual member countries of the Community suggests that extremely large funds would be needed to finance fiscal compensation. Only through a very effective regional policy could these differences perhaps be reduced to an extent that would be compatible with the existence of monetary union.[14]

The Delors report argues that while monetary union might create greater shocks for the less developed regions and countries of the EU, the general impact of the union would be more positive in the long run, resulting in reduction of regional disparities.[15] Furthermore, the report states that a comprehensive regime change in ERDF is the key for convergence of differences between regions and between countries.[16] The 1989–1991 reforms of the ERDF attempted to address these issues. However, the three regional objectives 1, 2, and 5b (see preceding discussion) remain rather vague because they only list the main problems to be addressed without setting any clear targets.

THE SOCIAL POLICY

Social policy in the EU evolved over two phases. The first phase began with the Treaty of Paris and continued until the SEA. During this period, the Treaty of Paris included provision for the High Authority to address occupational safety in the coal and steel industries and to sponsor research that would achieve better safety standards in these areas. The EEC treaty also addressed the need to achieve economic and social cohesion in the Community. The second phase began with the SEA and continues through the present, during which social policy has received more attention on the EU agenda. As Stephen Dearden explains:

> Although a number of Directives were adopted in the 1970s on various aspects of employees' rights, it is the passage of the Single European Act which has given new impetus to the evolution of EU social policies. However, central to this development has been the debate as to whether action should extend beyond the immediate needs of the establishment of the internal market. Concern has been voiced that an unregulated internal labor market will undermine the competitive position of those member states who have relatively high wages and social security without a more comprehensive approach. These aspirations find expression in the Social Charter, and in attempts to develop a European dimension for industrial relations.[17]

During the first phase, there was general concern to improve "health and safety at work, to facilitate free movement of labor, to improve the equality of men and women in the work place, to harmonize social security provisions, and to promote a social dialogue between management and workers at the Community level."[18] Articles 117–122 of the Rome treaty addressed these needs, and Articles 3 and 123–128 focused on the ESF, which was essential to the retraining and resettlement of unemployed workers and maintenance of occupations while enterprises changed their activities because of economic difficulties. However, the role and functioning of the ESF underwent significant revision. The financing of the ESF changed from reliance on levies of member states to financing from the Community budget. In addition, two sets of broad objectives were identified: (1) to facilitate employment adjustment resulting from EU policies, and (2) to overcome structural problems experienced by regions or economic sectors.[19] These goals required reallocation of some 90 percent of the Fund's resources to vocational training. During the 1970s, as unemployment became a serious problem for the Community, the Fund's resources increased fourfold by 1980.

The Paris Summit of 1972 was crucial for the social image of the Community. At this meeting, the leaders called for a proposal from the Commission on social policy. The Commission produced a Social Action Program in 1973 that was accepted by the Council of Ministers in January 1974, for implementation from 1974 to 1976. The policy goals covered three areas: (1) attainment of full and better employment, (2) improvement and harmonization of living conditions, and (3) involvement of management and labor in the economic and social decisions of the EC, and of workers in the operations of their companies.[20] However, as a result of the economic recession of the time, little progress was made on these fronts until the mid-1980s when the SEA was adopted.[21]

The second phase of the social policy began with the French concept of the Social Area in 1981, which the Commission president Jaques Delors endorsed in 1985. The argument was for greater equality in Community-wide social standards because in an increasingly competitive environment, caused by the creation of the Single Market, countries with lower standards of social protection would undercut other members.

The SEA made revisions to the section of the Rome treaty concerned with social policy. Article 118A requires member countries to encourage improvements in health and safety of workers by continuing the harmonization of policies. A second amendment, Article 118B, emphasized the need to promote a social dialogue at the Community level. Furthermore, the SEA also placed important proposals that have significant social policy implications (e.g., measures relating to free movement of labor and professionals) on the EC agenda. What eventually came out of these various efforts on social policy was the Social Charter of the EC. The Social Charter is the document of wide-ranging social commitments prepared by the Commission. The document, known as the *Proposal for a Community Charter of Fundamental Social Rights,* did not receive unanimous support of the EC members at the Strasbourg Summit of the European Council in December 1989. The strongest opposition came from the UK and was sustained at Maastricht in 1991. As a result of British opposition, the other 11 members signed a separate Social Protocol as a move to renew their commitment to EC-wide social policy.[22] The Social Charter specifies the following commitments:

1. *The right to freedom of movement.* This right enables EC citizens to establish themselves and to exercise any occupation in any of the member countries on the same terms as those applied to the nationals of the host country.
2. *The right to employment and remuneration.* This principle recognizes that any citizen of the EC has the right to employment and to fair remuneration of that employment. It aims at the establishment of a decent basic wage, receipt of a fair wage and the guarantee of an equitable reference wage for workers who are not in full-time employment of indefinite duration, and the maintenance of adequate means of subsistence in the event of attachment of wages.
3. *The right to improved living and working conditions.* This is directed against the threat of social dumping as discussed above.

4. *The right to social protection.* For example through minimum wage and social security.
5. *The right to freedom of association and collective bargaining.*
6. *The right to vocational training.* This right implies the organization of training leave that would enable EC citizens to be retrained or to obtain additional skills by taking advantage of the facilities for continuing and permanent training which the public officials, companies, and the two sides of the industry are called on to set up.
7. *The right of men and women to equal treatment.*
8. *The right to worker information, consultation, and participation.* This principle concerns the right of workers to be informed and even consulted about major events affecting their companies and work conditions.
9. *The right to health and safety protection at the workplace.*
10. *The right to protection of children and adolescence.* [sic] This principle sets the minimum working age at 16 and gives young workers the right to a fair wage, to be covered by labor regulations which take into account their specific characteristics and also to embark, after completion of statutory schooling, upon two years of vocational training.
11. *The rights of elderly people to receive an income that guarantees a decent standard of living.*
12. *The rights of disabled persons.* Every disabled person has the right to take advantage of specific measures, especially in the field of training and occupational and social integration and rehabilitation.[23]

The implementation of the Social Charter mainly depends on the member state governments, or the agencies within them responsible for the field of social affairs, and also on the two sides of industry (employers and workers). In evaluating the Social Charter, it should be kept in mind that this document does not have the force of law at this time.

The Social Charter after Maastricht

The Social Charter of the EU continues to cause divisions within the Union because of labor-management relations in each member state. There is no question that the Maastricht treaty significantly expands the scope of social policy. The allocation of the ESF now requires the consideration of the goal of economic and social cohesion. As we explained above, the Social Charter addressed the issues of the free movement of individuals, worker's rights, social protection by the social welfare state, the rights of men and women for equal treatment, living and working conditions, health and safety issues, and the rights of the children, elderly, and disabled. Given the extent of arguments for and against the Social Charter, especially with the UK choosing to opt out of the agreement, does the EU need a collective framework for its social policies?

In support of the Social Charter and its accompanying action program, one could argue that the overall policy recommendations offer the way forward in harmonizing labor-industry relations and reducing the gap between the regions by bringing together various policies such as social funds, health and safety, equal opportunities, and relatively comparable investment opportunities. On the other hand, the critics argue that this is rather impossible because labor relations in each country vary greatly. In particular, there are wide differences between labor rights embodied in legislation or attained through collective bargaining agreements. Critics instead call for a decentralized approach to labor-industry relations, with the establishment of minimum health and safety regulations.

Labor relations indeed vary greatly across the Community. For example, in the UK, the Thatcher government reduced the power of trade unions by reducing their rights to collective action.[24] With reduced trade union powers and weakened collective bargaining in the UK, a very competitive labor market now exists. In Germany, on the other hand, industrial relations remain corporatist with powerful works councils representing labor interests in industry's decision-making bodies, significantly influencing company decisions. In Italy, large companies face serious legal restrictions on their hiring and firing policies.

In terms of labor benefits (wages, work hours, holidays, etc.), the workers of Germany are better off than their counterparts in other countries, followed by the Danes and French. Among the newest members of the EU, Finland and Sweden also have generous worker benefits. The worst off are the Greeks, Irish, and Portuguese workers.[25] It is also important to note that the weakest labor laws exist in the UK and Ireland. Harmonizing these wide-ranging policies and practices is no small task and requires long-term commitment by officials at the EU, state, and interest group levels. For example, the Social Charter states that "information, consultation, and participation of workers must be developed along appropriate lines, taking account of the practices in force in the various Member States."[26] Yet national practices differ so much that it would be next to impossible to join them into a single EU policy, unless everyone agreed to abandon their long-lasting nation-specific practices. Moreover, we should remember that the Social Charter is a protocol and as such it is not part of the Maastricht treaty. It is a voluntary commitment on the part of the 11 Union members, which have signed it to work toward harmonization of labor-industry relations in their countries.

The decision of the British government to opt out of the Social Charter creates an additional concern for other members of the EU, who are concerned that the UK might be trying to gain unfair advantage over its EU partners by becoming a very attractive site for European investors because businesses would not pay the full price for labor costs.[27] These concerns are more relevant to the EU leaders as they face the task of reducing the size of EU's 20 million unemployed workers.[28]

In an attempt to address the EU's unemployment problem, the European Commission released a White Paper (*Tackling the Challenges and Moving into the 21st Century*) just before the Brussels meeting of the European Council on December 10, 1993, presenting a strategy to increase economic growth, with a goal of creating 15 million new jobs by the end of this century. This White Paper differs from the previous White Paper that gave rise to the SEA because it does not lay out a specific legislative program. It is simply a call to analyze the causes of the current unemployment, competitiveness, and growth problems and to discuss available policy options for the Community.

The White Paper identifies three types of unemployment requiring different corrective policies: (1) cyclical unemployment, which is caused by low economic growth; (2) structural unemployment, perhaps two-thirds of the total, caused by competition from low-wage economies, high cost of unskilled workers, and deficient training and overprotection of traditional industries; and (3) job losses caused by failure to adapt to technological changes.[29] The report argues that without drastically dismantling social protection systems and wage structures in the EU, the Community needs to reduce restrictions on hiring and firing; tie unemployment benefits to job searching; provide more flexible work hours and performance-related pay at the company level but not at the national level; subsidize expansion of social services in areas such as environmental protection, housing renovation, and community care; and reduce the cost of unskilled and semi-skilled labor through reduction in employment taxes. This last suggestion would be offset by budgetary savings and new taxes in areas such as carbon dioxide emissions.[30]

The report further specifies that the EU has to take medium and long-term measures to improve its competitiveness by making the best use of the Single Market, research and development, and education and training; encouraging development of small and medium-size enterprises; promoting global free trade; adapting to new technologies (particularly in information industries); and investing in other European markets.[31] (The emphasis on investment in information industries is discussed in greater detail later in the chapter.) The White Paper drew strong criticism from the British Prime Minister John Major, who said that Commission President Delors was trying to avoid criticism of the report by releasing it 2 days before the summit. On substantive matters, the British opposed Brussels' call for increased EU spending on roads, rail, and telecommunications, all of which are to be financed partly through the sale of new Brussels Bonds.[32] The British, and to some extent the Germans as well, also opposed the call for a stronger role for the EMI in the coordination of monetary policies and the management of the ERM. However, at the summit meeting in Brussels, the European Council endorsed the White Paper. The real test will come when the EU leaders must deliver an action plan to implement the proposed goals. The new president of the Commission, Jacques Santer, seems to steer a middle course for the EU in this matter. In his address to the EP on January 17, 1995, Santer called for a balance between "social and economic forces, as well as the environment."[33]

Education and Training

Education and training policies represent major challenges for the EU. Although both topics affect the lives of all EU citizens, Community-wide policies in these areas were introduced only recently, in conjunction with the Single Market, and have faced serious financing problems and political obstacles on the grounds of national sovereignty.[34] Prior to the SEA, the EU initiated a limited program for training to tackle unemployment problems in the 1970s. The European Center for the Development of Vocational Training (CEDEFOP) administered this program and had only limited support from some of the EU countries. However, the challenges of the Single Market, and now post-Maastricht Europe, required a more comprehensive policy package, which the EU's education ministers adopted on October 6, 1989, including the following programs:

1. ERASMUS (European Community Action Scheme for the Mobility of University Students): This is among the largest and most successful programs. Some 43,000 university students and 1,500 higher education institutions participate in it. During the initial phase (1987–1990) the EC allocated 85 million ECUs for this program intended for exchange of students and faculty as well as promoting joint curriculum development among universities.
2. COMETT (Community Program in Education and Training for Technology): The purpose of this program is to provide funds to encourage links between universities and industries to facilitate a higher level of training in cutting edge technologies. The original COMETT I (1987–1989) had a budget of 45 million ECUs and concentrated on five fields or "strands": (1) networking for university-industry training partnership; (2) financing for student internships in industry, in countries other than the student's, and assisting in industry-university exchanges of personnel; (3) joint university-industry training with transnational projects; (4) development of multimedia training systems; and (5) exchange of information between industry and universities.[35]
3. LINGUA (Community Action Program to promote Foreign Language Competence in the European Community): This program was approved by the Council in 1988 and was appropriated a budget of 200 million ECUs for the first 5 years. Government leaders believe EU citizens should know at least three Community languages[36] so they can become more mobile for job purposes and also help to build a "feeling of Europeanness" among different nationalities.
4. YES (Youth for Europe, or the Youth Exchange Scheme): In contrast to ERASMUS and COMETT, which address the concerns of students of higher education, YES is open to all young people in the EU between the ages of 15 and 25. With an initial budget of 30 million ECUs during 1988–1990, it encourages youth to spend at least a week in

another member country. The program is designed to promote greater understanding among the youth of the EU.[37]

In addition to these programs, the EC also developed smaller initiatives designed to promote vocational training of youth after their compulsory education and also to promote ties between the Community institutions of higher education and enterprises and their counterparts in the new democracies of Eastern Europe, as follows:

1. PETRA: This program was established in 1989 to promote 2 years of vocational training for youth after completion of compulsory education.
2. EUROTECNET: Another program for youth in vocational training in new technologies. It emphasizes cooperation in research and project demonstrations.
3. TEMPUS: This is a pilot program that the Community introduced in May 1990 following the breakdown of communist regimes in Eastern Europe. It covers joint projects in the European sphere between the EC universities and enterprises and their counterparts in east-central Europe.[38]

Through these programs, the EC, and now the EU, started to focus on the educational and other forms of training needs of European citizens, going beyond the Single Market.

INDUSTRIAL POLICY AND RESEARCH AND DEVELOPMENT

Unlike regional policy, industrial policy provides assistance to sectors of the economy, irrespective of geographical location, at least in initial policy choices. The Treaty of Rome made no specific reference to a Community-wide industrial policy. This silence is not surprising since industrial policies of the member states vary greatly: in France and Germany the state intervenes to shape industrial policy, whereas in the UK, there is a hands-off approach. However, with the launching of Project 1992, the Commission argued that to have a viable EU-wide industrial base, with a strong competition policy, coordinated policies were essential.[39] According to John Kemp, the Commission supported the idea of subsidiarity where "the EC would only become involved when national policies of the member states were ineffective, or harmful to other member states."[40] The Commission argued that policy coordination was necessary between industrial policy and other policy areas: common external policy, social and environmental policies, a research and development policy (R&D), and greater coordination of the member states' national industrial policies.

The EC adopted two main programs to support R&D at the European level: the Framework Programs, started in 1985 and run by the Commission, and the much less coordinated R&D programs known as EUREKA between 18 European countries and the EU.[41]

The Framework Programs started in 1985 with the introduction of the ESPRIT, European Strategic Program for Research and Development in Information Technologies. The second framework program entered into effect in 1987, lasted through 1991, and was followed by the third phase (1990-1994). The other R&D framework programs that were introduced under the second and third phases include the following: (1) RACE, Research in Advanced Communications in Europe; (2) BRITE, Basic Research in Industrial Technologies for Europe; (3) EURAM, European Research in Advanced Materials; (4) SCIENCE, Plan to Stimulate the International Cooperation and Interchange needed by European Research Scientists; (5) SPES, European Stimulation Plan for Economic Sciences; (6) STEP, Science and Technology for Environmental Protection; and (7) DELTA, Development of European Learning through Technological Advance.[42]

Currently, the EU research ministers are evaluating the Commission's proposal for the size and funding of the fourth phase of the Framework Programs which will cover the period from 1994 to 1998. The Commission's proposal calls for a budget of 13.1 billion ECUs (see Table 9.2) as compared to the 6.6 billion

TABLE 9.2 Fourth European Union research and technological development framework program, 1994–1998

R&D Program	Proposed Funding (ECUs million)	Percent of Total
Information and telecommunications	3,900	35.7
Industrial technologies	1,800	16.5
Environment	970	8.9
Life sciences and technology	1,325	12.1
Clean and efficient energy	1,050	9.6
Nuclear safety and security	495	4.5
Controlled thermonuclear fusion	980	9.0
Research for European transport policy	280	2.6
Socioeconomic research	125	1.1
Other Projects		
Cooperation with third countries and international organizations	790	
Dissemination and utilization of results	600	
Stimulation of training and mobility of researchers	785	
TOTAL	13,100	

SOURCE: *Financial Times,* October 26, 1993, p. 9.

ECUs for the third phase. Nevertheless, in real terms, the budget still remains at about 4 percent of the overall Community budget.[43]

The Commission's push for R&D was also a critical part of the Delors 1993 White Paper. The paper stressed that one of the main reasons for Europe's decline in competitiveness was the slowdown in infrastructure investment during the 1980s. To meet the challenges of the twenty-first century, the White Paper calls for new investments in information highways, pan-European transport, energy, and environmental infrastructure.[44] The development of new information technologies and highways would be financed by private capital, and transport and energy networks would be covered by a mixture of public and private sources. The paper also argues that the new information highways and technologies could not reach their potential advances unless the current industries are decentralized. Decentralization represents a major problem for several EU countries where information and telecommunication industries are state monopolies.

For the information industries, the Commission estimates a cost of 150 billion ECUs over a period of 10 years.[45] In addition, a task force would be needed to start the drive with a mandate from the EU countries. The transport and energy infrastructure, on the other hand, would require an estimated funding of 250 billion ECUs to establish better road, rail, airport, and gas pipeline infrastructures between the EU and her neighbors in east-central and southern Europe.[46]

ENVIRONMENTAL POLICY

The Rome treaty made no reference to environmental policy, and the topic did not enter the EC agenda until 1971 when the Commission gave its first detailed report on the environment to the European Council. At the subsequent 1972 Paris Summit, the Council agreed to adopt an EC environmental policy and to establish an Environmental and Protection Service.[47] Since then, the environmental policy goals have been defined in four different Environmental Action Programs (EAPs). Unfortunately, these programs did not represent a definitive commitment from the member states for implementation because each country has maintained its own set of environmental regulations. Nevertheless, the EAPs represent a growing emphasis, in an EU-wide approach, on how the EU could better coordinate its industrial policy and at the same time protect the environment. It has become clear that most environmental problems transcend national boundaries and cannot be dealt with at the national level alone. Furthermore, with the Maastricht treaty, the Commission is likely to attain more influence in the coordination and implementation of EU-wide environment policy.

The first EAP (1973–1977) set the main principles of the EC's environmental policy, which remain in effect: the polluter-pays principle, emphasis on preventive measures, and the need to consider the environmental impact of the Community's socioeconomic decisions. These principles received a similar endorsement in the second EAP (1977–1981). With the third EAP (1982–1986), environmental protection received a stronger emphasis. This program states that "an overall strategy has to be formulated in which prevention, rather than cure, should be the rule."[48] Later, the principle of prevention was included in the SEA and became a central issue in the fourth EAP.

The developments under the SEA are important for the future implementation of environmental policies. Even though Article 130 of the SEA, which deals with environmental policies, still requires unanimity by the Council of Ministers, Article 100A permits directives approved by a qualified majority. As David Vogel explains, this provides an alternative means of "enacting environmental legislation, one which deprived any single member state of the power to block approval."[49] The SEA also expanded the role of the EP in shaping EU legislation. The significance of this is that the EP has been more strict on environmental regulations than the Council of Ministers.[50] Finally, citizens' concerns over environment, following the Chernobyl disaster in the former Soviet Union and a massive spill of toxins into the Rhine River in 1986, placed ever-increasing pressure on EU leaders to respond to these challenges.

The fourth EAP (1987–1992) reflects these concerns and is a more comprehensive proposal with a greater emphasis on environmental management. This program emphasizes urgent action in the use of agricultural chemicals, treatment of agricultural wastes, protection of animal species, and general guidelines for product standards in an EU-wide approach.[51] In an attempt to stimulate action in response to these policy concerns, the European Environment Agency was established in 1990. The original task of the Agency was to collect data and publish reports on environmental issues and to publish a report on the state of the environment every 3 years.

According to Vogel, the EC enacted more environmental legislation from 1989 to 1991 than in the previous 2 decades combined.[52] The major factors behind this trend have been the SEA and the increase in public awareness as reflected in the rise in the number of environmental interest groups and green parties. In many areas, environmental standards in the EU have been strengthened to the extent that they now compare favorably with the U.S. standards. Furthermore, the EU has been very active in shaping global environmental policy. It participated in the 1987 Montreal Meeting and the 1992 Earth Summit in Brazil. As Vogel explains, at the prior meeting, 31 countries, including the EC, signed the Montreal Protocols calling for a 50 percent reduction in the manufacturing of chlorofluorocarbons by the end of 1999 and, soon after the meeting, the Commission went even further and announced that it intended to reduce production of these chemicals by 85 percent as soon as feasible and to ban all production by the end of the century.[53]

The present EU measures in environmental management can be divided into three categories. The first category is waste management. Efforts in this area date back to 1975 when the EC issued its Framework Directive 75/442 which required the states to ensure safe disposal of wastes. This topic gained more momentum with Project 1992 because the removal of border controls meant that policing of cross-border transfer of hazardous waste would become more difficult. As a result of these concerns, the Commission issued a paper on a "Community Strategy for Waste Management," which was then approved by the Council of Ministers in 1990.[54]

The second category of legislation pertains to water pollution. According to Hassan, the majority of EU water directives define quality standards for drinking water, standards for bathing (beaches), and control of clean water for fisheries.[55] But with regard to clean oceans, the EU needs to coordinate its policies with the neighboring non-EU countries. For example, there is concern over the future of the Mediterranean Sea, which requires cooperation between the EU and the nonmember Mediterranean countries—though it should be noted that the biggest polluters of the Mediterranean are France, Italy, and Spain. A similar concern is found in the Baltic Sea region.

Finally, the third category of environmental legislation refers to atmospheric pollution. Even though the EU started these regulations later than the United States, today it compares favorably with American standards. For example, the EU requires the automobile industry to produce cars that can run on lead-free gas. In addition, there are regulations on emission limits for carbon monoxide, hydrocarbons, sulfur dioxide, and nitrogen oxide.[56] In related areas of acid rain and global warming, the EU agreements, starting with the EC Directive 88/609, apply similar regulations to power plants and manufacturing industries.[57] Finally, directives have been issued controlling the use and marketing of dangerous substances like asbestos, PCB, and PCT.

CONCLUSION

The overall assessment of the EU's regional, social, industrial, and environmental policies is that the Europeans have made important gains in these areas. Despite different national standards between the 15 member states, EU-wide policies have been either adopted or initiated on a voluntary basis. Regions stand to benefit from the recent reforms in regional policy that permit multiregional development projects. The Social Charter provides an early blueprint for harmonizing social benefits across the Union based upon the EU's strong perception of a welfare state. Although British opposition to the charter still presents a major obstacle for its adoption as an official policy of the EU, the future of these efforts seems promising. However, the members' implementation of the EU Directives through national legislations are often slow in coming, which, in turn, contributes to the slowing down of the EU-wide implementation of policies.

ENDNOTES

1. Loukas Tsoukalis, *The New European Economy: The Politics and Economics of Integration* (New York and London: Oxford University Press, 1991), p. 41.
2. Dennis Swann, *The Economics of the Common Market* (London: Penguin Books, 1991), p. 289.

3. Stephen George, *Politics and Policy in the European Community* (Oxford: Oxford University Press, 1991), pp. 192-193.
4. Ibid.
5. Ibid., p. 194.
6. Tsoukalis, *The New European Economy,* pp. 210-211.
7. Judith Tomkins and Jim Twomey, "Regional Policy," in Frank McDonald and Stephen Dearden, eds., *European Economic Integration* (London: Longman, 1992), p. 105.
8. Ibid., pp. 107-108.
9. Ibid., p. 108.
10. Ibid.
11. Ibid., pp. 108-109.
12. Harvey Armstrong, "Community Regional Policy," in Juliet Lodge, ed., *The European Community and the Challenge of the Future,* 2nd ed. (New York: St. Martin's, 1993), pp. 147-148.
13. Ibid., p. 149.
14. As cited in Tomkins and Twomey, "Regional Policy," pp. 114-115.
15. Jaques Delors, *Regional Implications of Economic and Monetary Union: Report on Economic and Monetary Union in the EC* (Luxembourg: Office for the Official Publications, 1989).
16. Tomkins and Twomey, "Regional Policy," p. 115.
17. Stephen Dearden, "Social Policy," in McDonald and Dearden, eds., *European Economic Integration,* p. 82.
18. George, *Politics and Policy,* p. 203.
19. Dearden, "Social Policy," p. 85.
20. Swann, *The Economics of the Common Market,* p. 299.
21. For a detailed discussion of these years, see M. Shanks, *European Social Policy Today and Tomorrow* (Oxford: Pergamon, 1977); B. Laffan, "1983 Policy Implementation in the European Community: The European Social Fund as a Case Study," *Journal of Common Market Studies* 21 (June 1983).
22. Beverly Springer, *The Social Dimension of 1992* (Westport: Praeger, 1992), pp. 39-41.
23. EC, *1992: The Social Dimension* (Luxembourg: Office for Official Publications of the European Communities, 1990), pp. 83-85.
24. Dearden, "Social Policy," p. 97.
25. "Labour Conditions in the EC," *The European,* November 22-24, 1991, p. 24.
26. As cited in Edward Moxon-Browne, "Social Europe," in Lodge, ed., *The European Community and the Challenge of the Future,* pp. 157-158.
27. Ibid., p. 156.
28. "EU Urged to Catch up with the World," *Financial Times,* December 8, 1993, p. 2.
29. Ibid.
30. *Eurecom* 5.11 (December 1993), p. 1.
31. Ibid.
32. *Financial Times,* December 9, 1993, p. 1.
33. "Santer Steers Middle Course for EU," *Financial Times,* January 18, 1995, p. 3.
34. Glenda Rosenthal, "Educational and Training Policy," in Leon Hurwitz and Christian Lequesne, eds., *The State of the European Community: Policies, Institutions, and Debates in the Transition Years* (Boulder and London: Lynne Reinner and Longman, 1991), p. 273.
35. Ibid., p. 279.
36. Springer, *The Social Dimension,* p. 117.

37. Ibid. Also see Rosenthal, "Education and Training Policy."
38. Springer, *The Social Dimension,* p. 117.
39. John Kemp, "Competition Policy," in McDonald and Dearden, eds., *European Economic Integration,* p. 78.
40. Ibid.
41. The members of EUREKA are Austria, Belgium, Denmark, Germany, Finland, France, Greece, Iceland, Ireland, Italy, Luxembourg, the Netherlands, Norway, Portugal, Spain, Sweden, Switzerland, the UK, Turkey, and the EC represented by the Commission.
42. EC Delegation to the United States, *The European Community in the Nineties* (Washington, D.C.: EC Office, 1992), p. 15.
43. "R&D in a tussle over EC funding," *Financial Times,* October 26, 1993, p. 9.
44. "EC urged to catch up with the World," *Financial Times,* p. 8.
45. Ibid.
46. Ibid.
47. John Hassan, "Environment Policy," in McDonald and Dearden, eds., *European Economic Integration,* p. 122.
48. Angela Liberatore, "Problems of Transnational Policymaking: Environmental Policy in the European Community," *European Journal of Political Research* 19 (1991): 292.
49. David Vogel, "Environmental Protection and the Creation of a Single European Market" (Paper presented at the 1992 Annual Meeting of the American Political Science Association, Chicago, September 3-6), p. 11.
50. Ibid., p. 12.
51. Hassan, "Environment Policy," p. 124.
52. Vogel, "Environmental Protection," p. 14.
53. Ibid.
54. Hassan, "Environment Policy," p. 124; Vogel, "Environmental Protection," pp. 48-61.
55. Hassan, "Environment Policy," pp. 125-126.
56. Swann, *The Economics of the Common Market,* pp. 329-333.
57. Hassan, "Environment Policy," p. 126.

chapter **10**

External Economic Relations

The Single Market refers to the part of the SEA that aims at accomplishing the original goal of the Rome treaty: creation of a truly common market. This economic plan is known as the Internal Market, the Common Market, the Single Market, or Project 1992, and it has become one of the most studied subjects of recent years. Scholars and policy makers continue to debate the intra-EU and inter-EU effects of Project 1992 as the Union moves closer to completing the Common Market and pushes forward with further deepening of economic integration through the EMU.

In this chapter, we look at how the Single Market will affect the EU's external economic relations with the United States and Japan, other European countries (EFTA and east-central Europe), the Mediterranean Basin, and the Lomé (African, Caribbean, and Pacific) states. We believe that the policy packages adopted toward these states are crucial to understanding the EU's global competition with the United States and Japan.

THE EUROPEAN UNION, THE UNITED STATES, AND JAPAN

Whereas trilateral economic relations between the EU, Japan, and the United States constitute by far the world's largest economic exchange relationship, the Union generally views trade with these countries as less important than that with the old EFTA, prior to Austria, Finland, and Sweden joining the Union, and the east-central European countries.[1] The major reason is that the EU's combined exports to the United States and Japan are less than the exports to EFTA. The EU also exports less to Japan than to the east-central European countries. Finally, the EU, Japan, and the United States have been busy creating their respective zones of influence through regional trade blocs: the EU through the Single Market, the Euopean Economic Area (EEA), and the Europe agreements; Japan through the Association of South East Asian Nations (ASEAN); and the United States in North America through the North American Free Trade Agreement (NAFTA) (see Figure 10.1). Yet, there is one other important aspect of this triad relationship. In terms of direct foreign investment, the EU-US relationship is by far the most important in the world (see Figure 10.2).

As these figures clearly show, intra-EU trade is by far the largest among the competing trade blocs. Many scholars and policy makers worry that while the Single Market will undoubtedly promote economic growth for the EU, the nature of economic relations between the Union and its largest trade partners could go in two fundamentally opposite directions. Will the Single Market provide further opportunities for foreigners to penetrate a market that is larger than the United States, or will it result in "fortress Europe"?[2] The data in Figure 10.2 show that the triad of the EU-Japan-US accounts for roughly 80 percent of total outward foreign direct investment compared with a 47 percent share of world exports.[3] According to a study in *The Economist,* investment by the EU, Japan, and the United States was motivated during the 1980s by the rush of firms to position

FIGURE 10.1   International trade flows, 1992 (merchandise trade in billions of $US and as percent of world trade)

SOURCE: *Financial Times,* December 3, 1993, p. 15.

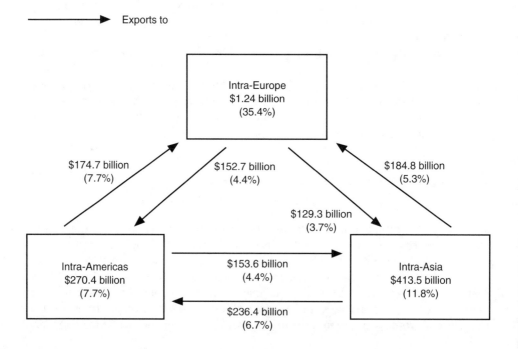

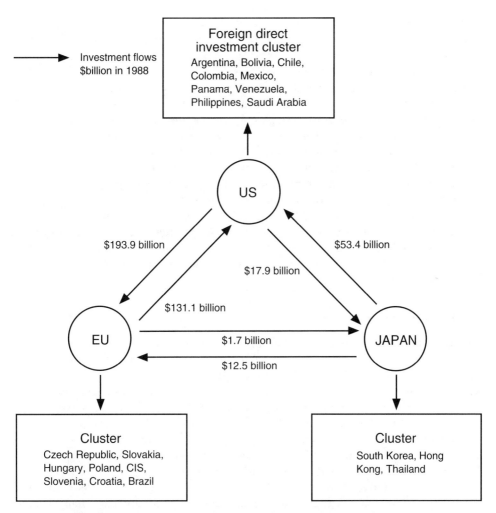

FIGURE 10.2   Foreign direct investment, 1988 (billions of $US)

SOURCE: *The Economist,* August 24, 1991, p. 57. © 1991 The Economist Newspaper Group, Inc. Reprinted with permission. Further reproduction prohibited.

themselves in the Union before the creation of the Single Market, by Japanese firms trying to escape rising costs at home, and by the growing importance of services in industrial countries.[4] Furthermore, the boxes in Figure 10.2 show how the big three are attempting to establish their areas of influence through investment clusters.

The challenge of the Single Market to the United States and Japan can be considered in terms of power relations in the world economy. First, the Single Market will increasingly position the EU members to act as a single voice in intergovernmental organizations like the GATT, which will affect the structural power of the other two members of the triad in the world economy. Second, as Michael Smith explains, "it [the Single Market] has more specific ramifications in the management of economic interdependence and the role to be played by the EU, [Japan], and the US in the evolution of the multilateral system."[5]

Hardly anyone disputes that the EU will be in a position to exercise increasing global economic leadership or at least share this position with the United States and Japan in a trilateral hegemony. Such a partnership is likely to be more cooperative than conflictual given the complex interdependent relationship of the economies of these countries. This does not mean, however, that disputes will not arise between the triad states. Rather, government leaders are likely to solve the disputes by avoiding serious damage to their economies despite pressures for more protectionism from some domestic interests in all three countries. The information provided in Figures 10.1 and 10.2 supports this point of view. Given the nature of commercial and financial transactions among the triad members, it is no surprise that the G-7 meetings[6] consistently ask for greater coordination of macroeconomic policies between these countries to promote economic stability and growth for the world. Let us now examine some of the major aspects of the EU's economic relations first with the United States and then with Japan.

EU-US Economic Relations

The U.S. Omnibus Trade Act of 1988 has the potential to provoke trade disputes between the United States and her trade partners. The Super 301 Provision of this act requires the administration to list publicly countries that trade unfairly with the United States, negotiate removal of such practices, and take retaliatory action if negotiations with those countries fail. U.S. trade partners have been highly critical of this policy, and their concerns were echoed in a GATT report in December 1988. They fear that different U.S. administrations could resort to the political use of Super 301 as leverage in gaining an advantageous position in their bilateral trade relations with other countries.

The primary dispute between the EU and the United States has been over CAP. One major issue in this area was over EU oilseed subsidies that haunted the GATT Uruguay Round negotiations for 5 years before it was resolved in November 1992.[7] This issue was the linchpin in the deadlocked GATT negotiations on agricultural trade that could have held up the entire Uruguay Round talks. The United States threatened to impose 200 percent punitive tariffs on about $300 million of EC agricultural exports, mostly in white wine, starting on December 5, 1992, unless the Community accepted reductions in oilseed subsidies. After painstaking negotiations, an agreement was reached in which the EU would limit the area of land for oilseed production rather than the total number of oilseeds produced.[8] Under this agreement up to 15 percent of that area is to be taken out of production during the first year, followed by a minimum of 10 percent in future years. In return, the United States agreed that oilseeds could be grown on land set aside for nonfood uses, such as fuel for vehicles. Furthermore, the EC agreed to cut the volume of subsidies for agricultural exports by 21 percent from the average of exports during 1986–1990 over a 6-year period starting in 1994. An important sticking point in these agreements is French displeasure. Under pressures from politically powerful farmers, the French government announced its opposition to the EU-US agricultural trade agreement as being incompatible with CAP and France's national interests. As we discussed in chapter 8, the French government further stated its intention to block the agreements unless the two sides achieved a favorable settlement for France.

Another trade dispute between the EU and the United States concerns the steel industry, with each side accusing the other of unfair trade practices. Both sides heavily subsidize their steel industries, the United States by use of import quotas and the EU by various policies implemented under the ECSC. A more recent episode in this dispute involves the announcement of preliminary countervailing duties on flat-rolled steel imports from six EU countries by the U.S. Department of Commerce in 1992 and again in 1994.[9] The Commission estimated that this action would cost the EU steel producers sales of some 2 million tons of steel worth nearly $1 billion and warned that the Union would retaliate if the Americans did not reverse their decision.

In a similar fashion, United States Trade Representative (USTR) Mickey Kantor announced in May 1993, that the United States would impose trade sanctions worth $20 million against EU firms in retaliation for the Union's refusal to grant the United States full access to the EU telecommunications procurement market.[10] The EU's Trade Commissioner, Sir Leon Brittan, responded angrily to the U.S. decision and on June 8, 1993, the EU retaliated. EU foreign ministers agreed on "mirror image" measures totaling $15 million per year against U.S. firms.

As these disputes demonstrate, the EU's economic relations with the United States have been turbulent in recent years. However, there are some indications that the Union is interested in improving these relations. For example, the Commission recently approved a positive report on the NAFTA as a goodwill measure to the United States in an attempt to avoid serious trade disputes with the two sides trying to reach a successful conclusion of the Uruguay Round negotiations.[11] Finally, regardless of how serious the trade grievances seem to be between the EU and the United States, the two sides have always been able to settle any trade dispute before it escalated into an all-out trade war (see Table 10.1).

The Future of EU-US Trade Relations. It should be emphasized that there are significant differences in the ways in which the EU and the United States address economic policies.[12] Within the EU, national governments will continue to "address and fulfill their obligations to ensure the preservation of their national democratic rights and cultural roots through subsidiarity within the [EU] confederation system before negotiation may begin externally. Louder and stronger voices coming from the US electorate to put 'America first' has placed new regional and national interests at the forefront for US lawmakers."[13]

Systemic differences between the EU and the United States, particularly in economic philosophies, will become more evident as the Western alliance adjusts to the disappearance of the Soviet threat. During the Cold War, these differences

TABLE 10.1   A sample of EU-US trade disputes, 1960–1989

Date and issue	Dispute	Resolution
Chicken war, 1962–1963	US chicken exports were hurt when West Germany raised duties on poultry as part of its obligations under the CAP	The US withdrew tariff concessions on EC exports of trucks and related items; although the chicken war is forgotten, the concessions are still withheld
US wine-gallon-tax system, 1963–1979	Tax discrimination against foreign bottled spirits indirectly protected the US alcoholic beverage industry	In the Tokyo round, the EC granted concessions on agricultural products in exchange for revisions of the wine-gallon-tax
Steel voluntary restraint agreements, 1982	EC shipments of subsidized and dumped steel to the US market added to the woes of US steel producers	Instead of countervailing and antidumping duties, the US and EC negotiated a VRA that effectively curbed EC steel exports to the US
Hormone-treated beef, 1987–1989	The EC banned imports of beef containing growth hormones	The EC will accept imports from US packagers that certify their meat as hormone free
Second Banking Directive, January 1988–June 1989	The EC initially asserted it would not license third-country banks if those countries failed to give EC banks reciprocal access	The EC will accept national treatment reciprocity provided that it results in equivalent market access
Technical standards, January 1988–August 1989	The US expressed concern about the exclusion of US firms from the EC standard-setting process	CEN and CENELEC, two quasi-public standards boards, will accept comments from ANSI, the US counterpart

KEY: VRA, Voluntary Restraint Agreement; CEN, European Committee for Standardization; CENELEC, Committee for Electro-Technical Standardization; ANSI, American National Standards Institute.
SOURCE: Reprinted from *National Forum: The Phi Kappa Phi Journal,* Volume LXXII, Number 2 (Spring 1992). Copyright © by Birol Yeşilada. By permission of the publishers.

were often overlooked as political and security matters dominated the West's agenda. In the post-Cold War era, we can expect the United States to push for trade and commercial policy based on laissez-faire principles with nongovernmental intervention in the private sector. The EU, on the other hand, will stress greater reliance on social market principles, as highlighted in the Social Charter. The European policies have generally been based on the desire to promote a more egalitarian distribution of national wealth. At the EU level, leaders continuously have tried to promote such policies through consensus and partnership among the member states, though this has not been easy, as highlighted by the UK's opposition to many aspects of the Social Charter. At each stage of economic

integration, particularly with the elimination of national frontiers to free movement of peoples, goods, and services, the Community had to come to terms with
the impact of its decisions on labor-management relations and the overall social
welfare of its citizens. Therefore, it is not surprising to see a similar approach
to global trade talks by the Europeans.

In the United States, on the other hand, the practice under the recent
Republican administrations was generally to view government intervention in the
marketplace as being fundamentally wrong and to pay less attention to an
egalitarian distribution of national wealth. This practice has not been substantially
altered under the Clinton administration. In international trade and investment
matters, the Americans continue to insist on a simple set of rules that would
guarantee free trade and open investments based on market forces. Furthermore,
the 1988 Trade Act includes Super 301 legislation, which gives the American trade
representative the authority to identify protectionist trade partners and to target
them for retaliatory measures. Over recent years, the enforcement of the Super
301 legislation has caused serious friction between the United States and its
trade partners.

What should be clear from the long and painstaking negotiations during the
Uruguay Round is that there is no common set of rules that are applicable to
all countries and economic systems. Neither the United States nor the EU is, or
should be, in a position to impose its own economic philosophies on a global
scale. Insistence on such policies would only serve to damage bilateral relations
between the EU and the United States at a time when economic interdependence
between the two allies warrants greater cooperation.

EU-Japan Economic Relations

The EU's relations with Japan, on the other hand, suffer from the series of
quantitative trade restrictions and Voluntary Export Restraints (VERs) that the
Union took over from its members as result of the Single Market. The VERs have
been particularly attractive in sensitive industries, such as cars and electronics,
in order to protect domestic industries through voluntary restraint on exports
by the foreign producer. In these areas, Articles 113 and 115 of the Rome treaty
played an important role.

According to the Rome treaty's Article 113, there was to be a common
external tariff schedule for the EU member states by 1969. This was achieved
in 1968 as part of the CU. However, Article 115 provided an escape clause in
permitting individual national trade policies as long as relevant parts of the
common policy remained on the EU agenda as unsettled. In fact, the complete
elimination of such nation-specific policies is not scheduled until the year 2000
when the EU is to lift restrictions on car imports from Japan. Various members
of the EU resorted to the use of Article 115 against the import of cars and
electronics from Japan and imports of textiles from the developing countries.[14]

This problem of projectionist trade policies continues to trouble EU-Japan
relations, but the creation of the Single Market presented an important opportunity

for the EU to abolish VERs and other quantitative restrictions on imports from Japan. VERs always cost the consumers rather than the domestic producers and foreign exporters of the same products. However, there will be pressures from EU producers to negotiate new EU-wide VERs with Japan, and the Japanese producers are likely to go along because they often benefit from the higher prices on the products that are affected by VERs and other quantitative restrictions. In an attempt to reduce serious trade friction between the EU and Japan, the two sides reached an agreement on a post-1992 policy in July 1992, which included the following:

1. Intra-EC trade will be liberalized by the adoption of an [EU]-type approval scheme by 1 January 1993, and all national import restrictions will be abolished by the same date.
2. Imports of cars from Japan will be unrestricted after 31 December 1999, and in the intervening period will be limited to the level of 1.23 million (approximately the 1991 level of imports).
3. Cars produced in Japanese-owned plants in the [EU] will have unrestricted access to the [EU] markets.
4. There is an understanding about the levels of Japanese imports to France, Italy, Spain, Portugal, and the UK from which it can be inferred that a deliberate attempt will be made by Japanese firms to reduce adjustment pressures in the markets from which national import restrictions have been removed.[15]

This agreement seems to allow for better relations in the future, but some outstanding issues remain in EU-Japan trade relations. The first is the continuous Japanese balance of payments surplus with the EU. Second, Japan's legal barriers limit EU exports to that country. Third, it is difficult for EU firms to sell consumer goods in Japan unless they have Japanese subsidiaries. The Japanese marketing and distribution system requires close collaboration between the producers, wholesalers, and retailers, which makes marketing and distribution costs higher for EU firms in Japanese markets than they are for Japanese companies in Union markets. Japanese companies maintain close collaboration with each other under the auspices of the Japanese Ministry of International Trade and Industry (MITI). Such collaboration inherently damages the non-Japanese firms' access to fair competition. This sort of activity would be illegal in the EU market.[16]

The Single Market provides an important incentive for all parties—the EU, the United States, and Japan—to improve their commercial relations. Each side stands to benefit from more open and free trade as well as from a foreign investment regime. One of the driving forces behind the Single Market is the improvement of EU firms' competitiveness in the world markets. Given the fact that the most competitive and technologically advanced industries are found in the United States and Japan, it would be counterproductive to restrict their access to EU markets.[17] More competition from U.S. and Japanese companies would promote greater efficiency and competitiveness in EU firms.

Furthermore, the extent of foreign investment flows between the EU and the United States suggests that protectionism would be counterproductive for both sides. The American firms already present in the EU are in a good position to benefit from the creation of the Single Market. Some 80 percent of the largest food processors in the Union are U.S.-owned, and other U.S.-owned companies, such as Ford, IBM, and General Motors, are pan-European in their operations.[18] Although the Japanese are not as well positioned as the Americans in the EU market, they are rapidly expanding their investments in such areas as banking, cars, electronics, and computer and information industries. Further progress in these and other ventures would promote better trade and financial relations between the three.

RELATIONS WITH THE EUROPEAN PERIPHERY COUNTRIES

Progress made in the Single Market has not gone unnoticed by the other countries around the EU during the late 1980s. The most important case is that of EFTA countries where applications for EC membership followed: Austria (1988), Finland (1992), Norway (1992), and Sweden (1991). Following the EU's acceptance of these applications, the respective governments of these countries put the membership issue to national vote in each country. With the exception of Norway, the citizens of Austria, Finland, and Sweden voted to join the Union as of January 1, 1995. Furthermore, almost all of the former Eastern European Bloc and the Mediterranean Basin of Europe have shown interest in improving their relations with the Union, and some of them have applied for full membership in the EU: Cyprus (1990), Malta (1990), Hungary (1994), Poland (1994), and Turkey (1987). Other countries, Albania, Bulgaria, the Czech Republic, Estonia, Latvia, Lithuania, Romania, Slovakia, and Slovenia, have either signed association agreements, known as Europe agreements, or intend to enter into such negotiations with the EU. These countries plan to apply for full membership in the Union in the future.

With regard to further enlargement of the EU, it is clear that the EFTA countries provided the most feasible cases for accession to full membership because of their high level of economic development. The procedure for this expansion deserves special mention. In a move that further stressed the close relationship between the two trade blocs, the EU and EFTA (Austria, Finland, Iceland, Liechtenstein, Norway, Sweden, and Switzerland) agreed to create a trade region, larger than the EU, known as the EEA. One member of EFTA, Switzerland, later chose not to take part in the EEA following a national referendum on this subject on December 6, 1992.

The EU was interested in expansion because this would enhance Union influence in Europe and in the world. Those who wanted to join the Union did so because of the expected economic benefits of Project 1992. In this regard, we need to pay special attention to the expansion of the Union in examining economic relations between the EU and periphery countries.

EXPANSION OF THE EUROPEAN UNION

EU officials expressed their view of expansion in the joint declaration of the EU heads of state and governments emerging from the Edinburgh Summit in December 1992 by stating that the Union intended to allow the accession to membership of the east-central European countries sometime in the future. At the Copenhagen Summit in June 1993, the EU further clarified this view by announcing that the next wave of expansion would include the EFTA countries and that the Union intended to improve economic and political relations with the other European countries that will eventually apply for membership.

The EU's strategic view on expansion of membership is reflected in an opinion paper prepared by the Economic and Social Council of the EC on January 25, 1989. This report argues that the EC finds itself in a global competition with the United States and Japan:

> even once it is reinforced by establishment of a barrier-free internal market, the [EC] will not be able to withstand competition from the two main strategic areas of America and Asia unless it expands its economic area and market. To create this strategic European area, the [EC] will have to turn to its neighbors: European Free Trade Association (EFTA), Eastern Europe, and the Mediterranean. In this latter region, the Community must rapidly make up for lost time: the Mediterranean is now a focus of US and Japanese trade, investment, economic aid, and above all, technological "colonisation."[19]

The recent efforts of the EU in providing economic assistance and leadership to the new democracies of east-central Europe through the establishment of the European Bank for Reconstruction and Development (EBRD), the proposed revisions of the EU's Global Mediterranean Policy, and participation in peace negotiations in the former Yugoslavia in partnership with the United Nations (UN), were all made with views such as those expressed by the Economic and Social Council in mind. While improvement of economic and political relations between the EU and its periphery are in the interest of both sides, the eventual membership in the EU for any candidate state depends on two factors: how well the candidate fares with regard to the conditions for membership and whether there exists a consensus among the EU members to grant membership to the applicant.

Article 237 of the Rome treaty states that any European country can apply to become a member of the EEC. Thus the first requirement for membership is that a country should be European. In addition, it must have a developed economy comparable to the member states' economies so that the expansion would not be an economic burden on the Community. Furthermore, whereas the Rome treaty did not specify any explicit political requirements for member-ship in the EC, the Birkelbach Report of 1962 stated that "only states which guarantee on their territories truly democratic practices and respect for funda-mental human rights and freedoms can become members of our Union."[20] Since then, the EC/EU has used this requirement in evaluating candidates for membership as part of the Maastricht treaty. As we will discuss later, this creates a delicate situation for weak democracies like Turkey and former Eastern Bloc countries.

In its relations with periphery countries, the EU also tries to improve ties by establishing association agreements. These agreements provide for greater economic and political cooperation between the Union and recipient countries. There are two types of association agreements extended to nonmember countries by the EU. The first type provides for economic and technical assistance by the EU and for improvement of trade relations in specified commodity categories. Countries in this category, the ACP (African, Caribbean, and Pacific countries) and most of the Mediterranean Basin countries, are not targeted for eventual accession to full membership. The second type of association prepares non-members for eventual membership in the EU or calls for the creation of a customs union between the nonmember state and the Union. Agreements with EFTA countries, and with Cyprus, Malta, and Turkey, and the Europe agreements with the east-central European states all fall into this second category.[21] It is expected that following the membership of three EFTA countries in 1995, the next phase of expansion will include the Czech Republic, Hungary, Poland, and Slovakia around 2000.[22]

EU-EFTA Relations

The EFTA countries are important for the EU economically and politically. Furthermore, they satisfy all of the conditions for membership in the Union. These countries are members of the democratic and capitalist half of the formally divided Europe, and their economies are highly developed. Their membership in the EU would contribute positively to the Union budget because they would not be drawing funds for various development programs and expensive economic and administrative restructuring to harmonize their systems with the EU. The importance of the EFTA countries to the EU is clear in trade relations prior to the 1995 expansion between the two communities (see Table 10.2).

The most important turning points in the development of EU-EFTA relations were the 1972–1973 free trade agreements (for the elimination of tariffs) and the Luxembourg Declaration of April 1984. Bilateral free-trade agreements were signed between the EU and EFTA states and most tariffs between the two communities were abolished by 1977, except for agricultural products. By 1983, all nonagricultural trade became tariff free. The resulting free-trade area was known as the European Economic Space (EES). The Luxembourg Declaration, which followed the first ministerial meeting further expanded on the EES idea. The Delors Commission then acted upon the plan. According to René Schwok, "The event that triggered the new development of the EEA was the speech of

TABLE 10.2 The European Union's external trade for selected regions (percent of total)

	1958	1980	1989
Imports by origin:			
EFTA	14	17	23
US	18	17	19
Japan	1	5	11
Eastern Europe	6	8	6
Exports to:			
EFTA	20	25	27
US	13	13	19
Japan	1	2	5
Eastern Europe	7	9	6

source: Eurostat, External Trade Statistics Yearbook 1989 and 1990.

January 17, 1989, by Jacques Delors to the European Parliament in which he proposed to EFTA 'a new form of association, with common decision making and administrative institutions.' At that time, Jacques Delors reactivated the EEA in order to avoid the [EC's] historic mission—political union—being endangered by neutral members. In January 1989, before the end of Communism in Europe, Jacques Delors was especially unenthusiastic about attempts by Austria, a neutral country, to apply for [EC] membership."[23]

With the collapse of communism in Europe, concerns about neutral countries' impact on EU security policies largely disappeared. After 16 months of negotiations, the two communities agreed to create the world's largest trading area, the EEA. The original agreement, initially encompassing 19 European states[24] and 380 million citizens, called for the free flow of capital, services, workers and most goods throughout the EEA as of January 1, 1993—at the time when the Single Market would take effect. This new trade area accounted for 46 percent of total world trade.

The original agreement stated that products originating in the 19 EU and EFTA countries would move freely throughout the EEA beginning on January 1, 1993. However, some restrictions on agricultural products, fish, energy, coal, and steel would remain in effect. At the same time, both the EU and individual EFTA countries would maintain their individual tariff schedules for imports from third parties. Furthermore, the EFTA countries would remain outside of CAP and maintain their own, even more projectionist, agricultural policies.[25] As the data in Table 10.3 show, farm subsidies in EFTA average much higher on a per capita basis than in the EU. The last three columns, in terms of per person, show how much each individual in each country is subsidizing farms, both in taxes and by spending more for food than necessary.

The agreement also specified that EFTA would adopt some 1,500 EU laws and rules on "competition, anti-trust, abuse of dominant position, public procurement and state aid, company regulations, consumer protection, education,

TABLE 10.3 Transfers to agriculture, 1991

	Total $billion	Taxpayer $ per head	Consumer $ per head	Total $ per head
EU	142	168	241	409
Austria	4.1	143	381	524
Finland	5.9	460	677	1,137
Sweden	3.6	100	316	416
Norway	4.2	493	494	987
Switzerland	6.4	236	689	925

SOURCE: "Survey: The European Union," *The Economist,* July 11, 1992, p. 22.

environment, research and development, and social policy."[26] As a control mechanism for compliance with these changes and also as a judicial body to settle disputes, an independent EU-EFTA tribunal would be established. Other points of the agreement include:

1. Institutions: Decisions in the EEA will be made by a European Economic Area Council of Ministers, which will meet at least once every six months.

2. Workers: From 1993, individuals should be able to live, work, and offer services throughout the 19 (now 18) countries. Professional diplomas, such as those of architects or physicians, will be recognized throughout the area.

3. Trucks: The EU agreed with Austria to cut truck emissions by 60 percent over 12 years. Other EU transport legislation would apply to EFTA countries, including EU rules increasing competition in the air transport sector.

4. Money: EFTA will put 1.5 billion ECU's in low-interest loans and 500 million ECU's in grants into a "cohesion fund" to help poorer EU members Spain, Portugal, Greece, and Ireland. The money must be used for environmental and educational projects.[27]

EFTA members supported the EEA because it accelerated accession to EU membership. Given the fact that about 61 percent of EFTA imports came from the EU and 55 percent of EFTA exports went to EU countries, these countries could not afford to be left outside the Single Market.[28] For the EU, the EEA stood to increase the EU's economic power base, and thus promote its status and influence in Europe and in the world.

Despite initial enthusiasm about the EEA, the agreement suffered some setbacks. First, the agreement was sent back to the negotiation table because of a reservation registered by the ECJ. The crucial concern of the Court was about the proposed joint EU-EFTA tribunal, which would include 5 of the 13 judges of the ECJ, to resolve EEA-related disagreements. This proposal raised the question whether the EU judges of the joint tribunal would still be allowed to rule on an EU case if a similar case was already decided by the previous body. The problem ended when the EU foreign ministers agreed to give the Commission more negotiating flexibility with EFTA by dropping the demand that EFTA countries apply EU laws uniformly under the EEA. The EU decided to drop the idea of the joint court envisaged under the EEA accord and proposed an arbitration procedure to settle any future disputes between the two communities. In return, EFTA members agreed to adopt future EU single market legislation.

The second problem with the EEA was the Swiss rejection of the accord. This rejection came after Austria, Finland, Norway, and Sweden ratified the EEA and the ratification process was fully underway in the EU member states. Furthermore, the EP had approved the agreement. The Swiss rejection destroyed the chances of the EEA's starting on the same day as the Single Market and required renegotiating of the original accord to exclude Switzerland from the document. The EU Commission proposed a revised document on March 9, 1993, and the foreign ministers of the member states of the EU and EFTA signed it on March 17, 1993. The revised accord allowed the Swiss to enter the EEA at a later date if they so desired and called for the remaining members of EFTA to cover 60 percent of Switzerland's planned contribution to the cohesion fund.[29] Related to this development, the tiny Liechtenstein needed to reformulate its own agreements with Switzerland if it intended to join the EEA.

Following these developments, the remaining four EFTA countries entered into membership talks with the EU and completed the terms for accession on March 1, 1994, (Austria, Finland, and Sweden) and March 15, 1994, (Norway). The delay in the Norwegian case involved resolving the controversy over fishing rights between this country and the Union. In addition, other disputes existed between these candidates and the EU: agricultural transition measures, contributions to the EU budget, and Alpine transit routes for international trucking.[30] With regard to agriculture, the applicants agreed to harmonize their agricultural prices with those found in the EU and to pay compensation to farmers where prices would fall sharply. The financing for this would come from national budgets.

As for financial contributions to the EU budget, Sweden wanted to avoid shocks that could result from sudden and large transfers to Brussels. At the end of negotiations, the EU agreed that budget contributions by EFTA countries could be phased in. Alpine trucking, on the other hand, became a serious environmental concern for both Austria and Switzerland. Switzerland decided to deal with this problem by banning all international truck-trafficking through its borders after 2004.[31] This decision threatened the volume of such traffic through Austria, and the problem would become even more significant after Austria's accession to the EU. Bowing to Austrian pressures, the EU agreed to Austria's transit controls until 2004 unless significant environmental improvements occur in the Alpine region.

Despite these substantive agreements, the problem of voting majorities in the Council of Ministers (see chapter 5) threatened to derail the entire enlargement plan, and the complete package required ratification by the EP and the citizens of the respective candidate states in national referendums. But necessary approval of the expansion was reached in the Council and the EP. It was agreed that the voting issue would be reexamined at the 1996 IGC. This conference would focus on the institutional changes necessary for an EU of 20 or more member countries. The applicants scheduled their referenda for June 12, 1994, (Austria) and October 16, November 13, and November 28, 1994, respectively for Finland, Sweden, and Norway.[32] On June 12, 1994, the Austrians voted by a 2 to 1 margin in favor of joining the Union. This vote provided some boost to the position of the pro-Unionists in other candidate countries, and the referenda were adopted by Finnish and Swedish voters in the fall. However, Norwegian voters rejected membership in the EU by a majority of 52.2 percent to 47.8 percent.[33] As a result of these referenda, the EU membership expanded by three on January 1, 1995. *The Economist* provides an excellent overview of the significance of the latest expansion for the EU:

> The accession of Austria, Finland, and Sweden to the European Union on January 1st has added around 7% to the EU's GDP and 6% to its population. It is a bigger and more populous economy than either America or Japan. However, the three countries of the North American Free Trade Agreement (America, Canada, and Mexico) have a combined GDP 4 % larger than the EU's and a mere 1 % more citizens. But whereas the EU is a single market, NAFTA is far less integrated. Workers cannot move freely between NAFTA countries; members of NAFTA still, unlike EU countries, take anti-dumping actions against each other; and America, Canada, and Mexico set their own tariffs, while there is a common tariff on imports to the EU.[34]

The impact of this latest enlargement on the EU's position in the global economy is substantial. As Figure 10.3 shows, the EU's share in global development assistance increased to 53 percent of world aid. The EU's currency reserves now account for 32 percent of global reserves, and the EU's auto production constitutes 27 percent of global production. Moreover, the EU's economic performance reached one quarter of world economic performance. In areas of exports, energy consumption, and contribution to global air pollution, the EU's share is around 20 percent.

Relations with East-central Europe

Recent democratization in east-central Europe served as a catalyst to refashion EU policies toward this region. Soon after the collapse of the communist regimes, the EU initiated an economic reconstruction program for the newly emerging democratic states. This initiative resulted, in part, from a call in July 1989 by

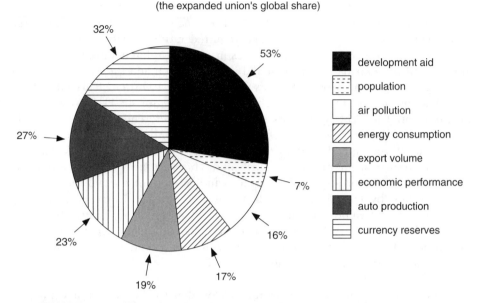

(the expanded union's global share)

32% 53%

27%

7%

23% 16%

19% 17%

- development aid
- population
- air pollution
- energy consumption
- export volume
- economic performance
- auto production
- currency reserves

FIGURE 10.3 The expanded European Union in the world

SOURCE: *The Week in Germany,* January 6, 1995, p. 1.

the G-7 countries to the Commission to coordinate the Western countries' support for political and economic reforms in east-central Europe.[35] The initial program, known as PHARE, called for assistance to Hungary and Poland. Later, the program expanded to include other east-central European states as they abandoned communism. The scope of the program also expanded from development credit to cooperation and reconstruction. Finally, the EU went a step further and proposed a global policy, similar in nature to the Global Mediterranean Policy (see the following discussion), which emphasizes the importance of establishing mutual association relationships with the east-central European states. The prerequisites for establishing such relationships, on the part of the ex-communist states, are political democratization and economic reforms toward a market system. According to Françoise de la Serre, "more than anything else, the experience the [EU] has accumulated in terms of trade and cooperation policy with third countries or in the field of operations (food aid, for example) has allowed it to become the privileged interlocutor for eastern Europe."[36] The program developed by the EU Commission to help east-central Europe has four major points:

1. Trade liberalization to establish a free trade area with Eastern Europe
2. Industrial, technical, and scientific cooperation
3. A program of financial assistance
4. The creation of a system of political dialogue.[37]

One year after negotiations started with the new democracies, the EU initiated Europe agreements with Czechoslovakia, Hungary, and Poland, known as the Visegrad countries because on February 15, 1991, a Hungarian-Polish-Czechoslovak summit was held in Visegrad (a small town at the Danube bend in Northern Hungary). At this summit, the Hungarian Prime Minister Jozsef Antall, the Polish President Lech Walesa, and the Czech President Václav Havel signed a comprehensive agreement to cooperate in their efforts to attain EU membership for their countries by the end of this century. While these agreements are similar in scope to the association agreements which helped Greece, Portugal, and Spain to join the Union, they have one important difference in that there is no timetable set for membership in the EU. Since the split of Czechoslovakia, the EU renegotiated the Europe Agreements with the Czech Republic and Slovakia. Since then, the EU has signed two more Europe Agreements with Bulgaria (1992) and Romania (1992).

The three agreements are similar in their structures but vary in content according to the specific needs of each country. For example, the agreements with Hungary and Poland stress that these countries are more dependent on agricultural exports and, consequently, are more vulnerable to EU's CAP restrictions than are the Czech Republic and Slovakia. Over time, these countries will adapt their administrative laws to comply with Union legislation—particularly the competition laws. In the meantime, the three countries will continue to receive financial assistance for technical training through the PHARE program and the EBRD.

In addition to the Europe agreements, there are interim agreements signed between the EC and Visegrad and other east-central European countries covering the trade and related questions of the association agreements. These did not require ratification by the EC's 12 national parliaments and became effective on March 1, 1992.[38] They are for a duration of 10 years, except that the agreement with Poland is for 5 years. They aim at the development and diversification of trade, the promotion of commercial relations, and economic cooperation between these countries and the EU. In essence, these interim and association agreements aim for normalization of the commercial and economic relations between the EU and the east-central European countries. However, there are certain problems in the way they are interpreted and applied by the EU. In a survey of the EU, *The Economist* explains:

> The essence of the Europe agreements is that they will "gradually" establish a free-trade area between the [EU] and [Visegrad countries] over a transition period . . . and that this mutual opening will be asymmetric—the [EU] will do more in the first five years, the trio in the second. . . . The commitment does not hold for farm products, which, in Hungary's case, currently account for one-quarter of its exports to the [EU]. Hungary will be permitted to sell just 5,000 tonnes of beef to the [Union]. This annual allowance will rise to 6,600 tonnes over five years. In the mid-1970s Hungary was selling a smaller [EU] some 100,000 tonnes of beef a year, paying whatever levies the [EU] was charging to bring imported beef up to the CAP price. [39]

Similar restrictions are also found for nonfarm products, such as steel, textiles, and clothing that fall into the sensitive industry categories of the Union. All of the Visegrad countries are affected by these restrictions.

Scope of the Aid Program. The scale of the economic and financial aid package for east-central Europe is very large. On December 18, 1989, the EU allocated 300 million ECUs, through Regulation 3606/89, for the financing of projects aimed at the economic restructuring of Poland and Hungary and, on September 17, 1990, the Council of Ministers passed Regulation 2698/90, amending Regulation 3906/89, to extend assistance to other east-central European countries.[40] Part of the aid package is nonreimbursable and the remaining is in the form of loans. For 1990, the nonreimbursable part was 500 million ECUs; for 1991, 850 million ECUs; and for 1992, the allocation was around 1 billion ECUs (see Table 10.4).[41] Loans, on the other hand, come in different forms and from a variety of sources. Initially, the Union granted a medium-term loan of a maximum amount of 870 million ECUs to Hungary and 375 million ECUs to Czechoslovakia, contingent upon credit approval by the IMF. The European Investment Bank (EIB) was given permission to grant loans to countries belonging to the PHARE program. Furthermore, the newly created EBRD, modeled after the International Bank for Reconstruction and Development (the World Bank), became operational on April 15, 1991, with a capital stock of 10 billion ECUs designed for assisting development projects in east-central Europe.

TABLE 10.4 PHARE aid granted in 1992

Sector	ECU million*
Agriculture	85.0
Private sector development, small business	91.5
Financial sector	5.0
Environment and nuclear safety	90.0
Social development, labor, and health	60.0
Education, training, research and development	140.5
Infrastructure: energy, telecoms, transport, etc.	70.4
Public administration and institutions, including customs, statistics, foreign trade	71.0
Integrated regional development measures	92.5
Humanitarian and emergency aid	156.5
GTAF and others	153.1
TOTAL	1,015.5

*The country allocation of this aid is as follows: Albania, 110.0 m; Bulgaria, 87.5 m; the Czech and Slovak republics, 100.0 m; Estonia, 100.0 m; Hungary, 98.5 m; Latvia, 15.0 m; Lithuania, 20.0 m; Poland, 200.0 m; Romania, 152 m; Slovenia, 9.0 m; Other ex-Yugoslavia, 49.0; Regional cooperation, 116.0 m; other programs, 48.0.
SOURCE: "EU Aid to the East," *The Economist,* April 10, 1993, p. 22. © 1993 The Economist Newspaper Group, Inc. Reprinted with permission. Further reproduction prohibited.

In addition to the PHARE program for east-central Europe, the EU also finances a technical training program for the economic restructuring of Russia and assists economic development in the Commonwealth of Independent States (CIS, ex-Soviet Union) through the EU's TACIS program (see Table 10.5). In 1992, the TACIS budget was 510 million ECUs, of which 450.1 million was distributed. Together, the PHARE and TACIS programs supply about 70 percent of the West's technical assistance to the former Soviet bloc.[42]

Extending the European Union Eastward

At the Essen meeting of the European Council during December 9–10, 1994, the EU leaders agreed to prepare six east-central European countries (Poland, Hungary, Czech Republic, Slovakia, Bulgaria, and Romania) for accession to full membership.[43] While the EU made this commitment, it also stated that accession negotiations with these countries would not start until after the 1996 IGC to review the state of the Maastricht treaty. The new president of the Commission Jacques Santer also reaffirmed the Essen decision in his address to the EP on January 17, 1995.[44] It is also important to note that, the host of the Essen Summit, German Chancellor Helmut Kohl, invited the heads of government of these east-central European countries to attend the meeting. Despite the initial enthusiasm, however, the EU also decided to lay down the groundwork for these countries to attain accession.

According to the EU decision, the Commission will produce a White Paper by June 1995, defining the main clauses of the *acquis communautaire* (the EU's

TABLE 10.5 TACIS aid granted in 1992

CIS Country	ECU million	Sectoral Distribution (all CIS)	ECU million
Armenia	9.5	Central government	36.8
Azerbaijan	12.5	Agriculture and food	59.7
Belorussia	14.6	Energy	119.8
Georgia	9.0	Transport	33.2
Kazakhistan	20.6	Telecommunications	6.8
Kirgizia	9.2	Privatization, finance, small business	80.5
Moldova	9.0	Human resources	41.5
Russia	111.0	Others	71.8
Turkmenistan	8.8		
Ukraine	48.2		
Uzbekistan	18.7		
Other non-national programs	179.0		
TOTAL	450.1		450.1

SOURCE: "EU Aid to the East," *The Economist*, April 10, 1993, pp. 22–23. © 1993 The Economist Newspaper Group, Inc. Reprinted with permission. Further reproduction prohibited.

regulations and laws) that the candidates must adopt before entering the single market of labor, goods, and capital. The Commission will then follow this White Paper with an annual assessment report of each country's performance. In addition, the EU asked the six candidates to expand their economic ties with the Union and with one another through promotion of investment and regional trade.

Reforming east-central European countries' laws and economies is not the only prerequisite for expanding the EU. As we explained in chapter 8, the EU might have to reexamine CAP before these countries enter the Union. Figure 10.4, providing comparative statistics for agricultural output and employment in these six countries and the EU, makes it clear that the six east-central European countries will increase the budgetary problems of CAP. It took the EU more than a decade to reform CAP and reduce its burden on the Union's budget. As we noted in chapter 8, the long-term cost of extending CAP to these countries would be 23–27 billion ECUs or a 70 percent increase in farm subsidies. Furthermore, four separate academic studies on an agricultural policy for a wider

FIGURE 10.4 Share of agriculture in east-central European economies, 1993

SOURCE: "Preparing to Join the Club," *The Economist,* August 20, 1994, p. 42.

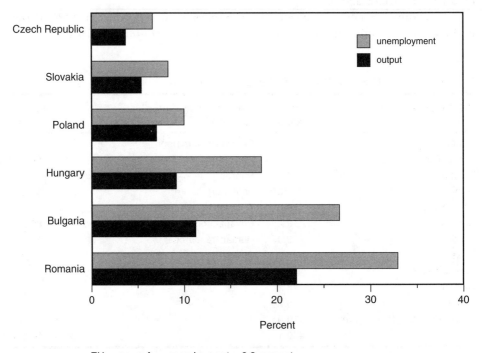

EU average for unemployment = 6.2 percent
EU average for output = 2.6 percent

EU assessed different options for the future and argued that reform of CAP was a necessary precondition to expansion of membership. The reports stated that necessary CAP reforms must include the following:

1. No support prices or support prices close to world market levels
2. Further decoupling of compensatory payments from production and their reduction over time
3. National responsibility for income support payments and payments for environmental services
4. Programs for action for the entrant countries ahead of accession, including such issues as implementing a strategy of low support and protection for farmers, improving competitiveness in the agricultural sector by widening the scope of private market participants, improving rural banking to overcome liquidity problems in agriculture, and establishment of common agricultural market among the six.[45]

Whereas these reports highlight potential agricultural problems, the outgoing EU farm commissioner, Rene Steichen, argued that the Union could expand its membership eastward without having to reform CAP.[46] Steichen maintained that the reforms of CAP, already achieved in 1992, satisfied the current needs of the EU, including the expansion issue. He rejected the cost estimation of enlargement and argued that "the extension of the CAP, with a transition period of about ten years and with price stabilization policies in place prior to accession, could be financed from the existing EU budget."[47] The position taken by Steichen is highly questionable given the history of agricultural policy problems in these east-central European countries. Unless these countries adopt very harsh economic adjustment policies to comply with new CAP regulations, their accession will cost heavy additional expenditures from the EU budget.

The European Union's Global Mediterranean Policy

The Mediterranean countries are the EU's third largest customer and its fourth largest supplier of imports, including roughly 20 percent of its energy needs. The Global Mediterranean Policy (GMP), adopted at the 1972 Paris Summit, has been the blueprint for the EU's relations with the nonmember Mediterranean Basin countries (NMBCs). This policy, aiming to promote closer trade and financial relations between the Union and the NMBCs, shifted the then EC's bilateral relations with each country in the region to the EU's multilateral approach treating the Mediterranean Basin as a single region (see Table 10.6).

There were political as well as economic motives for the then EC's approach to the Mediterranean Basin. The strategy called for using economic power to promote regional stability, to improve trade relations between the Community and the Mediterranean states, and to check Soviet expansionism in the region.[48] However, despite such ambitions several problems stood in the way of the GMP. First, the economies of the EC and the NMBCs were not sufficiently compatible

TABLE 10.6 Agreements between the European Union and the Mediterranean Basin countries

Association under Article 238		Cooperation Agreements		Preferential Trade Agreements		Nonpreferential Trade Agreements	
Greece	1961	Israel	1975	Spain	1970	Israel	1964
Turkey	1964	Maghreb[1]	1976	Israel	1970	Lebanon	1965
Morocco	1969	Mashrek[2]	1977	Egypt	1972	Yugoslavia	1970
Tunisia	1969	Yugoslavia	1980	Lebanon	1972	Yugoslavia	1973
Malta	1970			Portugal	1972		
Cyprus	1972						

[1]Algeria, Morocco, and Tunisia.
[2]Egypt, Lebanon, Jordan, and Syria.
SOURCE: Kevin Featherstone, "The Mediterranean Challenge: Cohesion and External Preferences," in Lodge, Juliet, ed., *The European Community and the Challenge of the Future* (New York: St. Martin's, 1989), p. 187. Copyright © Lodge, Juliet. Reprinted with permission of St. Martin's Press, Incorporated.

to promote the desired level of trade. Second, while the industrial products of the NMBCs received easy access to EC markets, agricultural goods were not included in the GMP because of the CAP. Third, even in industrial products, key exports of the NMBCs faced quota restrictions (e.g., textiles and clothing, shipping, steel, synthetic fibers, paper and paper products, machine tools, and cars) because the EC labeled these industries as "sensitive industries" that required Community protection. And finally, there was the question of the migrant workers from the NMBCs. The EC viewed this issue as a potential problem if not controlled.[49]

The problems of the GMP further intensified with the memberships of Greece, Portugal, and Spain in the Union. According to Alfred Tovias, these countries' membership resulted in making the EC more Mediterranean-like, resembling newly industrialized countries (like Israel and Turkey), with a very strong agricultural base.[50] Furthermore, studies have shown that the expansion of the Community into the northern Mediterranean and the adoption of various policies for the creation of a single market hampered the NMBCs' trade relations with the EC.[51] The problem is rather serious when we consider the structure of trade between the EU's Mediterranean members and the NMBCs:

> Despite some of the NMBCs' comparative export performance in certain agricultural goods, clothing and textiles, leather products, and footwear, they [NMBCs] have significant levels of export similarity indices with the new members of the [EU]. That is, these products are also produced and sold in [EU] markets by Greece, Portugal, and Spain. To make this issue even worse for the other Mediterranean basin countries, the commodities involved are in either low or medium demand in Commodity markets.[52]

As a result, the new Mediterranean members of the EU will continue to dominate the supply of these products to Union markets, thus reducing the likelihood of the other NMBCs increasing their exports of the same commodities.

In addition to trade, one other issue creates obstacles to the Union's relations with its Mediterranean neighbors, the problem of migrant workers in the various EU countries from the NMBCs. When the flow of workers reached its peak level in 1980, there were over 6 million guest workers and their families in the EC.[53] The largest number are workers from Turkey: 714,000 workers and their dependents, of whom 591,000 were found in Germany. At one time, the guest workers were welcomed in the EC states because they were willing to work in manual labor jobs the citizens did not want. However, after three serious economic recessions in the EC in 1974–1975, 1980–1983, and since 1991, the governments of the member states adopted strict controls for the influx of guest workers and refugees (particularly the asylum seekers in Germany). Militant right-wing extremists in the recipient countries began to target these foreigners for violent attacks, causing many deaths and serious injuries. Given the extent of the problems between the EU and NMBC, the Union decided to re-address its GMP in order to improve relations with these countries.

On April 25, 1990, the vice-president of the Brussels Commission, Frans Andriessen, stated that there was a need to re-address the GMP because "increasingly closer geopolitical rather than political links will be forged between the Mediterranean countries in the coming decades [and] the European Community will be involved in this process."[54]

In order to address these policy concerns, the Council called for a four-stage program: a blueprint for the construction of the new Mediterranean policy. The first stage called for adoption of an EU position paper setting out general guidelines for revitalizing the Mediterranean policy. During the second stage, a Mediterranean Forum, consisting of EC and the NMBC representatives, should be established to prepare specific guidelines for sectoral policies, for launching of major pilot development agreements, and for coordination and support over member states' policies towards the region. The third stage would involve the establishment of a center or agency which will provide technical support for the development agreements. And finally, the EU-NMBCs' joint development convention should convene to establish specific institutions for the above purposes.[55]

In accordance with the guidelines, the Commission, upon the request of the Council of Ministers, proposed a policy package on the GMP which included economic and technical assistance to the NMBCs, improving the nonmembers' access to EC markets, and promoting direct foreign investment in the Mediterranean Basin.[56] But how cohesive are the EC members on this issue? Since joining the Union, Spain, Portugal, and Greece have actively tried to influence EU policies toward the NMBCs to minimize the potential trade competition the new Union members would face from the nonmembers in the EU markets. In recent years, France and Italy also entered the argument on the side of their Mediterranean EU neighbors. The UK, the Netherlands, and Germany favor greater opening of conditions of access to the EU markets for imports from the NMBCs, whereas

France, Greece, Italy, Spain, and Portugal lean toward maintaining current trade flows. According to Alfred Tovias:

> Both Spain and Portugal will try to maximize trade diversion in wine, fruit, and vegetables by proposing modifications in the CAP, but not necessarily in the highly visible Mediterranean Policy. Both will strongly defend the principle of [Union] preference in agriculture, which can only mean more protectionism against other Mediterranean producers of fruit, vegetables, and olive oil. All this implies a further raising of fences between the [Union] and the Mediterranean Basin, a very dangerous strategy for the [Union] because of its energy dependence on the area as well as the importance of the basin's market for European goods and services.[57]

The positions of the three newest Mediterranean members regarding EU-NMBC relations are indeed crucial for the EU not only because of energy and market dependence but also because of geopolitical considerations. The recent Gulf crisis proved how important the region is for the security interests of the Union. The proposals of the Economic and Social Council and the EU Commission are aimed at minimizing such problems. Their efforts seem to have produced some modest results.

In September 1990, the Mediterranean members of the EC, led by the Italian Foreign Minister Gianni De Michelis, called for the establishment of a conference on security and cooperation in the Mediterranean,[58] modeled after the Conference on Security and Cooperation in Europe. The Italian and Spanish officials feared that growing economic and demographic disparity between the EC and the NMBCs would be damaging to the long-term interests of the EC. While they argued that such a conference should include all of the eastern Mediterranean states, even extending to the Persian Gulf and Iran, the French maintained that the cooperation ought to start with a more narrow focus, namely the Maghreb (Morocco, Algeria, and Tunisia). Despite the appearance of some differences in approach to the GMP, it is clear that Mediterranean Basin has once again become one of the important issues on EU agenda and the Commission prepared a draft plan, "Vers une Politiques Mediterraneenne Renovee: Propositions pour la Périod 1992-96," for renovating the GMP.

The EU leaders provided some answers at the June 1994 summit meeting in Corfu, Greece. At this meeting, the EU leaders invited the Commission to draft a new southern strategy for the Mediterranean Basin.[59] The Commission's response came in the form of a proposal for creating the biggest free trade zone in the world, including the EU and its North African and Middle Eastern neighbors. According to the EU Commissioner for Mediterranean Affairs Manuel Marin:

> . . . in broad terms, what we would be offering is something like the EEA. . . . The main difference would be that whereas four of the seven members of EFTA—Austria, Finland, Sweden and Norway—are poised

to enter the Union next year, membership would not be on offer to Euro-Med partners [except Cyprus, Malta, and Turkey].[60]

The Commission's proposal received support from the EU leaders at the Essen Summit. At this meeting, the EU reiterated its support for a Euro-Mediterranean partnership with a long-term goal of free trade. This goal will be reexamined at a Euro-Mediterranean ministerial meeting in the later half of 1995. Despite these decisions, whether the GMP will be revitalized to everyone's liking or not remains uncertain. It is quite possible that if Cyprus, Malta, and Turkey join the EU, the GMP with all of the above initiatives would suffer once more, just as it did following the memberships of Greece, Portugal, and Spain.

The Applications of Cyprus, Malta, and Turkey

Turkey applied for EU membership in 1987, and Malta and Cyprus placed their applications in July 1990. In terms of the conditions for membership in the EU, all three countries display some problems suggesting that the EU would not be in a hurry to accept them. On May 18, 1989, the European Commission concluded that the Union was not ready to enter into accession talks with Turkey because the Turkish economy was not as developed as the EU's, the Turkish democracy lacked extensive individual civil and political rights, and unemployment in Turkey posed a serious threat to the Union markets.[61] An additional and very serious problem in Turkey's case is the ongoing Greek-Turkish conflict over Cyprus, territorial waters, the Aegean airspace, the continental shelf, and the rights of the Greek and Turkish minorities in their respective countries. Given the extent of this conflict, Greece would veto Turkey's membership in the EU even if the latter were to meet all of the conditions for membership. With regard to Cyprus and Malta, the Commission report to the European Council at the Lisbon Summit in June 1992 made it very clear that these countries would not be among the first wave of countries joining the EU.[62] Let us now look at each case in light of the EU conditions for membership.

Evaluation of the Turkish case shows that on geographic grounds Turkey has always been considered a European country but that there is some debate on how European Turkey is. Turkey is a member of all of the Western European intergovernmental organizations—the OECD (1948), the Council of Europe (1949), NATO (1952)—an associate member of the EU (1963) and an associate member of the WEU (1992). The problems with restrictions on individual civil and political rights, found in the country's 1982 Constitution, do present an obstacle for its accession to EU membership. However, the postcoup political order in Turkey (since November 1983) is gradually becoming more reliably democratic, reflecting the increasingly pluralistic nature of the Turkish society.[63] Furthermore, in June 1993, Turkey became one of the few Western democracies to have a woman head of government. Supporters of Turkey's application argue that this country's membership in the Union would serve to strengthen Turkish democracy similar to the previous experiences with Greece, Portugal, and Spain.

The economic conditions in Turkey provide both positive and negative arguments for the accession to membership. The negative conditions are: high inflation, high unemployment, and low GNP per capita. Most importantly, Turkey would qualify for 5.4 billion ECUs from the EU budget as regional aid, based on the criteria used by the Union in paying out 7.4 billion ECUs of regional aid, also known as structural funds, to the member countries in 1991.[64] This figure is simply too costly for the Union at a time when the member states are facing recession and Germany is facing problems stemming from German unification. The high unemployment level, which was around 20 percent in Turkey in 1993, also concerns EU officials. The Union and Turkey have agreed, through the Ankara Agreement (an association agreement) of 1963 and the Additional Protocol of 1970, to allow free movement of labor between the EU countries and Turkey after a transition period, which ended in 1986. However, fearing that the Turkish workers would flood EC countries, the Community backed away from this commitment in 1987.[65] Finally, Turkey's exports of agricultural products and textiles to the Union are very similar to the exports of Greece and Portugal.

On a positive note, the Turkish economy is compatible with that of the Union. Since 1980, Turkey has successfully restructured and reoriented its economy from import-substitution to an export-oriented strategy. With a more realistic exchange rate regime, government export promotion policies, and liberalization of foreign investment, Turkey's economy grew rapidly, exports and direct foreign investment increased significantly, and the share of manufactured products in GNP and in exports rose substantially. As a result, the current account balance emerged from its perennial deficit in 1990.[66] Furthermore, strategic considerations also favor Turkey's position. The breakdown of the Soviet Union opened up vast economic opportunities for Turkey in the Central Asian republics. Given the racial, linguistic, cultural, and historical ties between the Turks and the peoples of Central Asia, Turkey has the potential to influence the future economic and political orientations of these new republics. The West also stands to gain by keeping Turkey closely tied to the Western world and serving as a bridge between the West and Central Asia.

In light of these complex issues, the EU is not likely to reject Turkey's application for membership. However, since immediate Turkish membership is also out of the question, the likely result was to extend the association agreement with a future date for Turkey to reapply for membership in the Union. A unique solution emerged in the form of a customs union (CU) agreement between Turkey and the Union.

However, the apparent problems with the Turkish accession became very clear during the meeting of the EU and Turkish officials over Turkey's desire to enter into a customs union with the EU. The Turks have been planning the customs union as a measure that would ease Turkey's accession to the Union. Yet, despite the decision of 11 EU members to sign the CU agreement, Greece vetoed it at the EU Council of Ministers meeting on December 19, 1994. This was the second veto by Greece to block EU economic agreement with Turkey. Earlier in 1984, Greece vetoed and effectively blocked EC economic assistance to Turkey in the amount of 400 million ECUs. The Greek objections on the CU emphasized Turkey's alleged human rights abuse against the Kurds and the ongoing Cyprus problem. It became clear that Greece would not drop its objection to the customs union until the EU would set a date to enter into accession talks with Cyprus.[67]

The apparent deadlock threatened to damage the EU's relationship with Turkey. However, as a result of intense negotiations between the Union and Greece, under the leadership of the French Foreign Minister Alain Júppe, the parties reached a compromise on March 5, 1995, and EU-Turkey signed the CU agreement the following day. In exchange for lifting the veto, the Greek government asked for specific concessions from the EU:

1. That the EU agrees to enter into negotiations with Cyprus for membership six months after the end of the 1996 intergovernmental conference on the Maastricht treaty
2. That Cyprus participates in dialogues with the EU on the same level as that between the EU and East European states
3. That the EU provides monetary compensation to the Greek textile industry which stands loose due to competition from Turkish textiles in the EU markets
4. That the proposed monetary assistance to Turkey over five years, 1 billion ECUs, be reduced.[68]

The EU agreed to items 1–3 which satisfied the Greek government. The CU agreement with Turkey cleared the Council of Ministers and needs ratification by the European parliament.

This agreement assures Turkey of a closer relationship with the EU than any other nonmembers except Iceland and Norway. It also delays the accession issue for the foreseeable future. Finally, it provides high visibility support for Turkey's secular government. If ratified, the CU agreement takes effect on January 1, 1996. It calls for free movement of ECSC products and reciprocal concessions on agricultural products; macroeconomic dialogue to ensure the best economic environment possible for the functioning of the CU; broadening of cooperation on social matters, trans-European networks, energy, transport, telecommunication, environment, agriculture, science, statistics, home affairs, consumer protection, and cultural cooperation; political dialogue; and cooperation in institutional matters through the organization of consultative relations between Turkey and the EU especially in areas of a transeuropean nature.[69]

Cyprus and Malta

The cases of Cyprus and Malta do not present economic obstacles for accession to Union membership. Both economies are rather small and could be easily absorbed into the EU economy. Moreover, both states are considered European. On the political side, however, the two cases differ considerably. While the problem in the Maltese case only pertains to the disproportionate representation of a small country in EU institutions (e.g., the EP and votes in the Council of Ministers), the Cypriot case remains highly volatile. As explained above, the agreement between the EU, Turkey, and Greece resulted in a customs union between the Union and Turkey. Furthermore, the EU agreed to set the date to start accession talks with Cyprus. The Cyprus government, which is dominated by Greek Cypriots, believes that both communities of the Island (Greeks and Turks) will benefit from EU accession. However, the Turkish Cypriots and Turkey strongly disagree. Since July 1974, when Turkey intervened to protect the Turkish Cypriot minority and to prevent union of Cyprus with Greece, the Island has been divided into a Turkish Cypriot-controlled North, the Turkish Republic of Northern Cyprus (TRNC), and a Greek Cypriot-controlled South, the internationally recognized Cyprus Republic. The TRNC is only recognized by Turkey.

There is no doubt that the Cyprus problem has been one of the toughest issues for international negotiators to resolve. For its part, the EU is attempting to provide some assistance in resolving this issue while preparing for future accession talks with the Cyprus government. Some of these efforts have centered around bringing together representatives of the two communities in some formal discussions. For example, the EC, headed by Ivor Roberts, sponsored an all trade union forum in Cyprus in January 1995, to promote better understanding between the Greek Cypriot and Turkish Cypriot labor leaders. If the joint declaration is any indication of the willingness of the Cypriots to work out a solution to this problem, the EU might be able to settle the conflict. The joint declaration calls for:

1. A federal and democratic political system for Cyprus
2. One type system of employment and labor relations
3. A unitary system of Social Insurance
4. Unified standards of wages and salaries
5. Complete safeguarding of the rights of freedom of movement and freedom of choice of employment in any part of Cyprus coupled with entrenched right of freedom of organization
6. No discrimination whatsoever in employment, or emoluments arising in connection with ethnic origin, religion, color, or sex
7. A unitary economy.[70]

European Union Relations with the African, Caribbean, and Pacific Countries

The centerpiece of the EU-ACP relations is the Lomé IV Convention, signed on December 15, 1989, in the capital of Togo by the then EC and 68 African, Caribbean, and Pacific states, most of which were former European colonial territories. The number of ACP countries increased to 69 in 1990. The Lomé IV Convention is in the tradition of the earlier agreements between the two sides: Yaoundé I (1963), Yaoundé II (1969), Lomé I (1975), Lomé II (1979), and Lomé

III (1984). According to Catherine Flaesch-Mougin and Jean Raux, the Lomé IV Convention was "a symbol of continuity, renovation, and innovation."[71] The history of the Lomé conventions resembles that of the GMP in that the initial enthusiasm quickly gave way to cynicism. The conventions neither changed the basic structures of North-South relations nor improved economic conditions of the ACP countries. From the ACP point of view, the erosion of trade preferences through the EU's General System of Preferences (GSP) and GATT, combined with the refusal of the Union to open its markets to more imports from ACP countries, seriously damaged the trade and industrial cooperation agreements of these conventions. Furthermore, according to John Ravenhill, the aid aspect gradually replaced the commercial cooperation as the cornerstone of the Lomé agreements, because aid is far cheaper for the EC.[72] This development is clearly different from the experiences of the GMP countries where commercial relations dominate the agenda.

Problems with Earlier Agreements. Trade had been a major disappointment with the former conventions. For ACP countries, trade was of crucial importance because the EC was the principal trading partner for most of them. The Lomé conventions granted unilateral free access for ACP products to the EC markets without being subject to tariffs, quotas, or other restrictive regulations. However, there was a serious restriction concerning agricultural products that fall under the CAP.[73] Furthermore, the EC reserved the right to change trade policies in case of serious economic or trade imbalances of the EC members. Such regulations proved to be detrimental for products like textiles and clothing when the EC decided to label these industries as sensitive industries, subject to special protection. The ACP countries viewed these special clauses as indications of growing protectionism in the EU.

Other issues that undermined EC-ACP trade relations were the extension of the EC's GSP to all Less Developed Countries (LDC) and the tariff reductions in the EC in accordance with the Tokyo Round GATT negotiations. The net result was an increased influx of non-ACP products into the EC markets, which undermined the market share of ACP states. The EC attempted to stabilize export earnings of ACP states through two arrangements: the Commodity Export Earnings Stabilization Scheme (STABEX of Lomé I) and the Mineral Accident Insurance System (SYSMIN of Lomé II).

There is no doubt that the STABEX addressed an important problem of the ACP countries. Most of these countries were exporters of a single primary commodity: In 1975, 50 percent of the exports of 33 of the initial 46 countries to the EC were single commodity exporters.[74] As a result, these countries were especially vulnerable to fluctuations in commodity prices in the world markets. The STABEX scheme provided funds to exporters of primary commodities in case of shortfalls of export earnings because of external factors. The funds were to be paid back at terms favorable to ACP countries, and there was no reimbursement required for the poorest countries. After the Lomé I Convention, 60 percent of the funds were provided without reimbursement.[75] However, STABEX only covered exports to the EC, or to other ACP markets (added in Lomé II), and only covered raw materials or products. In addition, STABEX funds lacked transparency and were often used to help recipient governments' balance of payments deficits. Thus, during the Lomé III Convention, the participants agreed to use the funds explicitly for the purposes specified in the agreements. Despite these drawbacks, the STABEX scheme was a relative success. After the signing of the Lomé III agreements, the EC also developed a new facility, the COMPEX, for the least developed countries not signatories to the Lomé agreements. The size of COMPEX is less than one-tenth of STABEX but it functions in a manner similar to the latter.[76]

Finally, Lomé I–III provided multilateral funds, mainly through the European Development Fund (EDF) and the EIB for financial and technical assistance to ACP countries. Lomé I specified 3.5 billion ECUs for this purpose. Lomé II raised this figure to 5.6 billion ECUs and Lomé III further increased it to 8.5 billion ECUs. Yet, these increases are in reality decreases over time due to high population growth rates and inflation in ACP countries and the fact that the number of countries signing on to the Lomé conventions increased. Thus, there is a decline in financial assistance in real and per capita terms from Lomé I to Lomé II and from Lomé II to Lomé III.[77] Lomé IV attempted to find acceptable solutions to these problems through a revised cooperation model to encourage economic, social, and cultural development of the ACP countries.[78] The Convention's duration is 10 years.

Lomé IV Agreements. Under Lomé IV trade provisions remain unchanged from the previous Conventions; that is, ACP countries continue to have free access to EU markets without reciprocity. The trade arrangements, however, have been adjusted to provide better conditions for some ACP products.[79]

In addition, the STABEX and SYSMIN schemes were overhauled and redefined. The EU added cocoa derivatives, essential oil products, and squid to the program and lowered the threshold limit for its implementation. It was also agreed that in the future, the system would apply to cover commodities that make up 5 percent of an ACP country's total exports to EU and other ACP states. This figure would be 1 percent for the less developed countries. These figures were 6 percent and 1.5 percent respectively under Lomé III.[80] Furthermore, under Lomé IV, STABEX allocation increased by 66 percent from Lomé III figures to 1.4 billion ECUs. SYSMIN, on the other hand, extended product coverage to include uranium and gold.

The financial protocol of Lomé IV provided for 12 billion ECUs (10.8 billion from the EDF and 1.2 billion from the EIB) for aid to ACP states. Even though this is a substantial increase from the 8.5 billion ECUs provided under Lomé III, it is considerably less than the amount requested by ACP countries (15.5 billion ECUs). This protocol also included structural adjustment support for ACP countries in the amount of 1.15 billion ECUs. Although this figure is rather small, the decision of the EU to include such financing, along with international debt rescheduling, showed that the Union was prepared to assert itself as a principal financial actor in international economic restructuring alongside the World Bank and the IMF.[81]

Despite significant improvements of the Lomé agreements, ACP countries face an uncertain future in their relations with the EU after the creation of the Single Market. As the Union places greater emphasis on the deepening of integration, assistance to the new democracies of Eastern Europe, and accession of EFTA countries to EU membership, the ACP countries' preferential position is likely to be undermined in a way similar to the problem faced by the GMP countries. Realizing these dangers, the Commission unveiled plans on September 9, 1993 to overhaul the Lomé Convention.[82] Commissioner Manuel Martin, who was responsible for the reform package, argued that it was "'vital to introduce tighter controls to counter inefficiency and corruption, while bolstering democratic reform and the private sector.'"[83] The proposed reforms call for funds to target civil society and strengthen democratic institutions and the rule of law in the ACP countries. The desire of the EU to promote the growth of the private sector was also clear in this declaration. Commissioner Marin stated that "'it may be unfashionable to say so, but we need to create a national bourgeoisie in Africa.'"[84]

CONCLUSION

In this chapter, we examined issues pertaining to the expansion of the EU and its other external economic relations. The analysis clearly demonstrates that the EU has become a major player in the international political and economic system. Through its expansion to include Mediterranean and Nordic countries, coupled with special trade and assistance agreements with almost all of the other European periphery states, the EU stands as the most influential economic power in post-Cold War Europe. Further expansion of the Union will contribute to this influence. The next wave of expansion is likely to include Cyprus and the east-central European states of the Czech Republic, Hungary, Poland, and Slovakia by the end of this century.

The EU also improved its ties to the nonmember Mediterranean countries and ACP states by providing preferential trade agreements and generous aid packages. Over the last 2 decades, these various programs underwent reforms to reflect the changing needs of the recipient countries. It is clear from the nature of these interactions that the overall impact of such programs is their contribution to the Union's international status vis-à-vis the United States and Japan.

ENDNOTES

1. Frank McDonald, "The European Community and the USA and Japan," in McDonald and Stephen Dearden, eds., *European Economic Integration* (London and New York: Longman, 1992), p. 199.

2. John A. C. Conybeare, "1992, The Community, and the World: Free Trade or Fortress Europe?" in Dale L. Smith and James Lee Ray, eds., *The 1992 Project and the Future of Integration in Europe* (New York: M. E. Sharpe, 1993), p. 143.

3. "Foreign investment and the Triad," *The Economist,* August 24, 1991, p. 57.

4. Ibid.

5. Michael Smith "The United States and 1992: Responses to a Changing European Community," in John Redmond, ed., *The External Relations of the European Community: The International Response to 1992* (New York: St. Martin's Press, 1992), p. 31.

6. The G-7 group includes the industrialized Western economies of the world: the United States, Japan, Canada, the UK, Germany, France, and Italy. The heads of government of the G-7 meet annually to review the state of the world economy and to attempt to coordinate their macroeconomic policies.

7. *Eurecom,* 4.11 (December 1992): 1.

8. Ibid.

9. Ibid., p. 2.

10. *Eurecom,* 5.6 (June 1993): 2.

11. *Financial Times,* "EC positive about Nafta agreement," May 13, 1993.

12. Jorgen Estrup, *The EC-US Trade Relationship: The Challenge of the Future* (Brussels: North Atlantic Assembly, Economic Committee, 1993), p. 1.

13. Ibid.

14. Peter Holmes and Alasdair Smith, "The EC, the USA and Japan: The Trilateral Relationship in World Context," in David Dyker, ed., *The European Economy* (New York and London: Longman, 1992), pp. 189-96.

15. Ibid., pp. 201-202.

16. McDonald, "The European Community and the USA and Japan," p. 207.

17. According to a study by the World Economic Forum and IMD, a Swiss business school, Japan has come on top in the survey of world competitiveness for the eighth consecutive year despite its declining domestic business confidence and increasing protectionism. The United States rose from fifth to second place. Germany and the UK dropped in the rankings to fifth and sixteenth positions respectively. France was ranked twelfth. See "Economic and Social Indicators," *The Economist,* June 26, 1993.

18. McDonald, "The European Community and the USA and Japan," p. 211.

19. EC, Economic and Social Council. "Opinion on the Mediterranean Policy of the European Community," *Official Journal of the European Communities,* No. C221/16 (January 25, 1989).

20. Laurence Whitehead, "International Aspects of Democratization," in Guillermo O'Donnell, Philippe Schmitter, and Laurence Whitehead, eds., *Transition from Authoritarian Rule: Comparative Perspectives* (Baltimore: The Johns Hopkins University Press, 1988), p. 5; and Birol A. Yeşilada, "Prospects for Turkey's membership in the European Community," *International Journal of Turkish Studies* (forthcoming, 1995).

21. Birol A. Yeşilada, "Further Enlargement of the European Community: The Cases of the European Periphery States," *National Forum* (Spring 1992): 21-25.

22. "Survey: The European Community," *The Economist* (July 11, 1992): 17.

23. René Schwok, "EC-EFTA Relations," in Leon Hurwitz and Christian Lequesne, eds., *The State of the European Community: Policies, Institutions, and Debates in the Transition Years* (Boulder: Lynne Reinner, 1991), p. 329.

24. These countries are the EC-12 and Austria, Finland, Iceland, Liechtenstein, Norway, Sweden, and Switzerland. Switzerland, however, later chose to withdraw from the EEA as a result of a national referendum on the subject on December 6, 1992.

25. *Eurecom* 3.10 (November 1991): 1; "Lest a fortress arise," *The Economist*, October 26, 1991: pp. 61 and 81–82.

26. *Eurecom* 3.10 (November 1991): 1.

27. "Pact Expands Europe's Common Market," *The Wall Street Journal*, October 23, 1991: p. A10.

28. René Schwok, "The European Free Trade Association: Revival or Collapse?" in Redmond, ed, *The External Relations of the European Community*, p. 58.

29. *Eurecom* 5.3 (March 1993): 1.

30. *Eurecom* 6.3 (March 1994): 1.

31. Ibid.

32. Hugh Carnegy and Ian Rodger "Outsiders hit by a strain of Euro-fever," *Financial Times*, June 3, 1994, p. 2.

33. "Norwegian PM Warns of Tough Times Ahead as Voters Spurn EU," *Financial Times*, November 30, 1994, p. 1.

34. "A Wider Europe," *The Economist*, January 7, 1995, p. 88.

35. Marc Maresceau, "The European Community, Eastern Europe and the USSR," in Redmond, ed., *The External Relations of the European Community*, pp. 97–98.

36. Françoise de la Serre, "The EC and Central and Eastern Europe," in Hurwitz and Lequesne, eds., *The State of the European Community*, p. 310.

37. McDonald, Frank and Keith Penketh, "The European Community and the rest of Europe," in Frank McDonald and Stephen Dearden, ed., European Economic Integration (London: Longman, 1992), p. 193.

38. Commission of the European Communities. Directorate General. *EC-East Europe: Relations with Central and Eastern Europe and the Commonwealth of Independent States*, November 1992.

39. "Survey: The European Community," *The Economist*, July 11, 1992: 26.

40. Maresceau, "The European Community, Eastern Europe and the USSR," p. 97.

41. Ibid., p. 98.

42. In 1993, the EBRD, headed by Jacques Attali, came under fire from the bank's 41 owners—governments and some pan-European institutions—and the media for extravagant spending on renovation of the EBRD's London offices, high pay of its personnel, private jets, lavish parties, and failure to put enough emphasis on development assistance to the former Soviet bloc countries. Under such criticism, Attali stepped down as the EBRD director on June 25, 1993. See "After Attali," *The Economist*, July 3, 1993, p. 73.

43. "Essen Summit Endorses Eastern European Strategy," *Eurecom*, 6.11 (December): 1.

44. "Santer Steers Middle Course for EU," *Financial Times*, January 18, 1995, p. 3.

45. "Seeking an Agricultural Policy for a Wider EU," *Financial Times*, January 16, 1995, p. 2.

46. "Steichen Sees no Need for CAP Reform," *Financial Times*, January 17, 1995, p. 3.

47. Ibid.

48. Roy Ginsberg, "The European Community and the Mediterranean," in Juliet Lodge, ed., *Institutions and Policies of the European Community* (New York: St. Martin's, 1983), pp. 161–162.

49. Birol A. Yeşilada, "The EC's Mediterranean Policy," in Hurwitz and Lequesne, eds., *The State of the European Community*, p. 361.

50. Alfred Tovias, *Foreign Economic Relations of the European Community: The Impact of Spain and Portugal* (Boulder: Lynne Reinner, 1990), p. 2.

51. For detailed discussion of issues surrounding the second enlargement and trade with the NMBCs see J. Donges, et al., *The Second Enlargement of the European Community*

(Tübingen: J.C.B. Mohr, 1982); Richard Pomfret, "The Impact of EEC Enlargement on Non-member Mediterranean Countries' Exports to the EC," *The Economic Journal* 91 (September 1981): 726–729; George Yannopoulos, "Prospects for the Manufacturing Exports of the Non-candidate Mediterranean Countries in a Community of Twelve," *World Development* 12 (December 1984): 1087–1094; and Birol Yeşilada, "The Impact of the European Community's Second Enlargement and Project 1992 on Relations with the Mediterranean Basin," paper presented at the 1990 *Annual Meeting of the Midwest Political Science Association,* Chicago, April 5–7.

52. Yeşilada, "The Impact of the European Community's Second Enlargement."

53. EC, *The European Community and the Mediterranean* (Luxembourg: Office for Official Publications of the Communities, 1984), p. 100.

54. Frans H. J. J. Andriessen, "Europe at the Crossroads," presentation given at the 10th Annual Paul-Henri Spaak Lecture at Harvard University on April 25, 1990, pp. 11–12.

55. Yeşilada, "Further Enlargement of the European Community," p. 24.

56. EC, "EEC/Mediterranean Countries: Refurbishing the Mediterranean Policy," *External Relations,* No. 1544, November 29, 1989, as cited in Yeşilada, "The EC's Mediterranean Policy," p. 369.

57. Tovias, *Foreign Economic Relations of the European Community,* p. 108.

58. "The Second Trojan's Empire," *The Economist,* September 29, 1990, p. 57.

59. "Brussels Urges Wider Trade Zone," *Financial Times,* October 20, 1994, p. 2.

60. Ibid.

61. EC, *Commission Opinion on Turkey's Request for Accession to the Community,* Sec. (89) 2290 final (Brussels, December 18, 1989).

62. EC, "Report on the Criteria and Conditions for Accession of New Members to the Community," *Agence Europe, European Documents,* No. 1789, June 27, 1992.

63. Yeşilada, "Prospects for Turkey's Membership in the European Community."

64. "Survey: The European Community," *The Economist,* July 11, 1992, p. 17.

65. Richard Pomfret, "The European Community's Relations with the Mediterranean Countries," in John Redmond, ed., The External Relations of the European Community: *The International Response to 1992,* (New York: St. Martin's), p. 83.

66. Birol A. Yeşilada and Mahir Fisunoglu, "Assessing the January 24, 1980 Economic Stabilization Program in Turkey," in Henri Barkey, ed., *The Politics of Economic Reform in the Middle East* (New York: St. Martin's, 1992), p. 207.

67. "Delay for Turkey's EU Trade Pact," *Financial Times,* December 20, 1994, pp. 1, 16.

68. Athens News Agency Bulletin, February 20, 1995.

69. EC, *Association Between the European Community and Turkey,* The Association Council. March 3, 1995, CE-TR 106/95.

70. Provided to the author by Ivor Roberts.

71. Catherine Flaesch-Mougin and Jean Raux, "From Lomé III to Lomé IV: EC-ACP Relations," in Hurwitz and Lequesne, eds., *The State of the European Community,* p. 343.

72. John Ravenhill, *Collective Clientelism: The Lomé Conventions and North-South Relations* (New York: Columbia University Press, 1985), p. 330.

73. Ellen Frey-Wouters, *The European Community and the Third World: The Lomé Convention and Its Impact* (New York: Praeger, 1980), p. 37.

74. Ravenhill, *Collective Clientelism,* p. 9.

75. Joanna Moss, *The Lomé Conventions and their Implications for the United States* (Boulder: Westview, 1982), p. 90.

76. Robert S. Walters and David H. Blake, *The Politics of Global Economic Relations,* 4th ed. (Englewood Cliffs: Prentice-Hall, 1992), p.54.

77. For a detailed discussion see Ravenhill, *Collective Clientelism.*
78. Cosgrove, Carol and Pierre-Henri Laurent, "The Unique Relationship: The European Community and the ACP," in John Redmond, ed., *The External Relations of the European Community,* p. 121.
79. Flaesch-Mougin and Raux, "From Lomé III to Lomé IV," p. 351. For a detailed discussion of the specifics of these trade policies see Cosgrove and Laurent, "The Unique Relationship."
80. Cosgrove and Laurent, "The Unique Relationship," pp. 351-352.
81. Ibid., p. 130.
82. "EC hopes to reform Lomé Convention," *Financial Times,* September 10, 1993, p. 3.
83. Ibid.
84. Ibid.

chapter 11

Common Foreign and Domestic Security Policies

$\mathbf{W}$e now return to the aspects of nation-state responsibilites that are at the very heart of what is called sovereignty. If the EU is to become a federal system of government, it will have to take over responsibility for foreign and security policy from the member states. Until that time, the EU will remain a confederation, with important economic and social policy responsibilities, as reviewed in chapters 7–10. But it will be confined essentially to the role of serving as a forum wherein member governments can discuss foreign and security (including internal security) policy matters. However, federalists hope that, in time, as integration deepens, the security element of each state will become less important than the overall security of the larger community. The members of the EU find themselves in a weak security community that is taking on more definite institutional shape. The second pillar of the Maastricht treaty, the CFSP, represents a major step forward in EPC, because it merges political and security matters. Given the increasing importance of the CFSP and other related matters to EU integration, we examine in this chapter the Union's attempts to formulate a CFSP and also assess how the member states cope with domestic security as borders disappear between them.

COMMON FOREIGN AND SECURITY POLICY

Today in international relations, the EU's powers stem from a transfer of power from member states to the Union. In power relations, this is also known as a limited surrender of sovereignty by the members to the EU.[1] As a collective body, the EU maintains diplomatic relations with sovereign states and has observer status in the UN and in the various UN agencies. According to Lodge, some 150 countries have diplomatic missions at the EU and, the Union maintains, in the name of the Commission rather than the EU per se, over 100 diplomatic offices around the world.[2] In these offices, the EU representatives enjoy the same diplomatic rights as regular diplomats of sovereign countries, and cooperate closely with the EU states' local diplomatic missions serving the purpose of cooperation in maintaining a common foreign policy position among the member countries.

Historical Background

During the Cold War, the security lines between East and West were clearly drawn, as the dominant members of the respective alliances provided the bulk of the capital necessary for maintaining the adversary alliances, as well as leadership in formulating foreign and security policies. According to Peter Ludlow, three major forces contributed to the foreign policy profile of the EU during the post–World War II era: "the external implications of the EU's internal objectives and achievements; the voluntary agreement of its member states to enlarge their power and influence in the world through common action; and, by no means least, the gravitational pulls of its regional and global environment."[3] The road to a common foreign and security policy, which is being discussed today under the auspices of the Maastricht treaty, has been rather rough.

During the 1950s, the experiment with the EDC ended in a disaster, but it demonstrated how the EU members have considered collective foreign and security policies. Therefore, a brief review of the EDC case would be helpful in understanding the Maastricht's approach to a common foreign and security policy.

After the outbreak of the Korean War in June 1950, Jean Monnet argued that the answer to the increasing Soviet threat in Europe could be found in pooling the military resources of the European democracies in a European Defense Community. The new Community was to have its parliamentary body, a joint defense commission, a Council of Ministers, and a Court of Justice parallel to the one found in the ECSC. The six members of the ECSC made rapid progress on this plan, and the EDC Treaty was signed in May 1952. With the signing of the treaty, Monnet argued that "'now, the federation of Europe would have to become an immediate objective.'"[4] It was clear that this proposed pooling of defense capabilities would inevitably restrict the independent foreign policies of the member countries. Therefore, integration in defense also necessitated some level of political integration. Italian federalist Altiero Spinelli convinced the Italian government that the only way to control a European army was to have federal European institutions. He then persuaded the other five partners. As a result, the six members of the ECSC asked the Assembly, in conjunction with the "coopted members of the Consultative Assembly of the Council of Europe,"[5] to draft a treaty for a European Political Community (EPC). The outcome was a quasi-federal constitution, drafted in 1953, that would complement the EDC Treaty. According to this plan, there would be one European Executive responsible to a European Parliament (composed of the Peoples' Chamber elected by the citizens and a Senate elected by the national Parliaments), a Council of

Ministers, and one European Court of Justice that would replace the parallel institutions found under the ECSC and EDC treaties.

This development was a remarkable step toward deepening integration among the six members soon after the horrors of World War II. The Parliaments of the Benelux countries, West Germany, and Italy ratified the EDC treaty but the idea came to an abrupt halt in the French Assembly on August 30, 1954. Several factors contributed to the French rejection. First was a general opposition to a supranational political community. Second was the opposition of the French left to the rearming of Germany. And third, was the opposition of the French right to placing French troops under foreign command.[6]

Troubles with developing a CFSP followed in the ensuing years. After Charles de Gaulle became president of France, he tried to promote cooperation in foreign policy in the Community on an intergovernmental basis. France launched the Fouchet Plan which called for coordination of foreign and defense policies outside the framework of the Community.[7] The EC continued to discuss the plan until de Gaulle vetoed the British application for membership in the Community, after which the Benelux countries refused to discuss the Fouchet Plan any further (see chapter 3).

A decade later, the EC moved to create a mechanism for political cooperation, known as the Davignon machinery, based on a plan proposed by the Belgian foreign ministry. This mechanism consisted of biannual meetings of the foreign ministers, though in practice, the meetings have occurred more often. Also, until the 1973 oil crisis, the matters pertaining to EPC and the EC were to be kept separate. As Stephen George explains:

> This reached the heights of absurdity in November 1973, when the Foreign Ministers of the then nine member states met in Copenhagen one morning under the heading of EPC, and then flew to Brussels to meet in the afternoon of the same day as the EC Council of Ministers.[8]

When the EC decided to enter into talks with the Arab world in 1974, this separation of EPC and EC matters finally ended. These talks demonstrated that it was no longer possible to separate political matters from commerce. Soon after, the Commission, which had been excluded from the EPC, became involved in coordinating links between the EPC and the Council of Ministers.

The merging of the EPC political and EC economic interests proved to be helpful in promoting the Community's status in the international system and provided a more viable mechanism for dealing with complex foreign policy issues. In 1980, the European-Arab dialogue resulted in the Venice Declaration by which the European Council made it clear that it recognized the right of the Palestinians to a homeland.[9] Other achievements of the EPC include the following: (1) a common EC stance in the CSCE in Helsinki in 1975, in Belgrade in 1977, and in Madrid in 1982; (2) a common foreign policy towards South Africa; and (3) a more harmonious position in UN voting, both in the General Assembly and in the Security Council.

The SEA further emphasized the necessity to coordinate EPC. It stated "that the EPC could include the 'political and economic aspects of security,' and that the European Parliament should be closely associated with the EPC."[10] Finally, with the end of the Cold War, a more multilateral approach to security and foreign policy in the EU gained momentum, with the following important developments in the international system affecting the EU's CFSP: (1) the changing role of the United States in the international system, associated with the decline in hegemony; (2) the collapse of communism in Central and Eastern Europe and the subsequent rise in regional conflicts, which have threatened to destabilize the international system; (3) the unification of Germany; (4) the Gulf War; (5) the crisis in Somalia; and (6) the war in the former Yugoslavia. The EU's response to these developments requires careful balancing of the member states' and the Union's roles in the relevant international security organizations: WEU, NATO, and CSCE (see Table 11.1).

Maastricht and the Common Foreign and Security Policy

The TEU establishes CFSP as the second main pillar of the Union. When considering the nature and purpose of the CFSP, it is crucial to note that this effort is an expansion of the EU's earlier trials during the 1970s and 1980s to coordinate external policies of the member countries. The specific objectives of the CFSP are provided in Article J.1(2) of the TEU:

TABLE 11.1   European Union members' membership in international security organizations

Country	WEU	NATO	CSCE
Belgium	Yes	Yes	Yes
Denmark	No (observer)	Yes	Yes
France	Yes	Yes	Yes
Germany	Yes	Yes	Yes
Greece	Yes	Yes	Yes
Ireland	No (observer)	No	Yes
Italy	Yes	Yes	Yes
Luxembourg	Yes	Yes	Yes
Netherlands	Yes	Yes	Yes
Portugal	Yes	Yes	Yes
Spain	Yes	Yes	Yes
UK	Yes	Yes	Yes
Austria	No	No	Yes
Finland	No	No	Yes
Sweden	No	No	Yes

SOURCE: Adapted from "Partners for What?" *The Economist,* September 24, 1994, p. 49.

- to safeguard the common values, fundamental interests and independence of the Union;
- to strengthen the security of the Union and its Member States in all ways;
- to preserve peace and strengthen international security, in accordance with the principles of the United Nations Charter as well as the principles of the Helsinki Final Act and the objectives of the Paris Charter;
- to promote international cooperation; and
- to develop and consolidate democracy and the rule of law, and respect for human rights and fundamental freedoms.[11]

Furthermore, Article J.1(3) elaborates that the EU, in pursuing these objectives, needs to establish systematic cooperation among its members and "by gradually implementing, in accordance with Article J.3, joint action in the areas in which the Member States have important interests in common."[12]

Defining and managing the CFSP lies with the Council and the presidency respectively.[13] According to Article J.3(1):

The Council shall decide, on the basis of general guidelines from the European Council, that a matter should be subject of joint action. Whenever the Council decides on the principles of joint action, it shall lay down the specific scope, the Union's general and specific objectives in carrying out such action, if necessary its duration, and the means, procedures and conditions of its implementation.[14]

Moreover, Article J.8(2) states that "the Council shall act unanimously, except for procedural questions and in the case referred to in Article J.3(2)."[15] Article J.3(2) specifies that "when adopting the joint action and at any stage during its development, [the Council shall] define those matters on which decisions are to be taken by a qualified majority."[16] Thus, the Council of Ministers clearly has a major role in defining the scope, the principles, and the objectives of the CFSP. However, the European Council has a decisive contribution to this process by providing the general guidelines of the CFSP. All of these policy-making steps require agreement between the member states. When the EU lacks such agreement, the members can follow their own policy preferences and the only restraint on their actions would be the threat of unilateralism (acting in the interest of a single member country rather than the common interest of all members) on the well-being of the Union.

The implementation of the CFSP is entrusted for 6 months to the presidency of the Council, as stated in Article J.5(2). In this capacity, the presidency is assisted, if necessary, by the previous and next member states holding the presidency.[17] Furthermore, the Commission is to be fully associated in such tasks.[18]

It should be noted that there is virtually no democratic control over the CFSP, even though the presidency is required "to consult the European Parliament on the main aspects and the basic choices of the common foreign and security policy and ensure that views of the European Parliament are duly taken into account."[19] This consultation does not mean that the EP plays a major role in formulating CFSP. At times of emergency, there would not be time for the presidency to have prior consultation with the EP. According to Lodge, "the Presidency will act on its own initiative, or at the request of the Commission or a member state, to convene an extraordinary Council meeting within forty-eight hours or, in an emergency, within an even shorter time."[20]

Thus, consultation with the EP would likely be after the fact and of limited assistance, a situation no different from the dilemma faced in democratic countries. Furthermore, it is quite possible for the member states not to honor their commitment to consult each other prior to taking unilateral action. As we discuss later, Germany's behavior prior to the Yugoslav crisis serves as an example of this problem.

In addition to the above clauses, Article J.4(1) calls for a closer cooperation between the EU and the WEU and among the EU countries of NATO. The same is also expected in the CSCE activities.[21] Nevertheless, such cooperation among the EU countries requires imaginative policy coordination because not all members are also members of the WEU and NATO. This problem becomes more acute with the accession of the neutral EFTA countries—Austria, Finland, and Sweden—to full membership.

The Western European Union

The WEU has been in existence since the mid-1950s. It was set up by the Treaty of Economic, Social, and Cultural Collaboration and Collective Self-defense which was signed in Paris on October 23, 1954, and came into effect on May 6, 1955. The Paris agreement was a modification of an earlier agreement, the Brussels Treaty, which was signed by Belgium, Luxembourg, the Netherlands, France, and the UK and laid the foundations of a European defense organization. The Paris accord also revised the Brussels Treaty to permit Italy and West Germany to join the organization. The preamble of the Paris agreement displays the purposes of the signatories:

> . . . to reaffirm their faith in fundamental human rights . . . and in the other ideals proclaimed in the Charter of the United Nations; . . . to preserve the principles of democracy; . . . to strengthen . . . the economic, social and cultural ties by which they are already united [by cooperating] to create in Western Europe a firm basis for European economic recovery; . . . to afford assistance to each other . . . in resisting any policy of aggression; . . . to promote the unity and to encourage the progressive integration of Europe.[22]

The subsequent protocols II–IV contained further provisions relating to the levels of forces and armaments of member countries and established the Agency for the Control of Armaments. The Brussels treaty was also very specific about the commitment to collective security of the member states. As Article V specified that:

> If any of the high contracting parties should be the object of an armed attack in Europe, the other high contracting parties will, in accordance with the provisions of Article 51 of the Charter of the United Nations, afford the party so attacked all the military and other aid and assistance in their power.[23]

The WEU consists of a council, a consultative assembly, a secretariat, the Standing Armaments Committee, and the Agency for the Control of Armaments. Between 1955 and 1984, the political achievements of the WEU were (1) facilitating the integration of West Germany into NATO and (2) serving as a link between the EU and the UK until the latter became a member of the Community. Otherwise, the WEU was not a major player in the Community's subsequent foreign policy making (EPC), and the organization remained inactive until 1984.

Frustrated with the U.S. nuclear missile and Strategic Defense Initiative policies, France started a campaign to reactivate the WEU. Another important reason for the French initiative was that at the time EPC excluded matters relating to defense and security. On October 26–27, 1984, in Rome, the foreign and defense ministers of the member countries agreed to reactivate the WEU. The Rome Declaration reaffirmed the WEU's commitment to strengthen peace and security, to promote the unity and to encourage the progressive integration of Europe, to cooperate more closely both among member states and with other European organizations, to make better use of the WEU framework in order to increase cooperation between the members in the field of security and to encourage consensus, and to improve the common defense of all the countries of the Atlantic Alliance since the two institutions were both designed to provide security to the West.[24]

In the years following the Rome declaration, important developments further strengthened the WEU. First, the SEA called for a greater collaboration in political and security matters, and the WEU was the logical place where consensus on security matters could be attained.[25] Second, the two newest members of the EU, Spain and Portugal, also decided to join the WEU. And third, the Hague Platform of October 26, 1987, which was adopted by the Council, outlined Europe's security interests. Tim Birch identifies four features of the Hague Platform that set the framework of future common European foreign and security policies:

> First, the Hague Platform emphasized WEU's potential value within the context of the Atlantic Alliance, in the form of consolidating the "European Pillar." Second, the Platform document acknowledged the British and French role in providing a nuclear "guarantee" to Western Europe. Third, members called for progress in the area of European Community. Fourth and finally, members called for closer military and diplomatic cooperation in the resolution of out-of-area crises.[26]

As the member states contemplated defense and security interests of the EC in the new Europe, two proposals emerged during the late 1980s from France and Germany, on the one hand, and Britain and Italy, on the other. The Franco-German plan called for a CFSP for the EC that would have a joint armed forces of at least 50,000 troops to serve as a nucleus of an independent Union defense force. In this plan, the WEU would become the institution for coordinating the EC's defense policy.[27] The British-Italian plan, on the other hand, proposed that the WEU remain separate from the EC. The members would form a Rapid Reaction Force, which would be used to defend the Community's interests outside NATO's sphere of operations.[28]

These debates resulted in a common view in the Maastricht treaty, which provides the most detailed declaration by the Union on the future role of the WEU in EU affairs. The declaration on WEU has two parts: (1) on the role of WEU and its relations with the EU and NATO, and (2) on expansion of WEU.

In the first part, the WEU members outline their need to develop a European security and defense identity through successive stages. This identity would enhance the European pillar of NATO, more as a cohesive unit than as separate members of the Atlantic Alliance, and assist in formulation of European defense policy. It calls upon the member states to promote WEU through such measures as synchronization and harmonization of meetings and working methods, cooperation between the Council and Secretary General of WEU on the one hand and the Council of the Union and General Secretary of the Council on the other, ensuring that the Commission is regularly informed and, as appropriate, consulted on WEU activities, and encouragement of closer cooperation between the parliamentary assembly of WEU and the European Parliament.[29] With regard to closer cooperation with NATO, the declaration states that the CFSP would require member states to establish closer ties between the secretary generals of the two alliances.

The operational role of WEU is also addressed in this declaration. It is stated that the alliance plans to establish a planning cell and closer military cooperation in logistics, transport, training and strategic surveillance; to hold meetings of WEU defense chiefs; and to create military units accountable to WEU.[30] The Franco-German effort at creating a joint military unit is within the realm of this declaration. Other proposals include "transforming the WEU Institute into a European Security and Defense Academy and enhancing cooperation in armaments with the goal of creating a European armaments agency."[31]

In the second part of the declaration, the members of the WEU invite the other EU countries to "accede to WEU on conditions to be agreed in accordance with Article XI of the modified Brussels Treaty, or to become observers if they so wish. Simultaneously, other European Member States of NATO are invited to become associate members of WEU in a way which will give them the possibility of participating fully in the activities of WEU."[32]

Following the signing of the Maastricht treaty, the WEU Council of Ministers for Foreign Affairs and Defense held a meeting in Bonn on June 19, 1992, and issued the Petersberg Declaration regarding their views on European defense and security matters.[33] This declaration emphasizes the importance of the CSCE in promoting peace and stability in Europe and calls for strengthening the CSCE's capabilities in conflict prevention, crisis management, and peaceful settlement of international disputes. It specifies that the WEU would support implementation of conflict-prevention and crisis-management measures, including peacekeeping operations of the CSCE or the UN Security Council. Furthermore, the declaration reaffirms the members' commitment to strengthen the European leg of the Atlantic Alliance and to invite other EU members and European members of NATO to join the WEU.

In accordance with these developments, nine WEU members held a meeting with six candidates for WEU membership (Denmark, Greece, Iceland, Ireland, Norway, and Turkey) in Rome on July 16, 1992. After a series of negotiations, the WEU decided on November 20, 1992, to admit Greece into its ranks. At the same time, Iceland, Norway, and Turkey were given associate membership in the WEU, and EU members Denmark and Ireland were admitted as observers to WEU.[34] Further developments followed soon after the expansion of membership. During the Defense Ministers' meeting of the 13 countries in the Independent European Program Group (IEPG) in Bonn on December 4, 1992, the participants agreed to transfer the IEPG's function to WEU. The Ministerial Council of WEU approved the transfer at its Rome meeting on May 19, 1993, and established a new structure within WEU, the Western European Armaments Group (WEAG), which inherited the previous work done by the IEPG.[35] A follow-up agreement allowed Denmark, Norway, and Turkey to participate in the new institution even though they were not full members of WEU. The significance of this development is that the new institution and its operating agreements with the nonmembers help promote "the objective of WEU's 1984 Rome Declaration—to provide political impetus for European cooperation in the field of armaments."[36] Finally, during the Council of Ministers meeting in Luxembourg on May 9, 1994, the WEU issued the Kirchberg Declaration which gave Bulgaria, the Czech Republic, Estonia, Hungary, Latvia, Lithuania, Poland, Romania, and Slovakia associate partnership in the WEU.[37] Although this move is aimed at improving ties with the former Eastern Bloc countries, the particular association status granted to these states is not as comprehensive as that with Iceland, Norway, and Turkey. According to the Kirchberg Declaration, the above mentioned east-central European countries may participate in the meetings of the Council and "associate themselves with decisions taken by the member states concerning humanitarian and rescue tasks, peacekeeping tasks, tasks of combat forces in crisis management, including peacekeeping."[38] Iceland, Norway, and Turkey, on the other hand, may nominate officers to the Planning Cell in order to "increase WEU's planning capabilities and to enable WEU to draw more easily on the Associate Members' expertise and resources."[39]

These developments need to be evaluated in light of the new security environment of the post–Cold War Europe. With the decision of the United States to reduce its military presence in the European theater, it became more apparent for the EU members that they had to coordinate their security and defense policies. According to Trevor Salmon, at the end of the 1980s, the Europeans provided the bulk of allied forces for Europe's defense: 90 percent of the manpower, 95 percent of the divisions, 85 percent of the tanks, 95 percent of the artillery, 80 percent of the combat aircraft, and 70 percent of the warships in European waters of the Atlantic.[40] However, as Birch explains, the WEU is far from having the necessary integrated military structure or the political will to become an alternative to NATO:

> . . . [First] Europe is not in a position to dispense with some of the "public goods" provided by the [US]. Second, there is the question of the economic costs associated with defense independence. . . .Third, movement towards the Unionist version of EDI [European Defense Initiative] will require enormous political will, and will have to rest upon general agreement regarding threats, preferable force-posture and common doctrines. Finally, divergence of interests among the principal European Powers will have to be overcome.[41]

Based on these observations, it is safe to conclude that the WEU will continue to function in conjunction with NATO. The EU members of these two security organizations share the burden of coordinating their policies, which is no easy task. A recent indication of such cooperation between the WEU and NATO came from the Noordwijk Declaration of the WEU Council of Ministers on November 14, 1994. At this meeting, the WEU defense ministers, including the representatives of the associate partner countries, reaffirmed their commitment to work with NATO to provide security and stability in Europe.[42] Moreover, as the membership of the EU expands to include neutral countries like Austria, Sweden, and Finland, defense cooperation within the EU becomes even more difficult.

In recent years, two international crises put to the test the EU's efforts to promote a CFSP: the Gulf War and the civil war in former Yugoslavia. In the next two sections, we examine the EU's response to these challenges.

The Gulf War.   After Iraq invaded Kuwait on August 2, 1990, the president of the Assembly of the WEU issued a communiqué, condemning the Iraqi aggression and demanding prompt withdrawal of Iraqi troops from Kuwait. He also called upon the WEU countries to respond to the crisis and asked the UN to take all necessary steps to defend the sovereignty of Kuwait. Yet, despite the urgency of the situation, it took the WEU countries 19 days before they met to discuss the situation. By that time, the United States had initiated its own diplomatic and military efforts to remove Iraq from Kuwait and asserted American leadership within the UN and NATO.[43]

The WEU Council of Ministers agreed to take all necessary steps to comply with the embargo on Iraq in accordance with UN Security Council Resolution 661. On the basis of their experiences in the Persian Gulf during the 1987–1989 operations, the WEU established an ad hoc group of foreign and defense ministry representatives to provide cooperation between the member states' capitals and the forces in the Gulf. By the end of 1990, the WEU had deployed 45 vessels (destroyers, frigates, corvettes, mine sweepers, and amphibious vessels) to the Gulf region. These vessels came from seven of the nine member countries. Only Luxembourg, which does not have a navy, and Germany, whose Constitution prevented deployment of German troops outside of Germany, did not participate in the Gulf operation.

The WEU also coordinated its members' response to the second operation in this crisis. On September 18, 1990, another meeting of the Council of Ministers decided to "strengthen the WEU coordination and to extend the coordination at present operating in the maritime field to ground and air forces and, within this framework, to identify the forms that these new deployments will take, to seek to ensure that they are complementary, to harmonize the missions of the member states' forces and to pool their logistic support capabilities as required."[44] When Desert Storm began on January 16, 1991, WEU members France, Italy, and the UK participated with aircraft. The next day, the WEU Council of Ministers held an extraordinary meeting and decided to provide full support for the operation. Parallel to the operations in the air and sea, ground forces from the WEU participated in the massive UN buildup in Saudi Arabia.

Following the successful operations in Kuwait, the WEU decided to continue to play an active role in implementation of the UN Security Council resolutions pertaining to the protection of the Kurds in northern Iraq and the Shiite Arabs of Basra. The naval embargo, which includes ships from WEU, was still in force as of early 1995.

The Yugoslav Crisis.   The breakup of Yugoslavia and the subsequent civil war in Bosnia-Herzegovina and Croatia represent potentially the most divisive issue for the WEU members. This crisis shows that WEU and the EC were not prepared to deal with a problem of this magnitude, and the subsequent disagreements among the Community's members over how to respond to the problem high-lights the member countries' inability to coordinate their national foreign policy priorities. Finally, disagreement over how to stop the bloodshed in these areas has also strained relations between the EC and its partners in the other major security communities, the UN and NATO. The crisis in the former Yugoslav republics is perhaps the most damaging test for the EC's ability to respond to security problems in the new Europe. In this regard, it is important to assess the EC's relative success and failure in resolving the crises in Slovenia, Croatia, and Bosnia-Herzegovina.

In Slovenia, the EC-sponsored mediation succeeded because the Serbs concentrated their attention on Croatia and Bosnia. Initially, Lord Carrington, representing the EC, organized a series of meetings with the warring parties. Yet, in late 1991, Germany went ahead of its EC partners and pressured the Croatians, the Slovenians, and the Bosnians to choose between independence from the Yugoslav federation and remaining as part of Yugoslavia. The German move came before the rest of the EC countries were prepared to undertake such an important responsibility. Soon after the German declaration, Croatia and Slovenia broke away from Yugoslavia and, subsequently, received full diplomatic recognition from the EC. According to Catherine McArdle Kelleher, "Foreign Minister Genscher, himself a convert to the recognition strategy pressed by German domestic sources, argued that recognition would allow comprehensive Community oversight over the pace and costs involved in the disintegration of the former Yugoslavia."[45]

Soon after, the Bosnians voted in a national referendum, which was highly divided along ethnic lines, to secede from Yugoslavia. Bosnian Croats and the Muslims favored independence, whereas Bosnian Serbs voted to remain part of Yugoslavia. The EC immediately recognized the independence of Bosnia-Herzegovina. The EC's recognition of these former Yugoslav republics was aimed at achieving two goals: to maintain a common policy among the EU countries towards Bosnia-Herzegovina, Croatia, and Slovenia; and to oversee the breakup of the Yugoslav federation in a peaceful manner. However, their efforts proved to be futile because civil war immediately broke out in these countries, though only briefly in Slovenia, as ethnic Serbs pushed to gain territories that could be joined to Serbia. In each case, the rebel Serbs received substantial support from the former Yugoslav army and quickly made territorial gains against the Croats and the Bosnia Muslims. Subsequently, the world witnessed numerous wartime atrocities of genocide, mass rapes, and massive destruction of villages and towns as the Serbs attempted to cleanse newly acquired territories from the Croats and the Muslims. The problem worsened as the other sides retaliated against Serbian populations in their respective areas and later when the Croats and the Muslims fought against each other over the control of Central and Southern Bosnia.

During these crises, the main international security organizations, the UN, NATO, and the WEU, attempted to bring about an end to hostilities by coordinating their political and military efforts. While they were partially successful in Croatia, the civil war in Bosnia-Herzegovina continues with no end in sight. Several factors have contributed to this failure.

First, the EC, the UN, and later NATO, failed to provide a common and effective position on the crisis. Time after time, these organizations failed to respond to Serbian actions in Bosnia even when they followed strong ultimatums from the West. The problem with the EC's efforts in Bosnia are effectively summarized by Kelleher:

> Europe's response in 1992 to the outrages in Bosnia reflected [internal] divisions and were particularly ineffective. Despite popular outcries and increasing popular pressures for European action, the general response within the EC and from member governments was expression of grave concern and the imposition of economic sanctions but great operational diffidence and constant delay. The EC was most engaged, but only with intermittent success, in the monitoring of a series of unsuccessful cease-fire attempts or in emergency humanitarian measures.[46]

Second, the EC sponsored the London peace process in the fall of 1992, which included the participation of the UN. In this setting, conflict management became an issue that required cooperation between the EC and the UN. When one considers the additional involvement of other actors, namely NATO, the United States, and Russia, in peace talks, it is not surprising that no one party was able to find a solution to the crisis. In the peace talks between the belligerents, former British Foreign Secretary Lord Owen represented the EC and former U.S. Secretary of State Cyrus Vance participated as the UN envoy. The Vance-Owen plan envisioned the partitioning of Bosnia-Herzegovina into cantons based on ethnic composition. Regardless of its merit, the plan came under serious criticism from all the warring parties and from the Muslim world. The Serbs did not accept it because it prevented their joining Serb-held Bosnian territories to Serbia. The Croats and the Muslims opposed it for its apparent reward for aggression by the Serbs. Eventually, this plan underwent a series of revisions as the war in Bosnia-Herzegovina continued to change the ethnic composition of the landscape. At the time of writing, the Serbs rejected yet another plan for partitioning of Bosnia-Herzegovina. Under this newest plan, the Serbs would keep 51 percent of the land (currently they occupy 70 percent) and a new Muslim-Croat confederation would receive 49 percent of Bosnia-Herzegovina.

Finally, as the war in Bosnia-Herzegovina worsened, it became quite apparent that the WEU lacked the necessary military structure to intervene effectively to stop the bloodshed. When human suffering reached new heights, the UN agreed to send peacekeepers, mostly from the WEU countries, to safeguard humanitarian assistance to the civilians. The only organization that had the military power to stop the war was NATO. No other organization has the integrated military structure, hardwear, and logistical planning and operation capabilities to deal with a crisis like Bosnia. However, NATO's intervention, directly or indirectly, meant involvement of the United States. Under normal circumstances, U.S. involvement would not be a problem for NATO. However, the Clinton administration's inconsistencies over its Bosnian policy worried the allies. Nevertheless, when the UN decided to impose an embargo on Yugoslavia and the ex-Yugoslav states of Croatia and Bosnia-Herzegovina, and to sponsor Operation Deny Flight and Operation Sharp Guard, NATO was asked to oversee such military operations. Once again, the success of the operations depended on cooperation between the UN, NATO, and the WEU.

Among these undertakings, the arms embargo has been criticized for punishing both the aggressors and the victims. The Bosnian government continually asked for the lifting of the arms embargo so that it could acquire the means for defending its people against the Serbs. The Bosnian Serbs, on the other hand, continued to receive supplies from Serbia, and at least on one occasion, from Russia. This policy resulted in tensions between the WEU countries with peacekeeping troops in Bosnia and the United States because the Americans occasionally pressured the UN to end the embargo on Bosnia.

Operation Sharp Guard's mission was to conduct operations to monitor and enforce compliance with UN sanctions, particularly against Serbia, in accordance with UN Security Council Resolutions 713, 757, 787, and 820. A combined task force was given the responsibility of preventing unauthorized shipping from entering the territorial waters of the Yugoslav Federal Republic. The operation was equipped with surface warships from Canada, France, Germany, Greece, Italy, the Netherlands, Norway, Portugal, Spain, Turkey, the UK, and the United States. In addition, eight fighter aircrafts from Italy and maritime patrol aircrafts from Canada, France, Germany, Italy, the Netherlands, Portugal, Spain, the UK, and the United States, supported by NATO Airborne Warning and Control System (AWACS), provide air support for this operation. By the end of March 1994, this operation had challenged 17,000 merchant vessels in the Adriatic Sea and on the Danube, halting 1,700.[47]

Operation Deny Flight, on the other hand, had a fourfold mission:

1. To conduct aerial monitoring and enforce compliance with UN Security Council Resolution 816, which bans flights by fixed-wing and rotary-wing aircraft in the airspace of Bosnia-Herzegovina
2. to provide air cover (close air support) at the request of and control by the United Nations Peacekeeping Forces in the former Yugoslavia (UNPROFOR) under the supervision of UN Security Council Resolution 836
3. to be ready to carry out, in coordination with the UN, air strikes on heavy weapons if they fire from outside (or inside) the 20 kilometer exclusion zone into Sarajevo or if they return into the exclusion zone
4. to be ready to carry out air strikes at other locations to aid UNPROFOR in humanitarian relief operations as authorized by the North Atlantic Council and in coordination with the UN.[48]

The aircraft for this operation came from France, Spain, the Netherlands, Turkey, and the United States. In addition, almost 4,500 personnel from 12 NATO countries (Belgium, Canada, Denmark, France, Germany, Italy, the Netherlands, Norway, Spain, Turkey, the UK, and the United States) were deployed in Italy and the Adriatic for this NATO operation. The most dramatic moment of the operation came on February 28, 1994, when four NATO fighters shot down four Yugoslav Galeb/Jastreb aircraft over Bosnia. Later, on March 12, 1994, NATO responded to the first UNPROFOR request to provide close air support by sending aircraft to give protection for French peacekeepers who were being fired upon near Bihac in Bosnia-Herzegovina. However, this did not result in attacks on the ground targets. Then, during the Serb attack on Gorazde in April 1994, NATO aircraft flew warning missions over Serbian positions. During this operation, the Serbs shot down a British Sea Harrier with a surface to air missile. That operation ended when the Serbs agreed to withdraw from Gorazde in the face of a NATO ultimatum.

The Serbian testing of NATO and the UN's resolve continued during Fall 1994. During these months, the Serbs launched a massive attack on the Muslim enclave of Bihac following a brief military success of the latter that resulted from a surprise offensive against Serbian positions. The Serbian counteroffensive also included attacks on Bihac from Serb-controlled areas of Croatia. When the subsequent UN and NATO threats against the Serbs failed to stop the Serbian attacks, the international media and influential political figures began to question the role of the UN peacekeepers and NATO airpower in Bosnia. In December 1994, the UN Secretary General Boutros Boutros-Ghali and the British and French governments went so far as to suggest the withdrawal of UN peacekeepers from Bosnia. During this time, the world witnessed a serious divide between some of the allies. For example, as the Clinton administration considered providing logistical support for UN withdrawal from Bosnia, key congressional leaders in the United States openly criticized the British and French governments' policies and called upon the U.S. administration unilaterally to lift the arms embargo against the Bosnian government. Senator Robert Dole argued that maintaining the arms embargo against all of former Yugoslavia amounted to nothing more than punishing the victims, the Bosnian Muslims, since the Serbs have access to heavy weapons.

Western allies' disagreement over Bosnia policy also appeared to sour relations within NATO. In an interview with the British Broadcasting Corporaton (BBC), the Turkish ambassador to NATO announced that Turkey did not intend to withdraw its 1,460 peacekeeping troops from Bosnia if the UN decided to pull out.[49] The ambassador also indicated that if necessary, Turkey was prepared to reinforce the Turkish contingent in Bosnia. The Turkish decision to defy possible UN withdrawal from Bosnia is due to historic ties between the two countries. For more than 4 centuries, Bosnia was part of the Ottoman Empire, and today some 5 million Turks living in Turkey are of Bosnian descent.

The inability of the WEU, NATO, and the UN to coordinate an effective policy over Bosnia also affected the European Council summit in Essen. At this meeting, the British and French leaders stated that there was a good chance to withdraw the UN peacekeeping force from Bosnia within weeks, unless the Serbs agreed to the UN-EU peace plan.[50] The host of the summit, Chancellor Kohl, on the other hand, expressed a strong interest in maintaining a consensus within the EU in favor of a diplomatic solution. At the time of writing, the so-called contact group over Bosnia, comprising France, Germany, Russia, the UK, and the United States, was holding talks with the warring parties to find a diplomatic solution to this crisis.

These developments show that the WEU and the UN lack the necessary integrated military command structure and the logistical means to cope with the crisis in Bosnia. The job has had to be carried out by NATO. Whereas such close consultation between NATO, the WEU, and the UN has meant slow reaction to Serbian actions in Bosnia, the military undertakings of the allies have not been without some limited success. First in Sarajevo, and later in Gorazde, NATO ultimatums, followed by close air support, resulted in lifting the Serbs' siege around these cities. Yet, in Bihac, the UN and NATO failed to stop the Bosnian Serbs. According to Kelleher, the EU and other organizations have failed in Bosnia-Herzegovina for the following reasons:

(1) The Yugoslav crisis occurred before any institutional structures and procedures for peacekeeping or peacemaking assistance were ready in Europe and when the United Nations was overburdened; (2) the complex civil structures and ethnic politics of Yugoslavia hinder attempts of outsiders to influence the situation; (3) the physical terrain of Yugoslavia is too intractable to permit intervention or even selective application of military sanctions; and (4) the instruments for restraining or punishing incidents of civil war are simply too rudimentary at this stage. . . . But the critical factors appears to be both the lack of political will and the failure to find multilateral agreement on direct, remedial action. There have been no European decisions towards peacemaking, only the unwillingness of a number of member governments and their populations to risk the lives of their military forces in direct intervention, and the inability to devise political and military incentives to induce an early end to the fighting or to the horrifying process of ethnic cleansing.[51]

The Macedonia Question.   The division among the EU countries over foreign policy coordination toward the former Yugoslav republics is also evident in Macedonia. Following Macedonia's declaration of independence from Yugoslavia, Greece blocked EU's recognition because Macedonia is the name of one of Greece's provinces. Greece maintained that Macedonia had territorial ambitions on the Greek province of Macedonia by virtue of its name; its constitution; its bank notes, which have the picture of the tower of Salonika; and its national flag, which bears the ancient Macedonian dynastic emblem discovered in northern Greece in 1975. Despite Greek opposition, six members of the EU (Denmark, France, Germany, Italy, the Netherlands, and the UK) established full diplomatic relations with Macedonia in December 1993 just before Greece took over the presidency of the Council in January 1994.[52] Belgium followed suit in early 1994. The crisis over Macedonia worsened in February 1994, when Greece moved unilaterally to impose a trade embargo against the former Yugoslav republic. This ban isolated Greece politically, which at the time held the presidency of the Union, presenting a major setback for the common foreign policymaking process foreseen in the Maastricht treaty. Moreover, Greece's actions appear to have violated the Maastricht treaty because under the treaty, member states cannot impose unilateral commercial sanctions except in cases of national security. Whereas Greece maintained that Macedonia represented a national security problem, the EU Commission rejected this argument and referred the case to the ECJ to force a reversal of the Greek decision.

DOMESTIC SECURITY

The Maastricht treaty contains provisions (see Title VI, Article K) on cooperation in justice and home affairs, known as the third pillar of the EU. According to these provisions, the members states' interior ministers are required to work together on asylum, immigration, frontier rules, crime, customs, and police cooperation regarding terrorism and drug control.[53] Furthermore, a new committee of officials would coordinate this work and prepare meetings of the Council of Ministers, which would then act on the proposals by unanimity. As Juliet Lodge explains, "it is instructive that the areas covered by judicial cooperation correspond closely to the preoccupation of the Schengen group [and treaty] and overlap with obvious concerns central to the completion and realization of the Single Market."[54] The reference to the Single Market is based on the four freedoms of movement (of goods, services, people, and capital) that are essential to the realization of such economic integration. Among these movements, the one by people presents an important security concern for the EU countries because it requires development of adequate policing at the common external borders to safeguard against illegal immigration, movement of criminals, terrorists, and drug traffickers.

The Schengen Treaty, signed in June 1990 and became effective in 1995, began as a Franco-German plan to abolish all frontier controls on the movement of people and goods and services between the two countries.[55] The Benelux countries joined France and Germany in 1985. The provisions relating to the free movement of goods and services became effective with the SEA, and the group then focused its attention to the issues relevant to the free movement of peoples. However, the signing of the treaty was delayed until June 1990 because of the insecure borders of the former East Germany. The treaty listed 45 countries whose nationals would be subject to border controls in an effort to curb immigration and to deal with refugee and asylum problems.[56] The group expanded with Italy's signing of the treaty in November 1990, followed by Spain and Portugal in June 1991. It is clear that the issues covered by the Schengen Treaty are addressed in the TEU. However, it is not clear when all of the EU countries will harmonize their immigration, refugee, and asylum policies.

In early 1992, there were 10.1 million legal immigrants in the EU, which is about 2.5 percent of the Union's population. Most of these immigrants came from North Africa, Turkey, Yugoslavia, and the Indian subcontinent[57] (see Figure 11.1). This number was increasing by an average of 400,000 per annum as family members of the present immigrant and asylum seekers entered the EU.

The real problem, however, is illegal immigration. Because of economic and political problems in Eastern Europe, North Africa, and the Mediterranean Basin, more and more illegal immigrants have been pouring into the Union. Despite border controls undertaken by the Schengen countries, the number of illegal immigrants in the Union increased to about 3 million in 1991. According to *The Economist,* some 1 million illegal immigrants were found in Spain and France, and the number in Italy alone could be close to 1 million.[58] The problem also exists in the North because Polish citizens use their free visa travel to Germany and then enter the illegal economy. The EU tried unsuccessfully to reduce the burden of foreign workers by offering them cash incentives to return to their homes. In Germany and France, which target Turkish and North African workers respectively, this policy had very limited success. As immigration pressure

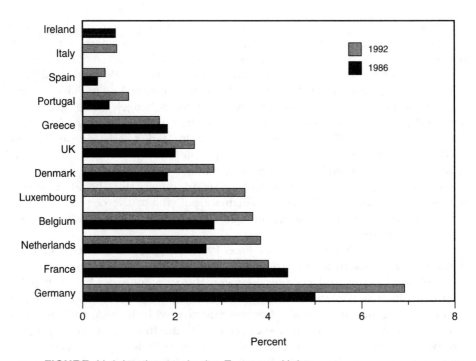

FIGURE 11.1 Immigrants in the European Union

SOURCE: "Open to Us, Closed to Them," *The Economist,* August 13, 1994, p. 43. © 1994 The Economist Newspaper Group, Inc. Reprinted with permission. Further reproduction prohibited.

increased on these countries, racial attacks on foreigners began a steady rise, particularly in Germany. In an attempt to reduce its burden of guest workers, the German government even abrogated its agreement with Turkey on free movement of workers.

Recently, the EU justice and interior ministers meeting in Luxembourg agreed on a joint approach to keeping unwanted foreign workers out of the Union and shelved discussion on a Commission proposal that non-EU nationals legally residing in one member country should be able to seek employment in other member states.[59] The ministers agreed to study the feasibility of the EURODAC network, a system for fingerprinting asylum seekers and suspected illegal immigrants at the port of entry. Furthermore, the ministers agreed that these restrictions could not be relaxed by national legislation, thus forcing conformity among the member states. There are, however, exemptions to these restrictions: EFTA countries' citizens, refugees, and asylum applicants; persons transferred within companies in the EU; investors; and students covered under youth exchange programs. Nonetheless, these recent developments highlight the sensitivity of immigration, asylum, and refugee policies in the EU. The problems associated with harmonization of internal security and justice are immense and would require more time than expected under the Maastricht provisions.

CONCLUSION

Our analysis of the EU's foreign and domestic security policies shows that these policy areas are probably the most disintegrated ones among all of the Union's policy dimensions. The least unified policy area is foreign security. Efforts have been made to make the WEU an alternative policy-making organization to NATO, though it is debatable whether the EU's NATO members desire such an outcome. However, the Union's response to recent foreign policy challenges in Bosnia demonstrates that the WEU lacks the necessary military structure to be an effective EU defense umbrella. In addition, not all EU countries are also members of the WEU. On the positive side, the WEU has come a long way since its inception. In recent years, the organization presented a united EU policy on the Gulf crisis, Somalia, and Macedonia. However, NATO still remains the only security organization that has the unified command and military structure to respond to threats to European security. The WEU, as it now stands, serves as useful policy bridge between the WEU and NATO members of the EU and also between the Union and the United States.

In domestic security matters, like free movement of labor and immigration policies, the Maastricht treaty contains a specific provision on cooperation in justice and home affairs, and it does look as though the member states' interior ministers are working together on establishing common EU policies on political asylum, immigration, border controls, and cooperation in police matters. However, these are very sensitive issues, and it will require much cooperation over time to harmonize member states' policies.

ENDNOTES

1. Juliet Lodge, "From Civilian Power to Speaking With a Common Voice: The Transition to a CFSP," in Lodge, ed. *The European Community and the Challenge of the Future,* 2nd ed. (New York: St. Martin's, 1993), p. 227.
2. Ibid., p. 228.
3. Peter Ludlow, "The Foreign Policy of the Union," in Peter Ludlow, ed., *Setting European Community Priorities, 1991-92* (London: Brassey's, for Center for European Policy Studies, 1991), p. 102.
4. Jean Monnet, *Memoirs,* trans. by Richard Mayne, as cited in John Pinder, *European Community: The Building of a Union* (London: Oxford University Press, 1991), p. 7.
5. Dennis Swann, *The Economics of the Common Market* (London: Penguin Books, 1992), p. 8.
6. Henri Brugmans, "The Defeat of the European Army," in F. Roy Willis, ed., *European Integration* (New York: New Viewpoints, 1975), pp. 38-49.
7. Stephen George, *Politics and Policy in the European Community,* 2nd ed. (London: Oxford University Press, 1991) p. 32.
8. Ibid., p. 219.
9. Ibid., p. 221.

10. Pinder, *European Community*, p. 193.
11. *Treaty on European Union,* Title V, Article J.1(2), (Luxembourg: Office for Official Publications of the European Communities, 1992), pp. 123-24.
12. Ibid., p. 124.
13. Lodge, "From Civilian Power," pp. 244-45.
14. *Treaty on European Union,* pp. 124-25.
15. Ibid., p. 128.
16. Ibid., p. 125.
17. Ibid., p. 127.
18. Article J.5(3).
19. Article J.7. Para. 1.
20. Lodge, "From Civilian Power," p. 246.
21. Ibid.
22. WEU, Preamble of the Paris Agreement, October 23, 1954.
23. Ibid., Article V.
24. WEU, Committee for Parliamentary and Public Relations,*Western European Union* (Brussels 1993).
25. Tim Birch, "Western European Union: Rhetoric and Reality," *American Review of Politics* Volume 15 (Autumn 1994), pp. 383-416.
26. Ibid.
27. Robert Jordan, *Atlantic Relations and the New Europe* (Occasional paper by the Eisenhower Center for Leadership Studies, University of New Orleans, March 1992), p. 23.
28. Ibid.
29. *Treaty on European Union,* pp. 243-44.
30. Ibid., p. 244.
31. Ibid., p. 245.
32. Ibid., p. 246.
33. *The New York Times,* June 20, 1992.
34. *Financial Times,* November 21, 1992, p. 2.
35. Willem van Eekelen, "WEU Prepares the Way for New Missions," *NATO Review* 41 (October 1993).
36. Ibid.
37. WEU, *Kirchberg Declaration,* May 9, 1994.
38. Ibid., Part II.
39. Ibid., Part III.
40. Trevor Salmon, "The Union, CFSP and the European Security Debate," in Lodge, ed. *The European Community and the Challenge of the Future,* p. 263.
41. Birch, "Western European Union: Rhetoric and Reality."
42. Chris Scheurweghs, "WEU Council of Ministers," NATO integrated data services.
43. David Garnham, "European Defense Cooperation," in Dale L. Smith and James Lee Ray, eds., *The 1992 Project and the Future of Integration in Europe* (New York: M. E. Sharpe, 1993), p. 210.
44. WEU, *Western European Union.*
45. Catherine McArdle Kelleher, "A New Security Order: The United States and the European Community in the 1990s" (Occasional paper of the European Community Studies Association, 1992), pp. 31-32.
46. Ibid., p. 32.
47. NATO/WEU, "Operation Sharp Guard Fact Sheet," NATO/WEU public data service.

48. NATO, "Operation Deny Flight Fact Sheet," NATO public data service.

49. BBC interview on December 6, 1994.

50. "Britain and France Firm on Bosnia," *Financial Times,* December 10-11, 1994, p. 2.

51. Kelleher, "A New Security Order," p. 33.

52. "Macedonia backed by half of EU," *Financial Times,* December 17, 1993, p. 3.

53. *Treaty on European Union,* Title VI, Article K.1-3, pp. 131-33.

54. Juliet Lodge, "Internal Security and Judicial Cooperation," in Lodge, ed. *The European Community and the Challenge of the Future,* p. 325.

55. Swann, *The Economics of the Common Market,* p. 170.

56. Lodge, "Internal Security and Judicial Cooperation," p. 321.

57. *The Economist,* June 1, 1991, p. 45.

58. Ibid.

59. "Twelve agree to policy on foreign workers," *Financial Times,* June 21, 1994, p. 2.

chapter 12

Conclusion

Throughout this text, we have shown that the emerging EU has followed an irregular course of integration. It has always found a middle way between integration that is strictly economic in nature and integration that is strongly political, and each integrative step has brought institutional changes that represent compromises between the principles of intergovernmentalism and supranationalism. In the 1950s, the effort to achieve a strongly political and supranational form of integration, in the form of the EDC, was rejected and ultimately replaced by an important step toward economic integration, the EEC, which assumed a more intergovernmental form. However, when the principal supranational agency of the EEC, the Commission, took steps in the mid-1960s to increase its own power, it was thwarted by the French president, who had a contrasting intergovernmentalist conception of political integration and who preferred not to move beyond the extent of economic integration envisaged in the Rome treaty.

By the 1970s, the Commission had receded to a more passive role, while the governments of the member countries, including the new entrants—Britain, Denmark, and Ireland—settled into a more intergovernmentalist mode of agenda setting and decision making, which featured the regularization of summit meetings of the heads of state and government in the European Council, institutionalized in 1974-1975. This was a period of learning and experimentation in the realm of economic integration, especially in the tentative steps taken toward the elusive goal of economic and monetary union. Finally, in the mid-1980s, with another new member, Greece, in place and two new members, Portugal and Spain, about to join, the governments converged on a package that developed the original Rome treaty idea of a common market beyond the CU that had been achieved two decades earlier. It also took some modest steps in the direction

241

of greater political union, particularly the extension of QMV in the Council of Ministers, to facilitate the implementation of further economic integration.

In the 1980s, the supranational institutions of the EC kicked back into gear, especially the Commission, from January 1985 under the dynamic leadership of Jacques Delors. It was Delors who spearheaded the public relations campaign in favor of the SEA and who, in the late 1980s, pushed budget reform, regional and social policy advances, and ultimately, EMU onto the extraordinary agenda, gaining the support of the European Council. Delors, with the support of President François Mitterrand and Chancellor Helmut Kohl, was able to overcome the opposition to his Social Charter and to EMU, of British Prime Minister Margaret Thatcher and her successor John Major. They could not stop the latest thrust of economic integration; Major succeeded only in getting the acceptance of Britain's right to opt out of the Social Charter and EMU.

More quietly, the ECJ, by successfully asserting its authority to interpret the treaties, had strengthened the likelihood that the single market legislation would be implemented by national governments and courts. And the EP had quietly been adding to its power by a combination of pressure on the governments to support formal accretions in the SEA and the Maastricht treaty, and by its restraint in actually exercising those powers, thus gaining the confidence of the other institutions. The EU came into being with the Maastricht treaty, which made the EP a coequal of the Council of Ministers regarding many legislative areas and extended EU competence in already existing areas of legislation as well as in some new ones. Most notable of the expanded powers under Maastricht were the planned stages for attaining EMU and the new pillars: CFSP and JHA.

But after the signing of the TEU, further political integration came under a cloud with failure of the first Danish ratification referendum of June 1992 and near failure in the September 1992 French referendum commissioned by Mitterrand. The British Parliament also refused ratification unless the Danes reversed their vote, which they did in 1993. But by this time, Britain had pulled out of the ERM in the crisis of September 1992, and Major was facing fierce opposition to ratification of Maastricht within his own parliamentary party. Although the TEU was eventually ratified by all 12 countries, and the EU moved ahead with the entry of three new members—Austria, Finland, and Sweden—the future of the EU was becoming a public agenda issue in France and Britain and looked like it might become one in Germany, as well as smaller member countries.

Yet the recent conflicts can be seen as another period in the evolution of the EU when resistance to economic and especially political union rises to force the process back to the middle ground, as happened in the 1960s thanks to de Gaulle and repeatedly in the 1970s as grand projects, such as EMU and steps toward Political Union, were rebuffed. Both EMU and Political Union came to be seen as more urgent with the sudden end of the Cold War in late 1989 and the recognition by both the French president and the German chancellor that steps must be taken to solidify Western Europe when new opportunities and distractions to the East, especially the unification of East and West Germany, could weaken the cohesion of the Community. The EMU, which appealed more to France on economic grounds than to Germany, was accepted by Kohl more on political grounds—as a way of tying his country's fortunes more irrevocably to those of his partners. But EMU will also mean a pooling of sovereignty over the capacity to make macroeconomic policy, which could mean a decrease in the already existing hegemony of the Bundesbank. Undoubtedly, if and when EMU enters into force, it will represent a greater degree of political as well as economic integration.

In international economic relations, the EU has become a major actor alongside the United States and Japan. On the one hand, competition with Japan and the United States has intensified on several grounds, as shown by trade in sensitive industries and the race for economic dominance in Eastern Europe and the Mediterranean Basin. However, despite intense competition, the Single Market, and eventually the EMU, are likely to promote better commercial and financial relations between the three economic giants. The fear of "fortress Europe" does not seem to be founded on rational economic grounds. The extent of direct foreign investment and trade flow supports the argument that protectionism is not likely to be the rule in future economic relations between the three giants.

The EU's relations with its European periphery highlight the inevitability of expansion of Union membership for several reasons. First, it is in the strategic and economic interests of the Union to maintain good relations with the nonmember European countries. Second, the EU needs to expand its economic base by absorbing new areas into its framework to compete with the United States and Japan—not only in regional terms but also on a global scale. Third, because the periphery states are interested in attaining the economic benefits of membership in the EU, it promises to reduce the danger of political instability and a return to authoritarian regimes in east-central, Eastern, and southeastern Europe. In this regard, it is important to note that even those countries that cannot become members of the Union, such as the non-European states of the Mediterranean Basin, are interested in establishing association agreements with the EU. Such agreements will give these countries preferential treatment over other trade partners of the Union, that is, the ACP countries. However, expansion beyond the EFTA countries will not occur immediately and will not necessarily include all of the other European states. Before any new poorer members are added to the Union, substantial progress has to be made in the deepening of integration between the members found in the Union as of the middle 1990s.

As least in the near future, the NMBC and ACP countries stand to lose in the Single Market as the EU shifts its attention to its immediate east. Both groups will continue to receive preferential trade and financial assistance from the Union, but the magnitude of these aid packages is not expected to increase substantially. Rather the future suggests that both regions will be increasingly marginalized in EU priorities. The possible exceptions are those NMBCs that have the hope of becoming EU members in the future: Cyprus, Malta, and Turkey.

In security matters, the provisions stated in the Maastricht treaty suggest that the EU remains a weak security community that requires intergovernmental coordination of common policies. In this regard, the member states are less willing to surrender additional sovereignty to the EU. The various provisions of the treaty do not prevent the members from following their own foreign policy preferences. Furthermore, while the members have strengthened ties between the EU and the WEU, it is not clear how NATO obligations of some countries will be reconciled. Thus, potential problems exist in formulating common external security policies. Recent experiences in the Persian Gulf and in former Yugoslavia support this observation. During the Gulf War, after the United States had asserted leadership, the EU countries managed to coordinate their policies effectively within the EU and between the WEU and NATO. However, inconsistencies during the Balkans crisis cast some doubt over the EU's ability to achieve a common foreign policy.

In domestic security matters, the provisions of the Maastricht treaty clearly call for cooperation among the member states in policy areas of political asylum, immigration, border controls, crime, customs, and police. Yet, while the interior ministers have agreed to improve cooperation in these policy areas, there remain many differences between national policies of the member countries.

As the successor to the EC, the EU of the 1990s has not yet assumed a shape distinct from that of its predecessor. The primacy of the intergovernmental bodies, especially the heads of state and government meeting as the European Council, will continue to be true of the EU for the foreseeable future. In today's interdependent world, domestic and foreign policy cannot be separated easily, nor can politics and economics. With the expansion of the EU's functions into areas of once-exclusive domestic policy competence, and with the increasing involvement of the EU in the political changes going on to the east and south of Western Europe, the highest political leaders of the member countries have compelling reasons to meet frequently and to try to coordinate their policies. The media and ever larger segments of the publics of the member countries closely watch the deliberations and joint decisions of the EU leaders, an inevitable outcome when the public increasingly goes to the ballot box to help settle EU matters. In the commitments made at Maastricht and in the proposals to complete EMU and Political Union, we can say that the European Union is *emerging*. Its future shape should become more distinct by the turn of the century, but it will remain a mixture of intergovernmental and supranational features. However, it will also be of greater relevance to the lives of ordinary citizens who will play a greater role in its future development than was true of its predecessor before the 1990s.

Index

About the Authors

David M. Wood is professor of Political Science at the University of Missouri-Columbia. He received his Ph.D. from the University of Illinois in 1960. Among his publications are two coauthored books, *Comparing Political Systems: Power and Politics in Three Worlds*, 4th ed. and *Back from Westminister: British Members of Parliament and Their Constituents*; and articles in scholarly journals, including *American Political Science Review; American Journal of Political Science; Political Studies; Legislative Studies Quarterly*; and *Parliamentary Affairs*. He specializes in the study of European political systems and comparative legislative behavior.

Birol A. Yeşilada is associate professor and chair of Political Science at the University of Missouri-Columbia. He received his Ph.D. from the University of Michigan in 1984. Among his publications are two coedited books, *The Political and Socioeconomic Transformation of Turkey* and *Agrarian Reform in Reverse: The Food Crisis in the Third World*; and articles and chapters in scholarly journals and research books, including *Polity; International Journal of Turkish Studies; The Cyprus Review; The State of the European Community, Vol. 1;* and *The Politics of Economic Reform in the Middle East*. He specializes in international political economy, European Union's external relations, the politics of EMU, the political economy of economic stabilization and adjustment policies of the IMF, and Turkish politics.